Skylights and Screen Doors

Dean J. Smart

ISBN 978-1-936680-02-3 Paperback
ISBN 978-1-936680-06-1 Hardcover
ISBN 978-1-936680-11-5 eBook

Printed in the United States of America

Published March 2011

MONT CLAIR PRESS
1094 New DeHaven Street, Suite 100
West Conshohocken, PA 19428-2713
(610) 941-6062
www.MontClairPress.com

364.1523

Dedication

For my family and Dun whose love,
guidance and inspiration
pushed me to finish.

A Note from the Author

This is a true story, just as I remember it.

As far as the trial testimony, I used secondary sources, not the official transcripts or the public record from the trial, but clippings from the time of the trial that I had placed in an old sneaker box. For the sake of time and for the reader, I often pieced together testimony from different sources. Some testimony may be disjointed or patched together from different times or days, as there was just too much to cover in the book. I was as accurate and true to the story as possible. I have taken the writers' liberty to create a better flow and reading experience.

Preface

Every day it's the same. I sit in front of the blank page on my computer screen, staring and waiting. I stare at the white drywall behind the computer. A white mist, like the whiteout of a blizzard, slips into my mind. It always starts with a haze—a kind of white-dot fog behind my eyes. It's as if windows and doors are lined up in a cloud. I open the door, and the scene comes to me.

I'm at school watching the students move between classes, and one of them sits down at the table next to me—the little one who has followed me around everywhere all year long. He looks up at me through his dark bangs, his brown eyes trapped in mine. He knows what's up: he knows I'm having "a day." He seems to be the only one that ever knows.

He throws his arm around me, still looking up and into me. "I love you, Mr. Smart, but, man, you worry too much." I look at his black terrycloth wristband draped over my shoulder, and all I can think of is Gregg.

"Love you too, Dun—thanks, man," I say to him. My dog barks at something out on the street, and I'm pulled out of the mist.

The fog returns after a while and I see myself holding a picture of Dun up to my father, as he lies in his hospital bed. Out of the side of his mouth that still works, he mutters softly, "Wow, Dean, he looks just like Eddie,

Eddie Marino." And I realize for the first time that Dun does look just like him — just like Gregg's old best friend, Eddie. A knock on the front door pulls me out of the haze, again.

I stare into the drywall behind my computer, waiting for another window or door to the past to open.

Part One

Under the Weeping Willow

Chapter 1

Mist And Memory

I stand in the doorway. I watch Dad in the kitchen. The silverware drawer squeaks as he pulls it open. He grabs a steak knife and scrapes it across the end of an old pencil, sharpening it. He turns to me, his moustache smiling. I watch the tiny woodchips land on the counter. He drops the knife and turns toward the window, holding up the pencil in the light, the light on the tip of it, and he stares at it for a moment. He walks toward me, the pencil firm in his hand. I stand up as straight as I can, my back pressed on the doorjamb.

"Stand up straight," he says, as he walks toward me. "Feet, flat on the floor." I press my back to the door. He kneels down, smiles at me and reaches across with the pencil. I feel him slide it across my hair as he marks the line.

I step away and watch as he goes over the line and darkens it with the pencil. He marks "Dean" on the top of the line, and the date. I look up at the two other lines, higher up on the inside of the doorway. Ricky's is on top; Gregg's, above mine. I reach up to it, touching the line, dark and pressed into the wood, embossed into the white-painted door frame. I feel the outline of the pencil, where it had been pressed in.

"Hey," he says, looking at me as I reach up, "you gonna go out and play?"

I run out the screen door, and it slams behind me. I run across the street, toward the woods, in the mist.

I'm running up and down a rock path in the woods behind my house in Hudson. Up and down between small rocky ravines beside Merrill Street. Up and down through forest and fog, chasing after friends playing enemy. I run and yell past cinnamon ferns and cragged rocks under pine and maple trees, screaming and chasing, while my feet pound down on the ground in the first winds of spring.

I'm searching the floor of the forest for a weapon — a sturdy branch to become my magical staff or sword. When I find the sacred relic, I will raise it up high into the air, causing my opponents to turn and run from its magnificent power to the center of a grassy field or on the rim of a fog-filled swampy bog. We will have a showdown, unless, of course, there is a mishap, and I break the artifact on some maple limb, pine trunk or moss-covered rock, giving my enemies the chance to intercept it. Then, there will be a fight to recover the relic, or I will scream, "Time out, not fair, I tripped," which everyone knows doesn't matter; clearly, the artifact will still be in play.

During the chase, any number of natural disasters or personal injuries can result in reversal or a complete time out. If some rare forest animal is spotted, like a deer or a stumbled-upon stick bug, time out is granted. If a thunderstorm forms and someone sees lightning or gets poured on, time out is granted. If someone falls and twists an ankle, scrapes a knee or gets injured in some way, time out is granted. Some participants pretend to be injured to gain possession of the relic.

This time, I'm not pretending. A sharp pulsing pain radiates from my left shoulder as something rips into my skin. I look back and search for the culprit, brushing my shoulder with my right hand as a second sharp pain rips through my lower back. I roll to the earth, frantically flopping in the pine needles and maple leaves, unaware that part of a beehive is stuck to the back of my shirt. The small chunk of papery hive is trapped at the ridge of my belt, between the flesh of my back and the cotton of my tee shirt. The hive is crushed when I roll around on it. Stinger after stinger pushes into my back, and I jump to my feet, wincing.

I begin running down the path that leads to my house, yelling and screaming, while the pain multiplies across my back. "Time out!" I yell, "The bees are killing me, time out!" I can feel several of them bouncing off the back of my head as they buzz in the air and chase after me. *How many are there?* I can't seem to outrun them and they continue to sting my back and bounce around my head. *Why are they after me? Are they trying to kill me?* My brother Gregg and a few of the neighborhood kids are running up behind me. I reach the edge of my driveway.

At the front porch of our small yellow cape, my mother swings open the screen door. "Bees on my back," I yell, "all over my back, Mom!" Behind me, the other boys have been watching. Mom says, "Show's over," and walks me into the house. In front of the bathroom mirror, where the lighting is bright, she begins pulling out the stingers, one by one, with a pair of tweezers.

"I don't know how you get yourself into these predicaments, freckle face." She says.

4

I watch her in the mirror as she works to pull out the stingers. Her hair is shorter than most of the neighborhood's other moms, but its size and girth are fashionably massive and quakes with each quick tug. I watch Mom in the bathroom mirror as she focuses on a tough stinger. I see a second reflection of Mom and me in the tinfoil bands of the wallpaper, then another, and another, the reflections finally getting so small you can barely see them, a thousand diminishing reflections of Mom and me.

Gregg, my older brother of three years, pops open the door, sticks his sunburned face through the opening and cracks a sly smile. I look up at his reflection, and his blue eyes light up the mirror. I know what's coming: he's a teaser. "Nice going, superhero," he says, "next time, use the weapon on the bad guys, not the trees—bumble-boy." I laugh, and he starts making buzzing noises at me.

"Okay, that's enough, Gregg," Mom says. She shuts the door, shooing him away. "The kids are going to pick on you for this one, you know."

"I know, Mom, I know."

She scrapes the last stinger out with the tweezers and then washes out the wounds with a hot soapy rust-colored facecloth that matches the wallpaper. She wipes off my back with a hand towel and says, "Tout finis," and then spanks me on the butt gently and pushes me through the bathroom's open doorway. "Go read under your tree for a while," she says. "We'll eat dinner soon."

My tree is the giant weeping willow that encompasses much of the small front yard, a twisted and drooped tree with branches and twigs that tumble back to earth, creating an enclosed canopy around its yellow trunk. Under the willow, it's like a cave that requires no building, nature's own shelter. Entering the "tree-cave" takes both hands, like opening a dozen heavy green drapes and stepping through them one at a time. I've made a circular clearing around the base and snapped out any twigs from the trunk, so I can sit comfortably without any branches brushing against my head. This is my special place where I think and relax in the silence.

I sit for a while with my back to the bark under the drooping tree, mostly hidden. From here, it's hard to see the outside world; I can only catch flashes of it when the breeze moves the branches. Neighbors drive by slowly in station wagons but I barely hear them. The tree stills me and slows the earth, altering time in some mythical way.

"How you doing, pal?" I hear Dad's voice call out to me from outside the tree-cave. He pokes his face under a high-hanging branch.

"All right, but the stings hurt pretty bad," I say.

"It'll feel better in a few days, son. Mom's starting the roast; do you want to play catch for a little while, monkey face?" I don't answer, but I see he is wearing his shorts and tennis sneakers. He's popping a ball back and forth into his mitt.

I decide to take him up on his offer and crawl out of my tree-cave to go play catch with him in the yard. "The key to it all, son," he says to me as I pick up a glove, "is that no matter what happens, buddy, you've got to keep smiling."

"I know, Dad, you tell me all the time," I say.

Dad and I toss the ball back and forth for a while and then Gregg walks out the back door with his glove and says, "I'm playing." He has his baseball hat on, and when I look at him, I remember back to the spectacular catch he made on Memorial Field during the championship game. I see him sliding across the infield gravel, his head and glove stretching out over the foul line; he jumps to his feet and whips the ball to first base for the out.

"Yeah, you can play," I say, "but no whipping it at me, all-star."

Gregg plays for the American Legion team. He wears a golden uniform, yellow cap and embossed golden team logo. Golden trophies line up on his bureau in our bedroom in the converted attic on Merrill Street. They read things like "Most Valuable Player," "All-Star Game" and "Division Champion." Some of Gregg's trophies stand a good foot high. At the top, they each have a little plastic baseball player taking a dramatic swing or reaching for a great catch. I have a trophy on my bureau, too; it reads, "Phillies, Third Place" — that's third place in a four-team league.

Gregg can zing it so fast that sometimes instead of trying to catch it I duck, cover my head and move away from it. His throws can really make your left palm sting and ring. "When's that roast going to be ready, I'm starving," Gregg says, as one of his hard throws gets by me and I chase it up the street.

"Pretty soon," Dad answers. "Get moving, Louie." I chase the ball that rolls across the pavement.

We play some pickle, waiting to be called in for the feast — Mom's incredible Sunday roast beef with homemade gravy. After dinner we watch the Disney "movie of the week" while Dad violently wiggles Jiffy Pop on an electric burner until the tinfoil dome fills with popped corn. We eat buttery popcorn and Hershey's chocolate bars and we wash them down with Coke on ice, and I almost forget about *bumble-boy.*

We live in Hudson, a small New England town that splits the Merrimack River. There isn't much to do in Hudson. It's a tiny New Hampshire town with mostly residential areas and two small shopping centers. There is a pond to swim at on hot summer days called Robinson Pond that is known for its leeches. I don't swim there much. There is also Hudson Speedway, a tiny oval where every Sunday evening many locals pray to the gods of oil, smoke and engine noise. We live at least four miles away, and every Sunday you can hear those cars go around again, again and again.

My street, Merrill Street, is shaped like a big "U." My house sits on the left-hand side of the U, last house on the corner. It's a small lot for a small cape. On the other side of the U is a dirt road that leads to the middle school and some baseball fields. The woods at the lowest part of the U are more interesting. In that small wooded area, there are several different types of terrain, all connected by aged paths and covered by tree crowns. There is one particular rocky outcropping of several large boulders that are very steep and perfect for rock climbing. There is a swamp, or bog, in the lowland region and several clearings of grass-covered field.

Hudson's a funny little place, a weird world all its own that I sometimes feel stuck in, like a lost toddler at an amusement park. I did get lost once at Benson's—that's Benson's Wild Animal Park, the coolest and the oddest place in town. A bizarre hodgepodge of "entertainments and amusements," Benson's is a place where Australian emus and Christmas elves converge, a place where roller coasters rumble above the red-boot house of the little old lady that lived in a shoe. A place where an American Indian totem pole stands next to a cotton-candy vendor's cart. A place where circus clowns and Santa Claus have lunch with lion tamers and eat hot dogs while watching people ride by on elephants named Betsy.

There's a perplexing path that meanders through the park, walking Benson's customers past all kinds of oddities. There's the little old lady that lives in the shoe, mechanically spanking her little boy's bare bottom. The path winds underneath her shoe, between the sole and the heel. Up another path, the lion tamer does his act with a whip and a stool. Down another path is Christmas Town where Christmas Carols are sung no matter the season.

The park is known, at least at our house, for its feces-chucking gorilla named Tony, a five hundred-pound silverback displayed in a giant circus wagon turned into a cage. On visits to Benson's, I would stare at Tony and he would stare right back. Then he would swing violently in his tire swing, giving customers nasty looks, charging them to get them to back away from his circus wagon, or whipping his own dung at them. Gregg had famously been hit with it during one of our early visits there.

Recently, they changed Tony the gorilla's name to Colossus. I've noticed that sometimes Colossus sits quietly slumped against the back of his cage, looking like he might cry. That's when I wish I could shoot the guy who brought him here with a tranquilizer gun and throw *him* into the circus wagon.

9

Hudson has its own neighborhood gorilla—Carl, the neighborhood bully. The chubby scrub with greasy hair and an unwashed jean jacket calls me "Dean the big bee baby" and torments me on the bus going to and from school. If this isn't enough, he trips me getting on and off the bus on the stairs. I fall pretty hard a few times, flat on my face, in front of the other kids. One day I finally stand up for myself. From the front seat, I whip an orange that strikes Carl directly in the forehead. Everyone, for the first time ever, laughs and makes fun of him. The bus driver even shouts, "Sit down, mister," when Carl tries to get up and whip the orange back at me. It feels pretty good, but I know I'm dead. He'll get me after school, on my walk home.

I spend the rest of the day clock watching. It's twelve thirty-four. It's one forty-eight. It's five past two. I get on the bus and I watch Carl pounding his fist into his palm and cracking his knuckles. He wiggles his head and stretches his arm and throws punches into the air. I get off the bus and hang back, watching from forty feet away as the clump of kids begins their walk up the hill on Merrill Street. Some of them walk backward and smile at me, their eyes gleaming. "Vultures," I think to myself. *They can't wait to see me get killed.*

At the top of the hill, ahead of me, the fight circle forms. Carl's fans are getting him psyched. He warms up and stretches like an Olympic boxer preparing for the championship match. "Stick and move," his coaches tell him, "stick and move." "Use the left." "Jab, jab, jab," they shout. I'm pushed into the circle and put my fists up near my face for protection. I think to myself, *I'm the puny safari hunter thrown into the gorilla's cage.*

The kids scream, "Fight, fight, fight!" Carl throws a left; I avoid it. Then he throws a right and it just misses my chin. I begin moving about. Without warning, a roundhouse right catches the side of my head, and as I turn away from it, it nails me in the ear and the back of my neck. I fall to the pavement. The crowd cheers. *I'm the puny safari hunter knocked down by the gorilla.*

I hobble home and Mom meets me at the screen door. I look up but she seems to know not to say anything. She gives me a quick hug, brings me inside and wraps ice in a face cloth. She places it gently on my red swollen ear. I head for my weeping willow.

You can tell whether or not you're in trouble by the tone of Dad's voice from the bottom of the stairs. If Dad calls us down by our full names, we know we have "had it," as he sometimes says. If Ricky gets a "Richard" from the bottom of the stairs, he's in for it. If Gregg gets a "Greggory" from the bottom of the stairs, he's in trouble. If I get "Dean John" from the bottom of the stairs, it's never good. If Dad yells your full name and adds "Smart" to the end, you're in really deep trouble. We all wait in fear. I think it's me for sure tonight, but it turns out I'm wrong.

"Greggory, get down here," he shouts. I breathe a sigh of relief; I bet Ricky does too, from the other side of the attic. Ricky is a lot older than Gregg and I and has his own small bedroom to the left of the stairs. He spends most nights out with his friends and is often discovered by Dad trying to sneak up the attic stairs after staying out and partying past curfew. But it's not him tonight; it's not me either. I wonder what Gregg did.

A few minutes later Gregg comes stomping back up the stairs, sighing. He slides into bed. From the other side of the room, I ask him, "What happened?"

"Nothing happened, brat, don't worry about it." He sighs again and rolls over. "But try not to get your butt whipped again tomorrow—all right, little guy." He adds.

I finally fall asleep after staring out the window at a white pine and listening to an owl's hoot.

The next afternoon at the top of the hill on Merrill Street the circle of destruction forms again. Carl apparently didn't get enough from yesterday's matchup and would like a rematch. I hear a familiar voice yell, "Hey, you want to fight, you little punk? Pick on someone your own size." It's Gregg, strutting up the circle from our house.

For the first time, Carl looks nervous. "Oh, have your big brother try to save your butt, huh?"

"I can't find someone my own size, because I'm the biggest kid on the block," he shouts to Gregg. "I'm even bigger than you, and I'm going to kick your butt, too."

It isn't much of a fight and ends with Gregg sitting on the bully's chest, his knees trapping the shoulders of Carl's scuzzy jean jacket. From this position Gregg has a discussion with Carl punctuated by his fists. "I think you should learn to shut your big mouth!" Left hook to the jaw. "I think you should learn to pick on someone your own size!" Right jab to the eye. "I think you should never touch my little brother again!" Left jab to the nose region. "If you do, this will happen every day!" Hard right hook to the mouth.

Finally, Gregg lets Carl up and he runs home, crying. I smile weakly and follow my brother back to the house.

Chapter 2

Druids and Moonies

Hudson, and my life for that matter, is home to several oddities. For instance, there is the flower man. Every weekend the flower man sets up shop in the parking lot of Ace Hardware on Derry Road across from Alexander's grocery store. He sells a large assortment of flowers, lining them up in white plastic buckets all around his big white van. His face bears a focused stern look, although, on very rare occasions, I see him smile slightly as we drive by. From the car window, his tight grey eyes look almost supernaturally powerful. But, to me, his most striking feature is his very long white hair, not grey hair, white hair, like Gandalf the wizard. He doesn't look nearly old enough to have grey hair, never mind white hair. I imagine he is a druid or warlock of some sort, using his "flowers" to create enchantments and potions. The flowers he sells are magnificent and come in every color of the rainbow. They have obviously benefited from the ancient power of his growth spell. As Gandalf travels his Shire, he exchanges gold pieces with his customers, his grey eyes searching the woods for hobgoblins.

Then, there are the "Moonies." Ricky swears the Moonies live in a mansion across from Alvirne High School just up the road from the flower man's bazaar. The mansion is on a small corner lot. The lot is highly landscaped and contains a large brick main house and in the back a small guest or pool house. A circular drive bordered by tall hedges is in front of the estate. The property is so over-whelmed with landscape plants and shrubs no one can see into the estate or what is going on inside the grounds. I try many times but can only catch a glimpse of the estate through its driveway openings. I am in love with the place and gawk at it every time we go by. The Moonie Mansion is my favorite house in Hudson, by far.

According to Ricky, the Moonies are a moon-worshiping cult from California. "They shave their heads and wear white robes and take donations at airports, like in the movie *Airplane*," he tells me.

"Well, they did all right for themselves—it looks like all that change added up to the nicest little mansion in Hudson," I say.

"Yeah but," Ricky adds, "the Moonies got kicked out of California because they kidnapped people and brainwashed them into being Moonies, like slaves." I think, *Kidnapping and brainwashing—how intriguing*. Ricky then says, "The Moonies leader, The Reverend Sun Young Moon, is worshipped like a god by his zombielike slaves." I think, *This is the craziest story ever. He must be making it up.*

"You're making it up, aren't you?"

"On no," Ricky replies, "it's definitely real." Then he adds, "The police and the FBI are watching them, don't worry."

For a while I don't believe Ricky, and then one day, driving by the estate with Mom, heading out on one of her shopping trips, I see the Moonies for myself. They are in the driveway, two of them, taking cardboard boxes out of the trunk of a black Lincoln Continental. They are bald and they have on white robes. There's another one, "Look, Mom, right there, a Moonie, he's trimming the hedges. He's bald with a white robe. Weird, Mom—look! Pull over, Mom, turn around and stop the car. Look at the Moonies!" She doesn't stop; nothing keeps her from Jordan Marsh, not even Moonies unloading mysterious cardboard boxes.

Having seen them, I think about them nonstop. *What goes on at the Moonie Mansion, I wonder, behind those beautiful trees and hedges? Do they have elaborate Moon ceremonies behind the shrubs? Are there fire pits and podiums on the brick pathways and patios?* I imagine the zombies chanting and wandering into various formations making hand signals led by their leader, The Reverend of the Moon. "We love the moon, the moon is our god, the reverend is our leader, and he is part of the moon." The ceremonies must go on for hours all through the night—white robes and firelight under the almighty moon, the reverend using his moon power to suck the thoughts from a recently captured moon rookie. I imagine the young abductee, her hands tied behind her back, as she tries to fight off the reverend's powerful moon magic. When she finally succumbs to the reverend's powers, the zombies celebrate in loud whoops and chants. They are all moon-struck, behind hedges in Hudson.

Just like the Moonies my mom's parents, my grandparents, are as odd as can be. Harold Bellevue, my grandfather, prefers to be called Harry. His wife Dorothy, my grandmother, prefers to be called Dot. As far as I can tell, that is the only thing Harry and Dot have in common. For instance, Harry likes to smile, have fun and make people laugh, while his wife Dot does not. Harry likes to sit in his little backyard on an aluminum lawn chair and hand feed the squirrels. Grammy Dot does not. But she does make us macaroni with a hamburger tomato sauce, which she calls dog food. She will flop it on your plate and either scowl or say something to aggravate my mom or someone else. Dot still remains somewhat likeable, however, mainly because she is good at playing the straight man to Grampy Harry's antics.

Grampy Harry has wooden legs. He lost his legs to diabetes and they are amputated just below the knee. Sometimes he puts his wooden legs on backward and walks into the room with a stroller and stands there with his feet on backward until someone notices, or he pops out his full set of dentures and mugs at us like one of those guys in a funny-face contest, or while everyone is sitting and talking he secretly undoes one of his legs and pokes us with it, while saying things like "'Bout time you get a leg up on the competition, sonny."

I wonder why Grammy Dot always seems so mad. Mom explains that Grammy hasn't been the same since Greggory, Mom's brother and Dot's son, died. Uncle Greggory, who my brother Gregg is named after, died in a car wreck when he was just twenty-three years old. I feel bad about this but still think Grampy has more to be mad about, with his wooden legs and all. Grampy is happy, so full of life, and his wife, well, she went the other way, it seems. My mom is like both of them, mainly enjoying life and being happy, but when she gets mad, I can see the Dot in her. She has had to deal with the loss of her brother as well and that can't be easy.

16

Mom is a shopaholic. On days when the boys go hunting—by boys, I mean Dad, Gregg, Ricky and sometimes my young Uncle Jeff—I go shopping with Mom instead. I went hunting once or twice and didn't enjoy it much. Sitting on a fallen tree trunk at the edge of a frozen swamp with a shotgun just didn't appeal to me. It's so cold and dark and Dad insists on being very quiet, while honking his duck caller and waiting for the birds to fly by, just so that we may blow their little heads off and watch them fall to their deaths. I tell Dad this just isn't my kind of fun. I argue that there really is no need to go hunting, when they sell meat, any kind you want, at the grocery store. I explain that it is unfair to the prey, that instead of using a gun you should use a spear or some rocks, or at the very most a simple bow and arrow. They disagree and go anyway, and I go shopping with Mom.

Mom's favorite shopping destination is the magnificent Jordan Marsh, just up the highway from Hudson, in Bedford, New Hampshire. This cement palace is huge, two whole floors with escalators, and it even has its own restaurant on the second floor, allowing Mom and me to stay inside the structure through lunch and dinner, if necessary. The bottom floor is all clothing, jewelry, perfume and makeup. The second floor is housewares, televisions, radios and toys. Mom spends most of her hours downstairs where she piles clothes in a shopping cart to try on. I spend hours upstairs messing with radios and studying the boxes of LEGOs.

I waste a lot of time riding up and down the escalators. I let the moving stairs carry me halfway up, then I turn around and run back down and do it again. There is a ridge on the escalators where the floor ends and the mesmerizing stairs begin to form and move upward or downward. I stand at this edge and let the front of my sneakers hang over it, while lifting up my toes. Then I lean forward and let my sneakers and toes catch the moving stairs as they pull me and whisk me up. This pleasant activity often blocks customers from getting on the escalators, then stuffy, overly perfumed employees shoo me away. I take naps on the leather sofas upstairs where Mom finds me and wakes me up, laughing. She says, "Time to go, freckle face, and wipe up that drool — that's a two thousand-dollar sofa."

One day, we are returning from one of our shopping trips. As we pull into the driveway, I can't believe my eyes. Hanging in a pine tree, not ten feet from our tiny porch entrance, is a tan deer, blood dripping from its mouth and forming a pool on the lawn. The deer hangs from the pine limb by its hind legs that are bound and tied to the limb with rope. It has only been recently hung, and it slowly spins toward us, enough for us to see its underside, which has been sliced from chest to crotch, its innards removed. I'm in shock; I can't move. "This just isn't right, Mom," I finally manage to say.

"No, it isn't, pumpkin," she replies, shaking her head. Mom turns the key and shuts the engine off, but we both just sit there staring at the poor thing through the windshield with our mouths wide open. Suddenly, Mom jumps from the car, slams the door, runs inside and yells to Dad, "William, get over here immediately." Mom only calls him William when she is scorching mad. Dad emerges from the bathroom where he has been showering. From the look in his eyes, he knows he has had it. Mom says, "You get Richard and Greggory, and the three of you take that goddamn deer off of that goddamn tree, right now, or you've goddamn had it, and put it where we can't see it."

Dad replies, "Now, calm down, Judith — it will only be there for a few days and then it's going to the butcher to make venison steaks."

Mom tends to repeat things people say that anger her, and she replies with, "A few days, a few days, a few days — you'll only have a few days left on earth, if you don't get the boys and get it out of the tree, NOW!"

Dad gives up, and says, "All right, Judith, we will put it out back where you can't see it."

From the little window in my attic bedroom, I watch Dad, Ricky and Gregg slowly lower the carcass down from the pine, then drag it across the lawn to a wooded area behind the house where it will be out of sight. The next day curiosity gets the better of me and I find myself in the backyard examining the carcass with a stick and pushing it slightly to make it spin, while flies feast on its black glossed-over eyeballs.

A day or two later, Gregg and Dad haul the body off to the butcher and Gregg returns with several trophies for his prize doe. The first trophy is the much-talked-about venison steaks, which I have heard about relentlessly since the shooting. "Oh, how delicious they will be," the boys taunt me. "So yummy and rare, bleeding on the plate," they all say. "We will have several weeks' worth." I decide I can let the grease and blood from the steaks bathe Mom's mashed potatoes in a feast of ultimate manliness. Meanwhile, Mom stocks up on chicken noodle soup so that I will have something to eat during the venison celebrations.

Gregg's second and most prized trophy is a hoof severed from the doe just below its knee. This is barbarically displayed on Gregg's bureau in the attic bedroom that we share. The hoof is placed front and center, in front of his many baseball trophies, so that I am forced to stare at it and think about it night after night while trying to fall asleep. When Gregg first brings it home, he chases me about the house with it while repeating in a creepy high-pitched voice, "Help me, Dean, help me." We all laugh. Later, when I'm in the shower, he sneaks into the bathroom and sticks the hoof up at me from around the shower curtain, while making moose calls. I can't stop laughing. That night as I get into bed I find the hoof under my pillow, and I whip it across the room at Gregg while we both crack up.

The last time I see Grampy Harry is in the rest home by the river on the other side of Hudson. *He is gone*, I think, even though he sits right in front of me covered in a tan blanket, sitting in an old wooden wheelchair with a wicker woven back. There is nothing left behind his eyes, and he sits frozen and speechless with an imprisoned gaze. He can't even control his body anymore, and he twitches, grunts and drools. Every so often, he tries to get up out of his wheelchair, but he falls back down. I feel like the world has done it, killed him, and he has just slowly broken down like the last days of spring that have to give way to summer.

One day, not long after, Dad tells Gregg and me that Grampy Harry has passed away and we need to be easy on our mother for a while. He takes us to Sears to buy new suits for the funeral.

Chapter 3

Speechless and Frozen

In Hudson, during the spring and summer months, we load into our gigantic car and head out for a night at the drive-in movies, just up the road, in Litchfield, New Hampshire. The drive-in is a fenced-off parking lot in the middle of the woods, off a back road. It usually features two movies, and I often fall asleep in the back of our station wagon on the pillows and blankets we bring along. There are also a couple of swing sets that a lot of the older kids hang out at, and make out at, during the movies. In the center of the parking lot, there is a concession stand that serves popcorn, soda, candy, hot dogs, hamburgers and fries. The parking area isn't completely level and features long rows of mounded dirt that cars pull up on to get a better view of the big screen. Next to each parking spot is an upright metal pole that holds the speaker box. The box is a stainless-steel square, with slatted vents and a black plastic volume knob. At its top and rear is a lip that allows you to hang the speaker box on your car window, trapping the cheap tinny sound of Hollywood inside your vehicle.

Mom is never satisfied with our parking spot. Inevitably, we find one and Dad puts the car in park, then one of us reaches out the window and grabs the speaker box and we set it on the window, and Mom inevitably says, "Oh, Billy, we need to move the car up a foot and a half at least." Dad moves the car and shuts it off again. Mom says, "Oh, that's no good, back us up about two feet." Dad does it, and then shuts the car off, and Mom says, "Let's move over to that spot, three rows up and to the left." The station wagon bounces over mounds of dirt, searching for the perfect position. This goes on for a good twenty minutes before the first feature begins.

Our wood-paneled wagon has newfangled power windows. Dad loves them, and so do I. I can't help but open and close my window repeatedly, watching it slide, like the doors of the space stations in *Star Wars*. Dad has ultimate control of all the windows from the front seat where he rules like the Galactic Emperor, over all four buttons. I open my back window, and he shuts it, and we go back and forth in a power-window war, laughing. I like to grab the speaker box when I can, just so I can use the space-station window.

After finally getting the car and Mom in the perfect position, I slide my back window down. It is a long reach tonight as the speaker box is a few feet away, forcing me to put my torso all the way through the window frame, both arms stretched to their limit. As I finally reach the box and grab it, Gregg says, "Turn it up and make sure it works or we'll have to move again." I crank the volume knob all the way up and begin sliding back through the window frame just as the power window begins to rise. I pull my stomach and chest back through the window frame, but it is too late. The rising glass has pushed up my arms at the shoulders, forcing me to drop the speaker box and trapping my head in the window frame, with the glass pressing tightly on my lower jaw. The window holds me there, the speaker box blaring from the gravel, my head held in an awkward position and my arms outstretched. I try yelling to Dad to open the window, but I can only muster several meek mumblings because I can't open my mouth. No one hears me over the blaring speaker box.

I keep trying to yell for quite a while but manage only a series of muffled "melps." Then I start banging on the car door and kicking my feet at Gregg in the backseat. He doesn't look at first and thinks that I am fooling around. He says, "Cut it, dork." I continue banging, kicking and trying to yell. Finally, Gregg notices my odd predicament and points it out to Dad who immediately opens the window. Everybody laughs, including me. We realize my knee must have been on the switch to the power window while I reached for the speaker box. I could have freed myself at any point but didn't realize it.

My favorite part of the drive-in is the intermission. During the intermission, dancing hot dogs, hamburgers, french fries, candies and sodas sing their tribute on the big screen and we all line up at the concession stand, as we wait for the next feature. The intermission show is often more entertaining than the first movie, as all sorts of Hudson folk stand in line wiggling their way through the repeated S-shaped metal divider.

I hear the horns blowing outside the concession stand. Horn blowing is just another form of drive-in entertainment. Sometimes, during the movie, for no apparent reason, one person blows his horn, then another, and before you know it everyone is honking. Sometimes it goes on for at least five minutes. Then it will finally stop and a few moments later somebody hits his horn again and the whole beeping episode starts over. At least one hundred cars, in the middle of the forest, headlights facing the giant screen, are like honking geese heading south.

On this night I walk over to the concession stand and have the feeling every person in every car is staring at me. They are looking at me through their steamy windows, allowing them to see me while I can't see them. I walk past the grills of every car in town, positioning myself perfectly between car doors so I don't get too close to the steamy tanks. I feel like an invader, walking past their living room picture windows while trying not to peek in. The sound of all the little speaker boxes reverberating off all the vinyl and plastic is like a thousand news reports being played in sync from every television in town.

❖❖❖❖❖

I lie in bed in Hudson, trying to fall asleep. I'm alone in my attic bedroom. Gregg, being three years older than me, gets to stay up later than I do. I lie there watching the ceiling and its attic angles or staring out the window watching the wind sway a white pine. My bed is to the far left of the window at the peak of the house. Gregg's bed has the spot closest to the window; my bed rests on the wall near the door. It's really only a half wall, with a steep pitch jutting upward above my bed. On the other side of the room is an identical wall and along the pitched part I see something dart across in the moonlight.

I rub my eyes and look again, nothing. I must be getting tired. I shift my eyes to the window and the pine tree and shrug it off. After a few moments, I catch something move again in the shadows of the pitched wall. *Whoa, what was that?* A few moments go by and I feel "safe" again, so I roll over and stare at the ceiling. I lie motionless, as my eyes watch a small black flashing orb move quickly along the ceiling from the doorway to the window and back again. My breath comes to a halt, my body stiffens and my eyes bulge. I wait to die: there is a flying demon in my room. My eyes dart about the room. *Is it gone? No, there it is again.* The black orb zings across the ceiling, moving erratically, back and forth across the room. I can't move, I can't yell, I just watch, speechless and frozen.

Then, just as suddenly, it stops and I breathe again. I tell myself to jump out of bed and run downstairs or it's going to get me, but I can't move an inch. I try and try again but I can't move. I can't even open my eyes to check if the thing is back. I hear it or think I hear it again. This time there is a rumbling sound. Suddenly, I hear a thud, followed by a long silence. I convince myself to take a peek. Just one eye opens only a sliver for one millisecond and then I shut it. Nothing—maybe everything's all right now. I force myself to take one more peek, but all I see is the ceiling, window and doorway. Bravely, I open both eyes and wait in the darkness.

The silence is broken by a screech that echoes up the stairway to the attic and throughout the entire house. It's Mom yelling. The demon orb must have escaped my room and is now after her, downstairs. Another yell makes its way up the stairway. It's Dad, and he sounds startled. Mom yells, "Get the broom, get the broom, Billy." The demon is attacking my mother and father, but I still can't move or talk or go to help them. I hear a great commotion from the living room downstairs, as Mom and Dad do battle. *A broom, that's all they got?* I think to myself. *No one slays a demon orb with a broom. I've got to help them.* More banging and screeching echo up the stairs, as I lay stiff, trapped in my bed. I hear someone open the basement door and run, heavy footed, down the basement stairway. Mom screams, this time longer and sustained. I can't take it anymore. I jump out of bed, grab Gregg's aluminum baseball bat and bolt down the stairs like lightning in the clouds.

Mom is in the dining room, swatting at the stained-glass light fixture that hangs by a chain over the dinner table. The light fixture bounces and flutters like Muhammad Ali's speed bag, but somehow it doesn't shatter. Dad swings open the cellar door violently after banging his way up the basement stairs. He is carrying a small green filament fishnet. *A broom and a fishnet!* I head to the stained-glass light fixture, wielding Gregg's bat. As I prepare to park it, Mom yells, "No, wait, it's just a bat."

I say, "I know it's a bat. I'll get it, don't worry, Mom, back up."

She yells at me once again, "Dean, it's a bat!" *Why does she keep telling me this? I know it's a bat; I'm holding it in my hands.*

"Look out, I'll catch it," shouts Dad, and we both back away from the swinging lamp, as he approaches with his fishing net.

That's when I see it. On top of the lamp fixture sits a very tiny dark grey bat, the flying kind! It's not a demon orb after all, just a little bat. Dad takes a great swing at it, but misses. Gregg walks in and we watch as Dad chases the creature back and forth from the dining room to the living room, missing each time with his fishing net. Even when the tiny bat does get caught in Dad's net, it manages to fly through the holes and escape. Finally, Dad trades the net in for Mom's broom and props open the front door that leads to the porch. Dad pushes the bat through the front door, but the bat manages to fly back into the house. It perches again on the stained-glass light fixture, tilting its head at us, as if to say, "You guys could never catch me." Then it flies out the door on its own and glides off into the night.

Across town there is an old abandoned Victorian house. It is white with black shutters and with some work would have been very nice, but it is in disrepair. The house is located on Derry Road across from Alexander's Shopping Plaza and only a few steps away from where the flower druid works every weekend. For years the house just sat there with boarded-up windows and overgrown shrubbery. The rumor on Merrill Street was that the widow of a prominent town doctor had lived in it until she passed away and left the house to relatives who, in turn, left it abandoned. One of the kids said the house would soon be demolished to make way for a cosmetology school.

Gregg's friend, Mike, lives in the neighborhood adjacent to the old white Victorian. One night he and Mike and a few of their other friends find their way into the house and decide to explore it. They equip themselves with makeshift weapons and flashlights and wander through the big rooms of the house, undetected. Word gets out and all the younger kids on Merrill Street are envious and amazed by their bravery.

A few houses down from our cape, in a small, modern ranch, live the Townsend twins—Ronny, a tall and lanky boy, and his younger brother by moments, Ben, who is shorter and stouter. The three of us hang out with Danny Dexter, a skinny tough kid from a part of the neighborhood where the streets are named after letters. Dexter lives on D

Street, a few blocks away from Merrill Street. One Saturday afternoon the four of us decide that we are tough enough and old enough to bike across town with some equipment and try to explore the abandoned Victorian. Backpacks, flashlights, slingshots and magical staffs pedal past the stone library and make their way up busy Derry Road. The quest is on and the four of us are hoping to make a name for ourselves.

Once we arrive at the old house, we realize that getting in isn't going to be easy. We are sure to be seen by one of the neighbors, as the Victorian is located very close to several smaller houses, and it's still daylight. We take a quick look around and then pedal behind the grocery store to make our plans, while we wait for dusk. The four of us sit on a small outcropping of rocks, behind Alexander's on the edge of the woods. We start an equipment check. Three flashlights, one stick, a slingshot, four ball bearings, two marbles, three backpacks, one Swiss Army knife and four bikes shimmer on the grass near the edge of the woods. Next, we devise our actual plan of entry. Ronny, being the biggest and oldest, will lead and have the jackknife. Dexter will go second and carry the slingshot and ammo. Ben will go third with just a flashlight, and I'm going to guard the rear with a stick. We decide to enter the old Victorian the same way the older guys did, through the basement bulkhead. If there are any problems, we are to meet back here at the rocks, and if someone gets caught, no one should "rat" on the others who escape.

We quietly drop our bikes on the shadowed gravel driveway and tiptoe around the back of the house. Ronny leads and heads closer to the basement doors, taking a few steps at a time, as we, in turn, follow him sequentially, like spies, infiltrating the enemy's stronghold. I lean against the old house, hiding in its shadows, as the four of us encircle the wooded doors of the bulkhead. Ronny leans down and grips the handles to the double wooden doors and silently gives them a pull. The doors don't budge, "Locked," he whispers. *Good news, I'm not going to jail tonight.*

Dexter whispers, "The garage, let's try the garage."

We snake around the garage, but it's locked, too. We file up the side porch and crouch near a side door to the main house. Ronny turns the doorknob and pushes the door, which opens slowly. We stare at each other in a state of shock, as we realize the door is open and we can get in easily. We shuffle back to the dark graveled driveway and kneel down near our bikes. Someone says, "Let's just go in, real quick, check the place out and then we'll scram real fast and go home."

"I'll stay here and keep a look out and, umm, I'll watch the bikes and, umm, I'll hoot like an owl if someone is coming — all right, guys?" I respond.

Someone says, "That's not the plan. We're all going in, now let's go."

We move and dip back to the side doorway and peer inside. Ronny heads in first, followed by Dexter, Ben and me. The flashlights click on and shine yellow circles into a small entry room. The walls are a dirty white and the house smells musty. We huddle close together and move through the entranceway into a large main room. We shine the flashlight on an old stone fireplace, some crumpled-up newspapers, several charred pieces of wood in the fireplace, an empty paper bag from McDonald's, a *Playboy* magazine and some built-in glass shelving. While the others poke around in the fireplace with one of the staffs, I grab the

Playboy, fold it in half and stuff it into the back pocket of my Levi's. I think about how I am wicked late for dinner, pork chops, and how Mom must be wondering where in the hell I am. I'm sure she has already yelled my name across the block several times.

We meander about the first floor of the Victorian and find ourselves near the steep stairway that leads to the second floor. We crouch and inch our way up the creaking wooden steps, weapons in hand, waiting to find something horrifying. We find three empty rooms and a small bathroom. The only item of interest is in the bathroom in a mirrored cabinet—a small round tin of facial powder with one of those cottony puff things inside. We begin to laugh at the tin and ourselves. Suddenly, there is a loud thud from downstairs, and I drop the tin of powder to the floor. We all stand up perfectly straight and look white as ghosts. There is nothing to do but run down the stairs as quick as we can. I bolt past the fireplace and the glass cabinets, through the entryway, and make it through the side door we came in. Ronny and Dexter are already peeling out of the driveway, as Ben and I head for our bikes. Both of us jump at the sound of the door slamming itself shut in the heavy wind. We laugh and pedal away, our hearts still racing. I feel at least a half an inch taller as I quickly race home.

My heart is still pounding as I walk through the side door of our yellow cape. I notice that Dad's wagon isn't in the driveway and there are no plates or food on the table. Mom hardly notices that I've walked in. *I must have missed dinner completely—I'm in so much trouble!* But Mom barely looks up from the stove as I enter. She flips some pork chops into a frying pan, as she says, "Hi, pumpkin."

"Hey," I respond sharply. *Here it comes, I can feel it, I've had it, she knows.* Chops begin to sizzle.

"Where you been, monkey face?" *It's over: she knows where I've been and I should just confess.*

"Out playing, Mom, out playing, in the woods, out playing, you know, bike riding and, umm, out playing." The sizzling from the frying pan is louder.

"Well, go clean up, change and get ready for dinner," she says.

"All right, Mom." I say. *Whew, made it.*

I feel her eyes on me as I walk through the dining room, toward the attic stairs. She calls out, "What's that in your pocket, monkey face?" My hand instantly reaches for the back pocket of my Levi's, as a flash goes off in my head. *It can't still be there, can it?* Yes, it is still there; the *Playboy* magazine from the old Victorian sticks out of the denim, like the flag on a sinking ship. Despite feeling a bit taller, I'm grounded for two weeks.

Chapter 4

The Blizzard

There's a great storm approaching. I hear everyone talking about it. The biggest storm in the history of America, they say. A blizzard of frozen destruction will blanket New England and the Northeast. The super nor'easter is coming with great winds capable of ripping the roofs off homes. The storm will take whole houses into the Atlantic Ocean. Whole cities will be covered in snow so deep no one will be able to walk or drive in it. The television stations tell us to stock up on firewood, food, water and any medicine we might need.

The forecasters in New England are rarely correct on such predictions. This time, however, my grandfather, United States Air Force Lieutenant Colonel Richard J. Smart, says the forecast is absolutely correct. The colonel has called all his children and told them to head to his farm in New Sweden, Maine, for safety's sake. Many of my aunts and uncles are not going to the ranch, as the colonel has asked. Dad and Mom seem to be going back and forth on the subject. Dad is on the fence; he's not sure if he wants to take that long drive up. But our cape doesn't have a fireplace, and if the power goes out and then doesn't come back on for a few days, it's going to be very cold.

I am listening to them argue the subject, back and forth, as I spit yellow phlegm into a white Tupperware bowl next to my bed. My bronchitis doesn't seem to be getting any better. I get out of bed and yell down the attic stairs, "Mom, start the water, please." I cough up brown phlegm into the bowl and crawl back into bed, shivering. I wait and then hear the tub water turn on. *We should go to the farm in Maine. I could die in the cold.*

My mother calls from the bottom of the stairs. "Come on, Dean, it's ready." I grab the Tupperware bowl and wobble down the cold stairs. The mucus slides back and forth in the plastic bowl with each step I take. At the bottom of the stairs, I hand the bowl off to Mom. "Medicine first," she says as I walk past. I pull the refrigerator door open and grab the bottle of pink antibiotic. The thick, pink, foamy substance needs to be shaken well.

Gregg walks into the kitchen as I begin pouring the medicine into the tablespoon over the sink. He gently bumps me with his shoulder from behind and says in a loud voice, "Hey, look out now, don't spill any." Then he starts laughing and I join him. "Do you want to go to Maine, little guy?" He continues, "I do, because if we do, then we won't have to go to school for the rest of the week." He adds, "Plus, it will be cool up at the farm in the snowstorm."

"Yes, I think we should go too, Gregg." I answer. I swallow down two full tablespoons worth of the pink antibiotic that's supposed to taste like bubblegum, but tastes of something else, something horrible. Mom walks into the kitchen and hands me back the white plastic bowl. "Better get in there before the steam disappears. I'll be in, in a minute." She says.

The bathroom is filled with steam, and I sit on the edge of the bathtub. The tub is filled to the brim with steaming hot water. I hold the Tupperware bowl between my knees and spit phlegm into it, as the steam sets into my clogged lungs. I take deep breaths trying to clear them out. I breathe deeply and drain some of the water from the tub, so I can add more hot water for the steam I need. If I'm going to Maine, I need to bring one of the models I haven't built yet because Grampy will help me build it, as he always does, and Grammy will make me toast with her homemade butter, with cinnamon and sugar on it. *I love that farm in Maine.* I drain the tub completely.

The snow is already starting to accumulate on the driveway and on Merrill Street. It's decided: we are going. I hear the wind whipping outside the window of my bedroom, as I begin to gather toys and books for the trip. I search for and find an opened plastic model of a battleship. I grab my baseball cards and a few of my books on World War II, some plastic army men, and I'm ready to go. I stand by the attic window and see white flakes flash by sideways in the gust.

Gregg piles up our luggage near the side door with the little stairs and porch. We all sit in the kitchen and start to wonder where Dad is, because he left to pick up my prescription from the drugstore quite a while ago. I'm still in my pajamas, which have their own little slipper socks attached with plastic foot bottoms. Over my pajamas I wear a heavy cotton robe to keep from getting a chill. Periodically, Gregg checks outside in the driveway to see how much snow is accumulating. It's getting dark and the snow is piling up. After an hour or so, I hear the sound of Dad's tires crunching in the snow at the end of the driveway. He backs in the big white wagon with faux wood paneling, to make it easier for us to pack the car.

Mom snaps my winter boots shut over my pajama slippers. A huge, plump, red-and-blue down snowsuit goes over my pajamas and robe, but this isn't enough polar protection for Mom; she adds itch-inducing wool mittens, rendering my hands useless. The final touch is the most annoying hat item ever created, a winter wool cap with two huge earmuff flaps, tied under my chin in a bow. The only part of my flesh still visible is a tiny expanse around my nose, cheeks and eyes. Mom giggles as she unzips the unusually large collar on the back of the snowsuit, revealing the built-in hood with yet more strings, which she pulls tight and ties around the wool hat. I try to move and end up bouncing about the room and then off the walls, like a hot air balloon trapped inside the Boston Garden. Mom and Gregg laugh as I walk like a clumsy spaceman in slow motion with my arms raised. I bounce myself off the doorway, continuing the skit on the way out to the car.

I sit on the vinyl bench seat in the back of the wagon, unzipping my snowsuit, while Dad and Gregg arrange and then rearrange the luggage in the very back of the wagon. Dad fiddles obsessively with the configuration of the luggage, trying three or four different arrangements until Mom urges him to finish quickly. Finally, with the luggage just right, Dad gets behind the wheel and we pull out of the snow-covered driveway. Dad stops for coffee and donuts in Hudson, and then we finally begin our trek to the northernmost tip of Maine.

I watch the snow whip around the evergreen trees and rock outcroppings on the side of the highway as we drive by. On occasion, Mom says either "careful" or "easy" to

Dad, as red brake lights and giant plow trucks slow our progress. Dad repeatedly sighs and comments on the movements of the other cars. He talks directly to the cars and says things like "What are you doing, now?" and "Take a hike." He even names the other drivers or their cars on occasion by saying things like "Go jump in a lake, Harry."

I wait until we cross the border into Maine before I allow myself to fall asleep. Getting any decent sleep is difficult, as crammed into the backseat, Gregg's legs and my legs shuffle, push and kick for position. The wagon speeds up and slows down every few minutes, forcing my head back and forth, bringing me back to earth each time. For hours, I alternate between two worlds: one of vinyl seats, blankets and blizzards and one of a wheezing fevered rest.

A cough wakes me up and I reach for the white plastic Tupperware bowl at my feet. My eyes squint in the morning light as I spit the first round of phlegm into the bowl. "Morning, pumpkin," Mom says, as she hands me my antibiotic.

I look through the windshield wipers and see the snow and wind still blowing toward our wagon. I stare at the speedometer and Dad is only going thirty miles an hour.

"How long until we get to Grampy's, Dad?" I ask.

"Could be a while, son, the roads are horrible." He answers.

We're off the big highway now and on the long hilly back road that heads toward the farm. I know from past trips that the bigger the hills get, the closer we are. On this stretch the hills are still kind of small which means we have a ways to go.

Gregg wakes up and wipes the fog off his window. "Wow, look at all that snow." He says. The roads are slippery, and on occasion Gregg and I can feel the back end of the wagon begin to fishtail. Mom wants to stop at the next town and get some breakfast and coffee; Dad wants to keep driving. We end up stopping at one of the last "McDonald's" off the long hilly road to the farm. The snow isn't letting up; it's getting heavier as Dad pulls out of the parking lot, the wheels spinning on ice as the back end of the wagon slides back and forth.

I fall asleep after breakfast, and when I wake a few hours later I'm amazed at the amount of snow that has blanketed the hilly landscape. On the side of the road there are huge snowbanks that have been created by the snowplows. They are at least three or four feet high on each side of the road, making the road look like a chute with the wagon trapped inside. The hills are growing larger as we enter potato-growing country. Farmhouses and barns are surrounded by snow-covered hills and are separated by acres of fields. We pass cars and trucks that have been abandoned next to the high embankments of snow lining the side of the road.

The hills are getting very large now and the tension in the wagon begins to grow as the snow refuses to let up. Dad is getting tired and continues to sigh on a regular basis. Frustrated, he begins "talking" to a grey Buick as it tries to climb a large hill. "Get moving," he says. The driver of the grey Buick is going too slowly, and we end up right behind him as both cars struggle to get up the hill.

Gregg and I look out the rear window of the wagon. A plow truck is moving its way up the hill behind us. "Plow at the bottom of the hill, Dad, we've got to make it up or we will slide down and hit him!" Gregg yells to Dad.

Dad quickly glances into the rear-view mirror and shouts at the Buick, "Get moving, Louie, come on, gun it!" The Buick manages to just reach the top of the hill but is almost at a standstill. At the pinnacle the Buick taps its brakes, forcing Dad to do the same, just as he is about to get the wagon over the top. Dad shouts, "You bastard, don't stop now!" The wagon's wheels are spinning but somehow we make it to the top, just as the road levels out. "God bless America!" Dad cries, and we all shout and cheer.

Our cheering stops, however, as we see how many cars and trucks are stuck in snowbanks on the other side of the hill. Some of them are stuck sideways, their rear bumpers directly in our path. It's too late; our car has already started to slide. "Hold on," shouts Dad, "we're heading down!" We close our eyes and don't open them again until we are at the bottom of the hill, only to find ourselves facing another giant incline. We start up the slippery slope but begin to go back almost immediately. A red car just ahead of us is sliding backward toward us. Mom whispers, "We're in trouble now, Billy!"

We slide down the icy slope in the wagon, which feels like a huge toboggan. Father's foot frantically pounds the brake pedal with little effect as we begin to gain speed. Deftly, he maneuvers us around one of the stuck cars like a gold medal luger in the Winter Olympics. "Nice going, Dad!" I scream. Mom's right foot nervously shakes back and forth, as she chews her nails. Gregg has braced himself on the back of Mom's seat with his feet. I close my eyes and prepare for the inevitable collision, as we slide perilously downward. Amazingly, Dad whips the wagon around yet another car's rear end and we slide safely into the valley.

Dad's face is glowing. He revs the engine to try for the next hill, "Yee-ha!" he screams like a maniac. "Hold on, we're going up!"

Mom yells, "You'll get us all killed, Billy!" Sure enough, less than halfway up the hill, the wagon begins to slow and then stops completely. We start to slide down the mountain backward, the four of us screaming like kids on a roller coaster. Gregg and I look out the rear window and can't believe our eyes.

"We're going to hit the plow!" I scream. The huge metal beast is taking up both lanes of the road as it snakes its way around the stranded cars. I close my eyes and brace for the impact.

"Hold on!" Dad yells and then cuts the steering wheel sharply. The wagon fishtails to the left and we miss colliding with the plow by fractions of an inch. We come to a halt as we clap, yell and celebrate the fact that we are still alive.

Dad has had enough. He drops the transmission into drive and follows the plow back up the hill, using the rock salt it deposits on the snow-covered road for traction. This time we make it all the way up. Dad stays close to the plow for the rest of the ride to New Sweden.

"We're here, buddy." Gregg says as he nudges me awake. I pop out of my blankets and wipe the fog off the window with the palm of my hand. We pull into the long driveway and pass by the wood-carved sign that reads "Double Eagle Farm and Antique Shoppe." The double-headed eagle on the sign is partially covered in snow as it sways in the blizzard's wind. The carving depicts the eagle in midflight, swooping down as if to attack. The eagle has four eyes, each with a look of strength and determination. The meticulously carved double-headed eagle, its wings spread wide and its golden talons protruding into the storm, welcomes us to the peaceful farm. It's a great sign and one of the many reasons why I love coming to Grampy Smart's farm.

In front of the house, Grampy is shoveling the walkway that leads to the side entrance of the farmhouse. He stands tall, wide and strong in the whipping snow, a shovel gripped in his big right hand. On his head is a large, tan, rimmed military hat, the type drill sergeants wear, with a golden strand around it, tied up front in a perfect little bow. Grampy approaches the car, his heavy boots stomping through the snow like the feet of an angry giant.

"Jesus, Mary and Joseph, soldier, where in the hell have you been—we've been waiting for hours!" Grampy is at least a foot taller than my father and one hundred pounds heavier. "Well, don't just stand there, disembark for Christ's sake!" He wraps his huge arms around my father, like a great black bear wrestling in a hug. Then he sticks his huge head and sergeant's hat through the opening of the car door. "Women and children first, women and children first," he calls out, a tiny smirk beginning to form on the corners of his stern lips. "Get moving, soldiers!" he says, as the smirk widens.

I quickly gather my stuff that is thrown about the backseat of the car. I can smell the fire burning inside the house on the wind that bellows through the front door of the wagon. Grampy hugs us all and then helps Dad and Gregg grab the bags out of the back of the wagon. Mom and I grab the smaller things from inside the car, and we all push our knees through the snow toward the side door of the farmhouse. Grampy walks behind me and says, "Now be careful, little one, you've got to look out for snow snakes up here—they get pretty big up here in Maine, with their white scales and red eyes!" I laugh and then something bites me on the ass and I jump and turn around. I see Grampy's giant hand with his fat fingers in the pinch position moving away from my butt. I laugh, as he says, "Snow snakes, see, I told you!"

We make our way to the side door that houses the antique shop. "Careful with your bags, don't knock anything over," the colonel orders from under the brim of his hat. The room clearly used to be a porch or entryway until it was converted into a little room and stuffed with artifacts on tables and shelves. On one side of the room is a large dark hardwood hutch that houses a collection of tiny porcelain Hummel figurines, a few teakettles, cups and saucers and an assortment of plates, vases and bowls all splintered with time. Writing desks with lion ball feet and wood-carved bookshelves line another wall. On top are stacks of china, old records and leather-bound books with pages that are edged in gold. Dark paintings of many different shapes and sizes cover the walls, some with elaborate golden hand-carved frames, others with no frames at all. Old wooden trunks that look like treasure chests and silver-embossed platters mingle with crystal brandy decanters and carved glasses, which sit next to iron painted mechanical toy tractors and trucks and a big copper goose weathervane. A couple of German cuckoo clocks, with little carved doors that release tiny moving and cooing birds that really coo, hang next to blue and white Asian painted plates that depict pagodas, bridges, fishermen and gardens of pine and willow. "Watch the luggage," Colonel Grampy repeats kindly, as I pass a small rickety table covered in blue and pink stained glasses and bowls. I wiggle my bags and blankets through the maze of porcelain and carved wood into the kitchen where Grammy and Aunt Carrie await.

I hug Grammy next to the thick rustic dining table. My face is trapped in her bosom and my forehead rests on a silver dragonfly brooch with tiny emerald eyes. As she lets go, she asks, "How you feeling, Dean?"

"Still sick," I reply, as I walk toward Aunt Carrie for a hug. Both Grammy and my young Aunt Carrie look alike, short, soft and wide, and I can't clasp my arms all the way around either of them. We all sit at the table and Dad tells them about the ride up, while I slurp chicken noodle soup. The adults pour drinks and head into the living room. Gregg and Carrie head upstairs, but I'm not invited, so I hang back in the kitchen to finish my soup.

Gregg and Carrie, despite being nephew and aunt, are about the same age and are very close friends. They both love strong rock music, the type that people call heavy metal. They say "dude" and "cool" a lot while they talk. Every time they see each other for the first time in a while, they have this ritual of playing each other their newest favorite songs and artists. Ten minutes after they go upstairs, I hear music coming from Carrie's room and I decide to follow. Halfway up the stairs, I hear them laughing and coughing behind the heavy wooden door, while a guitar riff repeats over a heavy bass-driven rhythm. I get up my courage and knock.

There is a sudden commotion in the room — a scuttle and some scuffling combined with some frantic whispering and then Carrie says, "Hold on, I'll be right there." I stare at the bumper sticker on the door that says ENTER AT YOUR

OWN RISK, while I wait for them to open up and let me in. "Who is it?" Carrie asks from behind the locked door.

"It's me," I say, as I hear Carrie let out a heavy sigh and the latch is released.

I turn the knob and push through the door into Carrie's den of rebellion, a rock-and-roll revolt against the colonel's militaristic structure. A thick, pungent, almost skunk-like smoke fills the air in the room and penetrates my lungs. Incense burns on a makeshift coffee table, an old linen chest in front of a couch. The couch faces the stereo system where a wax record spins.

I look over at Gregg. His feet are propped up and crossed on the linen chest, and I notice that lying next to them are three sticks of dynamite taped together with a timer and wires. Next to the dynamite are a clear-glass paperweight and a large-cut crystal ashtray. I walk over and grab the sticks of dynamite and Gregg says, "Careful with that," and chuckles. I can tell by the weight of the dynamite in my hand that it's fake, but the timer and wires are real. The sticks of dynamite are made from paper towel tubes and are covered in red tissue paper.

"Where did you get this?" I ask Carrie.

"I made it in art class," she answers, proudly.

"Cool, it looks real."

I put the dynamite back down on the linen chest and grab the glass paperweight. It's clear, has a large fracture on it, and inside, trapped in the glass, written in cursive and made out of white powder is the Coca-Cola logo. I place it back on the table next to the cut-crystal ashtray.

I wake to the sound of war. A trumpeted reveille is blaring up the stairs. The tune is extremely loud and my sleep can't deny it. I toss over and look out the window as the sun just splits the earth's edge and the morning's first beams hit a group of spindly apple trees, its branches covered in snow. *There it is again.* The horn repeats its sharp notes that spread and reverberate up the stairs of the old farmhouse. It's first thing in the morning, and Grampy is gathering his troops.

I head downstairs and realize the house is trapped in a cloud. A weird light comes through the windows like fog. The big shield above the fireplace, with its set of two-handed bastard swords, reflects and mirrors the muted light. On the mantle, the faces on the dark woodcarving of the seven deadly sins look like they came up from hell, as the strange light hits them. I walk over to the window and see that the snow is covering the glass. Nothing in the landscape is visible except for the meek traces of shadow from the outside world. "Crazy," I mumble to myself, "just crazy."

Chapter 5

Apple Blossoms and Marble Chips

I'm standing in the playground during my last recess in Hudson. I lean on the chain-link fence and watch maple buds and the fresh shoots of the yew shrubs that surround the school drink up the last of the great snow. The dim of a long winter is giving way to sunshine and I watch the grass green with spring. The melting snow reflects the sun into my oversized glasses, as I squint and stare at the aged library in front of me. I'm facing away from my classmates, who don't seem to notice. *They never do*, I think to myself.

I wonder what it will be like in the new town we're moving to. Gregg is not at all happy about the idea, and I can't say that I blame him. He's popular, so why would he want to start all over with new people? I, on the other hand, could use a fresh start. I stare down at the plaid pattern of my ugly brown shirt. *This stupid cowboy shirt*, I think, *it's got to stay here in Hudson if I'm going to have any chance at all. Who wears cowboy shirts?* I look down at the annoying white polished buttons, and think, *Unreal*. I look down at the sewed-in, ropelike piping lassoed across my chest. *Yee-ha!* I shout in my head. I think I must look like the redheaded cross between John Wayne and the freckle-faced kid from *Mad* magazine. *No wonder I'm not cool,* I think to myself, staring at the old library. Gregg always wears Levi's and black rocker tee shirts. I cross my arms and place them on top of the chain-link fence, sigh deeply and rest my chin back on my forearms.

"Hey, Dean," a soft voice comes from behind me. *Oh great,* I think to myself, *this must be the last harassment, of my last recess.* I stare at the library and ignore the voice, hoping it will go away.

"Hey, Dean, I know you hear me," the soft voice says. *That's the voice of a girl,* I say to myself. *I wonder what she wants.* I quickly turn my head around to the left and my body jerks back toward the fence, trapping my cowboy shirt cuff in the metal edging of the chain link. I tug hard but it doesn't come free. The girl starts to giggle. I tug hard again and it still doesn't come free. The girl giggles again. I give one final spasmodic tug and it rips free, and I spin around like a dorky square dancer and see her laughing so hard she has to cover her mouth with her hand.

It's Christine, the smart redheaded girl that always sits in the front of the classroom, flanked by a pair of friends. *What does she want?* I ask myself. *She never talks to me, no girls do.* I look down at the playground's pavement and white-painted hopscotch court.

"Dean," she says, "I wanted to give you something before you left."

I cross my arms and sigh. I think to myself, *She's going to kick me right in the nuts.* I close my eyes and await the impact. I feel the weight of her freckled arms as she lays them over each of my shoulders. She presses her body hard against mine and every part of my body tightens, as I await the devastating crunch of her knee. Then she lays it on me.

It's not a crunch but a kiss, warm with spring sun, her thin lips pressed against mine. The contact lasts for less than a second, and when I open my eyes I see that her eyes are closed, her head tilted awkwardly to the left. She opens her eyes slowly and lets go, then turns and runs to the other side of the playground where her waiting friends greet her with smiles and giggles. The bell rings and we line up to march back into the school. I hear the three of them whispering at the front of the line, but I can't stop smiling and my eyes feel dizzy. *Last recess,* I think, *best one ever!*

I turn around in the backseat of the wagon and watch my old life whizz by. First the playground, then the old library, then the Moonie Manor glides away, as we make our way north up Route 102. As we head past the speedway, I start to really worry about what it is going to be like in a whole new town. "This freaking sucks," I mutter to myself, a bit too loud, as I catch Dad looking at me sternly through the large rear-view mirror.

"Where's Gregg?" I ask, trying to change the subject.

"He's at his friend's house." Dad answers. "He'll come to the new house later, when he's done saying goodbye."

"I'm not done saying goodbye." I mumble to myself, thinking about Christine and my first kiss. Dad doesn't hear me. I turn around and look over the vinyl backseat at cardboard boxes taped at the top and labeled neatly by Mom, "Upstairs Kitchen" and "Boys Bedroom." Hudson fades away behind a hill as I watch through the back window. All at once it hits me that we are really leaving. I don't want Dad or Mom to see me cry and quickly wipe away the tears that are starting to form.

Yellow lines flash by as Dad slows the wagon and takes a left. I read the green street sign on the corner, High Range Road, as the old wagon winds us up another hill. "Almost there." Dad says, as he takes a right onto Adam's Road.

I turn around in the backseat and face forward as the car makes it way down our new street. An old tan farmhouse sits on the right side at the top of the hill near the road sign. Across from the farmhouse is a huge McIntosh apple orchard in spring bloom. The stunted apple trees sprout thousands of tiny white flowers off twisted and craggy branches. Row after row of apple trees force a whispered "wow" out to me.

Mom lets out an appreciative sigh. "How pretty."

"You know, Judy," Dad says, "you can see the orchard from the house."

"Ma, after I help you unpack, can I go for a bike ride?" I ask.

"Sure you can, honey, if we are done before dark."

The orchard ends at a little pond that drains and crosses in a stream under the road before our house. Dad turns the steering wheel to the right and we head up the steep incline of the new driveway. Our new house sits on a hill and looks a bit intimidating as it stares down at us. It seems to be held back by a long horizontal row of railroad ties that end flush at the driveway. "It's big, huh." I say.

"Oh yeah," Dad replies proudly, "it's got two real fireplaces, son."

Behind the house and all around the drive are towering white pines that drape the house with a sky full of green. Tall pines crowd us, as we make our way up the low driveway. I finally understand why Mom raised such a fuss about having the house repainted from a gray slate blue to a sunshine-like yellow—so that it would clearly stand out against the evergreen backdrop. The contractor and Dad were not pleased with the repainting ordered from Mom, but that's just how she is; if she wants the new house repainted yellow, it gets repainted yellow, despite being freshly painted blue, weeks earlier. Dad stops the car in front of the railroad ties, and I hear Mom sigh again, but this time it's a sigh of frustration. "The painter still isn't finished," she says, "William, look." She points to a section on the left side of the house that's still blue.

"He'll finish, Judith, don't worry." He plops the wagon's transmission into park.

Dad quickly whips the trunk open and begins handing out boxes. He hands Mom a small box labeled "Downstairs Kitchen" and she carries it toward the house. Next, he hands me a large box that reads "Boys Bedroom." He grabs the largest box, "Upstairs Kitchen, Pots and Pans." I follow him to the front steps of the house as he juggles the heavy box. The steps are made of railroad ties and backfilled with tiny white pebbles that crunch under my sneakers.

Mom stops at the front door, places her box on the steps and begins fishing in her pocketbook for the key. I stand behind her, waiting. Dad comes clanging up the stairs behind me, juggling the heavy box of pots and pans. He presses the box into my back and shakes it, causing the pans to clang off me. I start giggling as Dad pretends to be annoyed with Mom. "What's the holdup?" He asks. Mom pulls out the key and tries it. It doesn't fit and we laugh. "Let's get moving, Louie." Dad says. She tries the next key and has no luck. I'm turning red now, and Mom is laughing so hard her hands are shaking and she drops the key ring. "You're slower than molasses," Dad whines. Mom finally turns the knob and opens the door on the fourth try.

"You're a bunch of fruitcakes!" she shouts as she opens the door. She swings the box through the open doorway, steps in and yells, "The dingbats are home!"

I step through the doorway and catch my breath. The entry foyer is bigger than any I've ever seen. Just beyond, a staircase leads to the second story, then splits and changes direction halfway up, creating a little landing, just like in the big houses on television. As I stand and stare, Dad brushes past and heads up the stairs with his pots and pans still clanging. "What are you waiting for—Christmas?" He asks as he gets to the top.

I figure my bedroom must be upstairs somewhere, but when I carry my box up the stairway I find myself in what appears to be a living room. Mom has furnished it with a gigantic round couch covered with a palm-tree print. In front of the couch is an ultramodern glass-top coffee table with circular steel legs. "Mom," I yell, "where's my bedroom?"

"Down here," she calls from the other side of the house, "on the left." I head down the hallway toward her voice, as I peer over the low railing into the foyer below.

My new bedroom looks cool and features more of Mom's outlandish modern furniture. The twin beds are decked out in a futuristic swirled-print bedspread and pillowcases in varying shades of blue. The beds form an L in the corner, connected by a large wood table with stainless-steel corners and built-in stereo speakers. *Cool.* Each bed has a set of big matching triangular pillows that are propped up against the wall, making the beds look like long sofas. *Really cool*, I think, as I take it all in.

Mom walks in with a big white trash bag in her hand. "What do you think about your room, pumpkin?"

"Really nice, Mom, and the beds are wicked cool."

She drops the trash bag in the corner near the closet. "This is for all the trash from the packing—okay, honey."

I shake my head yes, "Thanks, Mom."

I plug in the stereo and put on the Rolling Stones and begin unpacking my clothes into a new black lacquer bureau. I rip open box after box until I finally get to the last one. Tearing off the packing tape that holds it together, I spread open the cardboard flaps and stare down at its contents in horror. *The monstrosity lives,* I think to myself, *everyone run for your lives!* I force myself to look again and see it laying there, folded perfectly, its pearly little buttons winking at me in the sunlight. I rip it out of the box and hoist it high into the air. As I hold it there, a flash of brilliance comes over me. I whip the shirt across the room and it lands right on top of the trash bag. *Good, right where it belongs.* I stomp over to the shirt, grab it and stuff it way down into the trash bag, then cover it up with packing paper, tie the top shut and turn up the radio.

I finish unpacking and stare out the window, listening to the Stones. The house is so high up on a bluff that from the window I can see the very tops of three pine trees that grow on the side of the hill. The side of the hill must be thirty or forty feet below the window. *It's like I'm in a skyscraper or something.* I stare at the swamp at the bottom of the hill. The three pines seem to hold the hill back and stop it from falling into the swamp.

I head down the stairs and find Mom unpacking the pots and pans in the kitchen. "I'm done now, Mom. Can I go for a bike ride?" I ask.

"All cleaned up, too?" She asks.

"Everything, except for the trash bag," I answer.

"Well, bring it out here with the others, and then you can go, okay?"

I head to my room and grab the trash bag, thinking about the monster that's stuffed down in the bag beneath mounds of paper. *It's gone, gone for good,* I think, as I walk the bag out to the living room and toss it on top of the other bags. I run down the stairs and find my old red bike resting against a wall in the utility room. I wheel it through the den and into the foyer and just as I'm about to open the front door, Mom's voice booms from the landing. "Dean John Smart, get your butt up these stairs immediately!" She is holding the cowboy shirt in her hand, dangling it above the foyer. *Oh, no – the monster lives!*

I try to defend myself but it sounds feeble, even to me. "I didn't mean to throw it out," I sputter.

"What a bunch of baloney, you didn't mean to throw it out! I suppose it jumped out of the box and threw itself away, huh? Am I supposed to believe that? You get in your room, mister – you're grounded."

An hour later, after conjuring up a tearful apology, I'm pedaling in circles around the bottom of our new driveway. There's so much to do here – so many new things to explore. I decide to get off my bike and check out the small stream that drains the pond across the pavement. I watch the silver water flow through a metal pipe that goes under the street. I stare at spiderlike bugs that skim and jump across the top of the water as they make tiny ripples. I hop across the stream on some flat boulders half submerged and zigzag my way down the banks until I get to a section that's too wide to cross and is loaded with prickly bushes. The stream turns to swamp as it widens and is covered in grasslike stumps. It's getting darker, so I jump my way back to my bike. As I hop on the seat, I hear some kids playing and talking up the street. They sound pretty close, maybe a few houses away. I decide to go the other way. Maybe it's still light enough for me to check out the orchard.

Just as I arrive, the sun falls behind the pines and maples that border the back of the orchard. I drop my bike and stare at the apple trees. I'm surprised to see that they have almost no leaves and their branches are covered in tiny white flowers with a bit of a soft red in their centers. Row after row of distorted trunks and twisted branches overwhelm me. They remind me of the old trees that always front the yard of haunted houses. I decide it's too dark and too freaky to take a walk inside the orchard. Instead, I just stand there for a while. As it gets darker, the orchard seems to glow ever so lightly. *Weird*, I think, *it's glowing — very strange*. I watch awhile longer as the tiny flowers light up the night. Finally, even standing there is too creepy. The strange uncontrollable glow of the orchard forces me back on my bike, and I head up the street, toward our new house.

I decide to check out the other direction. I pass by our driveway and start pedaling up a big hill. Halfway up, the hill is beating me. I start to run out of air, as a big truck whizzes by. I hop off my bike and walk it to the top. I'm huffing and puffing, as my glasses slide down my nose on sweat. Then, on the wind, I hear the voices of the kids I heard before. I turn and spot them sitting on the front steps of a big yellow house at the top of the hill. They are older than me—high school age, maybe. They stare at me as I get back on my bike. The biggest one with long hair says something to the others. All three start laughing. One of them with blond hair has a handful of little rocks and he's whipping them and pinging them off the walkway while he laughs. "Ten points," I hear him say to the others, looking in my direction. *Uh-oh.*

I peel out, pedaling as fast as I can down the street. I'm too slow and the barrage begins. A marble chip pings the pavement on my right and bounces into the spin of my front spoke. Another chip lands far ahead of my bike. A third whizzes by my head. I catch one on my leg and realize they are honing in. I start weaving the bike back and forth in S's to avoid the bombardment. Suddenly, I'm hit, smack-dab in the forehead, *Damn.* I make a sharp S turn and it causes the handlebars to swing back toward me and lock up. I dump the bike, roll on the pavement and sit up as quickly as I can, feeling my forehead for damage. My hand drips red with blood.

I look up at the kids and they have their mouths wide open in shock. "Oh shit!" the big one says. And all at once they scatter, running into the backyard and woods behind the yellow house. I jump up, grab one of the marble chips off the street and whip it as hard as I can at them. But, they're too far away and my weak throw bounces miserably nine feet away in the grass.

I pick up my bike and mumble angrily to myself, "Frigging dickheads, I'm gonna need stitches." I coast back down the hill, one hand on the handlebars and the other on my forehead that won't stop bleeding. I drop my bike at the bottom of the driveway and walk up the hill to the front door.

"Mom, I got hurt." I cry, as I walk up the foyer stairs. She comes out of the kitchen and lets out a gasp. "Ahhhhh, what happened?"

"Fell off my bike, Mom. I'm okay, don't worry." I make my way to the bathroom to get a towel.

She follows me in, cleans out the wound with hot water and soap in front of the mirror and says, "It's just a little cut, but it bleeds a lot, huh, pumpkin, not deep, no stitches, don't worry. How do you get yourself into these predicaments, monkey face?"

"I don't know, Mom," I say, "I don't know."

Gregg sticks his head into the bathroom and says, "Nice going, bonehead—way to ride, should we call you Evel Knievel from now on?"

"That's enough, Gregg," Mom says. "He's been through enough today, all right."

Just then, the doorbell rings. It goes through like five tones, sort of like a cuckoo clock. Bing, bong, ping, dong, ding. "Doorbell's cool." I say to Mom, as I wash the blood off my hands in the sink.

"I wonder who it is," she says, as she walks out of the bathroom and heads to the front door.

I stand at the top of the stairs and look down over the balcony. As Mom swings the door open, I can't believe my eyes. *It's the frigging dickheads.* Mom smiles sweetly. "Well, what can I do for you, young men?" she asks.

"We wanted to talk to your son, if it's okay, ma'am," the big sweaty kid in the jean jacket says. The blond kid looks up at me and smiles, as he takes off his baseball hat.

"Oh wonderful, how nice," Mom says, as she looks up at me. "Come on down and say hello to these nice boys, pumpkin."

I turn around, whip the towel into the bathroom, clench my teeth and stomp down the stairs. Mom gives me one of her looks.

"Hi, I'm Dean," I say to the largest one in the jean jacket, as I extend my hand. He's a monster, twice as tall as me easy. He grabs my hand while I look way up at him.

"Pat," he says slowly, like Frankenstein's monster, as his grip crushes my small hand. I manage to slip out of his grasp.

Gregg heads down the stairs and introduces himself and before I know it the foyer is filled with handshakes all around. It turns out Gregg and Pat are the same age and that all three of them live close by. "We're playing wiffle ball tomorrow, up at my place," Pat says. "It's the next one on up the road. Come on over."

"Sure," I respond, still mystified by the end to a day I never expected.

Part Two

When the McIntosh Flower

Chapter 6

Wiffle Ball and Waterfalls

Mom and Dad are out having dinner and Gregg's girlfriend from Hudson is coming over for a visit to our new house. When she shows up, Gregg runs down the stairs. I watch his blue eyes light up like a neon sign, as he sees her come through the front door. I sit on the couch in the TV room downstairs where I have a good view of the two of them standing in the foyer. I watch Gregg kiss her softly and hold her in his arms for a long time. She is something else, a beauty with big dark brown eyes and dark straight hair, long and shining. I can't take my eyes off her. I open them wide and blink them repeatedly. Her tight jeans trap me. Gregg must know I'm watching. He calls out to me, "Hey, buddy, we're going upstairs to, umm, listen to some music, all right?"

"All right, Gregg, see you later." The two of them run up the stairs and I'm left alone. I hear the music start playing.

I decide to head to my writing spot. It's on the main floor, at the end of a hallway that appears to lead to nowhere, just past the den. The hallway is cozy and I feel good in it; it's my own special place in our new house. I sit down at the small desk and stare into the freshly painted white wall, Grampy Bellevue's old typewriter in front of me. There's not much ink left on the ribbon and some of the keys clash before they strike the paper. I try to tap out a few sentences but can't get my mind off Gregg and his girlfriend. *I wonder what they're doing up there.*

I decide to find out. I walk up the foyer stairs. I stand at our bedroom door for a second and hear them giggling to the music. I "accidentally" open the door and just sort of walk in. "Dean!" Gregg yells, "You've got to knock!" They're stretched across Gregg's twin bed and they both scramble to pull up the covers, but not before I see things, her things, flashes of them tangled between the bedspread and sheets. Gregg is smiling. He looks happy, despite my interruption. "All right, junior, you've seen enough." He says kind of smirking. "Now get out of here, Dean, I mean it." I think to myself, *He must really like this girl.* I take one last look at her and walk back out the door, the image of her half-naked in Gregg's bed stuck in my mind. *I wonder if he's in love with her.*

I go back to my desk in my strange little hallway to nowhere. I stare at the texture of the white drywall directly ahead of me. The white of it seems to send me into some sort of dream state where I can imagine things more vividly. My dream moment is interrupted by the sound of Dad's car pulling into the driveway. I yell a warning up to Gregg, "Dad and Mom are home!"

Later, as we lay in our beds, Gregg sits up and says, "Hey, junior, you still awake?"

"Yeah, Gregg, why—what's up?"

He looks me right in the eyes and smiles. "You know, buddy, you didn't have to do that," he says.

"Sorry, Gregg, I didn't mean to barge in on you guys. I'm sorry, buddy." I think to myself, *Oh, man, he's pissed at me.*

"Oh no, not that," he answers. "That's not a big deal. I meant that you didn't have to yell up and tell us that Mom and Dad were home. Nice job, Dean. You saved my ass! Thanks, buddy."

"No problem, Gregg." Gregg lays his head back down on his pillow.

"You really like her, huh?" I ask.

"Yeah, she's really nice, man. *Really* nice, you know what I mean?"

"Yeah, she's nice all right. *Really* nice." I start laughing.

"Oh yeah, buddy, you think so, huh, you *really* like my girl, huh? I think—it's time—time you get the finger of death." *Oh, no,* I think to myself, *not again.* The finger of death is Gregg's new finishing maneuver that he uses whenever we wrestle or fight. He got it from an old karate movie that featured a hero who used the "finger of death" to destroy his opponents. In the movie, the hero would hit his enemies with just his pointer finger, extended from his fist and supported by his thumb. Once he hit the bad guys with this move, they totally dropped or went flying through the air, even though he had barely tapped them.

Gregg jumps out of bed, his "finger of death" poised above me before he strikes. He leaps on top of me and pins my elbows to the bed under his knees and begins his finger torture while he lets out a sinister laugh. He taps the center of my chest with his extended pointer finger over and over until it "kills," but both of us can't stop laughing. He taunts me in his karate voice while tapping, "Oh, little junior likes my girlfriend, does he?" He keeps tapping and we start laughing really loud. "You die," he says, "you die, my girlfriend liker."

"Enough!" I say. "I can hardly breathe, from laughing."

Dad opens the door, and yells, "What the hell is going on in here — get to bed, you two, it's late."

We both answer, "Okay, Dad." Gregg jumps off me and I catch my breath. After a few minutes, he looks over at me and says, "Seriously, buddy, thanks — good night, man."

"Good night, Gregg."

He comes home early one night after going to Hudson. He stomps up the stairs in the foyer and goes straight into our bedroom without saying hi. Mom and Dad don't seem to know what to do. I jump up and run into the foyer and say, "I'll go." I'm up the stairs before they have a chance to say anything.

I open the door to our bedroom and find him sitting at the end of the bed near his pillow, his head down. He looks up at me and I can see his face is red and he has been crying. "Get the hell out of here, Dean," he says. I'm not sure what to do, so I stand there for a second, looking at him. His head drops lower and I watch a tear fall onto the blue bedspread. "Get out!" he yells.

"All right, buddy," I say, and I walk toward the door and turn the doorknob.

He sputters out, "She broke up with me and I didn't even do anything." I stand still and turn around to face him. He repeats back at me, "I didn't even do anything."

"Wow, crazy." I answer. "What happened?" I ask him while he cries.

"Nothing, Dean, that's the thing." He answers and wipes his tears with the back of his hand.

"Crazy." I sit down next to him on the bed.

"That's not the worst of it."

"What?" I ask. He huffs a breath and tries to spit it out.

"She's . . . she's . . . ," he can't seem to say it, and starts crying even more, "she's going out with my best friend." He sighs very hard. "I got to be alone for a while, buddy," he says, and he taps me on the back.

For a while it seems like nothing can help Gregg or make him smile, so I'm relieved when one day he asks if I want to go play wiffle ball. I follow him to the field near our new house, hoping a game will bring him out of his misery.

The wiffle-ball field is really just a large rectangle of grass that ends opposite a big red barn. At the other end is Adam's Road. We walk up the hill and stand together at the edge of the field. An old radio hanging on the siding of the barn sings the Doobie Brothers over and over. The neighbors, the same kids that threw the pebbles at me, see us standing there and ask us to play with them.

We choose sides and Gregg says he'll pitch. Kenny, Pat's much smaller brother, takes infield and I take the outfield. Kenny says, "We'll rotate every inning, okay?" We agree and he hands the plastic slotted ball to Gregg who has no trouble retiring the side.

I'm the first up to bat for our side. Of course, I strike out. Kenny bats next and manages a single. Gregg is up to bat, facing big Pat, and I'm glad to see him smiling again. He takes a couple strikes and smiles back at me and winks. On the next pitch he knocks it over the field, over Adam's Road and onto Kenny's lawn across the street, for a two-run homer. *Way to go, Gregg!* I watch as he rounds the foul line near third base. As he crosses home plate, he high-fives me and gives me a hug, as if we just won the World Series. We keep playing until darkness covers the field.

School in Londonderry is not the same as it was in Hudson. The students are all divided up into small groups. There are the preps, the jocks, the rockers, the punk kids. It's a big puzzle that my piece somehow doesn't fit in. Seems to me, they are also bigger than the kids at my old school, cooler too. I arrive, unnoticed, the pearl buttons of my cowboy shirt reflecting everything around it, sitting alone in the back corner of a quiet classroom.

My grades drop. I score an F in math class and I am afraid to show my report card to Mom and Dad. It's printed on a computer, not handwritten like at my old school. I sit with it in the strange little hallway to nowhere, wondering what to do. I search around for an ink pen that is half out of ink, one that will write a light grey. I need the perfect pen that will match the tiny computer-generated ink dots and turn my "F" into a "B." I find one somewhere that seems like it'll work. I practice copying the F over and over onto thin tan math-class paper. I realize I'll need an eraser, just in case I make a horrible mistake. I need a good one that can erase ink. I check in an old art kit stored in the closet of my bedroom, and find one that seems pretty good. I practice changing Fs to Bs on a separate piece of paper, while my report card lays hidden in the bottom desk drawer. I reason that if I get caught I'll get grounded forever, but I'm going to get grounded for the F anyway.

I open up the bottom drawer of the desk and pull out the report card. Carefully, I press the pen tip to the top of the F and gently make the F into a squared-off B. I lift the pen off the paper and look at it. The shape is nearly perfect, just like the "real" computer-generated ink-dot Bs. But, as my eyes back away from the report card to get a look from a distance, the outer loops of the B that I created look too dark, compared to the ink on the rest of the report card. *Oh, man*, I think to myself, *I'm going to get busted.*

I pull my head back for a longer view. The new B still looks too dark. "Damn," I mumble to myself. Then I think, *Wait a second, maybe I can lighten it — yeah — with the eraser!* I sit back down and grab the eraser, *I've got to be gentle, I can't tear the report card.* I lightly drag the eraser just over the part of the B that I added with the pen. It lightens up the ink just a bit. "Yes!" I shout at the end of the hallway. "Just a little bit more." I drag the eraser over the B until I'm totally satisfied. *Wow, it looks great, totally real, I did it!* I study my handiwork for a few minutes, then stuff the report card back into the bottom drawer of the desk and wait for supper.

I sit down at the kitchen table and slide the report card over to Dad before Mom has a chance to bring in the dinner plates. Dad is in the habit of sitting at the end of the glass table. Sometimes, he goes over his paperwork, drinks coffee and smokes. Tonight he is sitting and staring out the sliding glass door to the backyard and the woods behind it. I watch him grab the report card off the table and put his reading glasses on. "You've got to sign at the bottom," I say to him.

My heart is pounding, as I watch his eyes go over the report card. Finally, he places it back on the table and he reaches in his shirt pocket for his favorite gold pen. I think to myself, *Magnificent, he can't tell.* He twists open his pen and lowers it toward the report card — then, to my horror, he lifts the pen back up and looks me square in the eyes. *I'm dead. He knows.* Slowly, his mouth opens to speak.

"Son," he says, "you have to — keep these grades up, monkey face." He signs the bottom of the report card with a flourish and slides it back across the table in my direction. He lights a cigarette and stares out at the backyard.

The next morning I hand in the report card. I'm sitting in math class and staring out the window, and I see Dad's wagon pull in the school driveway. I watch him park and stride toward the main office in his light-blue polyester suit and wide plaid tie. He has a serious look on his face. *Uh-oh, this can't be good.* A moment later a voice comes over the intercom. "Dean Smart to the office, please."

Every kid in class responds with the traditional, "Ooowww!" A few say, "Oh Smart's in trouble!" One shouts, "The new kid's busted!" I walk to the office and hear them snickering from all the way down the hall.

I have to sit through a stern lecture from the principal, but somehow, Dad doesn't seem as angry as I expected him to be. We walk to the car in silence, but there's a little spring in his step. I slide into the front seat of the wagon next to him.

"What the hell were you thinking?" Dad finally asks, trying to sound stern. He puts on his huge mirrored Clint Eastwood sunglasses and turns his head to check the rear window. He turns the key in the ignition and backs the wagon out of the parking spot.

"I don't know, Dad, it was stupid."

"Well, you got that right; it was stupid. You can't forge things — people go to jail for that, you know."

"I know, Dad, it was stupid. I'm sorry."

"I don't know how the hell you came up with this crazy scheme, son."

"I don't know either, Dad, I don't know either." On the whole ride home I'm waiting to hear his punishment or waiting for him to start screaming, but he just keeps listening to the radio, as we drive past the apple orchards. Every once and a while he looks at me and chuckles to himself through his Paul Newman moustache.

Finally, he says, "Wait until your mother gets a load of this one. Oh, she's going to love it." We both start laughing as we pull into the driveway. I think to myself, getting out of the car, *I'm not even getting grounded, I can't believe it.*

I am, however, forced into a nightly study group with Mom at the kitchen table. We work some nights until dark. It takes several long "nights of division," but I eventually turn my F in math class to a C- for real. For what seems like weeks, Mom and Dad tell anyone who will listen about their scheming little forger. They all seem to get a kick out of it.

One day I'm wrestling with one of the neighbors before a wiffle-ball game. We're only "fake wrestling" but I land on my arm the wrong way and end up with a hairline fracture. They put me to sleep at the hospital, and when I wake up, my arm is in a cast and I learn I'm not allowed to play ball for a month and will have a cast on my arm for six months, maybe more.

After a few days of nothing to do, I'm bored. I wander around down near the culvert and the swamp, searching for something interesting. I hop across the stream and swamp, jumping across hummocks. The hummocks look like heavy metal hairdos that pop out of the water. I step on top of their heads and travel over the water. I soak a sneaker every once in a while when the hummocks sink on me. I pull my sneakers out of the cold water and shake them off and continue back and forth across the bog. I challenge myself over and over again with more difficult routes and farther jumps across the hummocks on the swamp. Sometimes my sneaker sinks so deep in the mud that when I try to pull my foot out, there is a sloshing sound and all I pull out is a drenched sock.

I find a concrete waterfall, past the swamp, where the bog and stream drain out and fall into a small sand-bottomed pond. The waterfall is man-made and constructed of high and thin concrete slabs, built into an edge, at the low end of the orchard. On the top of the concrete walls, there is a small V-shaped duct that the water flows through, from the pond above it. I sit on the concrete edge and watch it drain while I eat tart McIntosh apples from the orchard until my belly aches. There are little crayfish at the bottom where the swamp water splashes. I can't catch a single one of the tiny lobsters with my hand. I end up watching the apple cores float around as the water splashes off the concrete waterfall, while trying not to get my cast wet. A mist rises and rains, and I head home.

Gregg gets his driver's license and buys himself an old beater, a Volkswagen Beetle that's rusty, orange and without heat. One night he's out at a party and has too many drinks, and on his way home he drives the Beetle into a pond. Gregg tells the police that there was a bee in the car that caused him to drive off the road. He makes the police laugh when he says, "Look, there's a huge orange *beetle* in the pond." He tells the tale so convincingly that all he gets is a pat on the shoulder from the police and a stern lecture from Dad.

Dad is mad at Gregg but can't help but be impressed with his smooth-talking coolness. The next night at supper he tells Gregg he should sell insurance, as he does, and that he will help pay for the car repair. "Just keep smiling, Greggory, the car will be all right." Dad turns to Mom and says, "Like father, like son—huh, Jude?"

"Yeah, the nut doesn't fall far from the tree." Mom answers.

Gregg gets his car back and I don't see him a lot that summer. He barely ever plays wiffle ball with us anymore. He gets a job clearing brush up at the orchard near our house, and at night he's off doing his own high school things.

We don't get to spend much time together until just before Christmas when Mom and Dad take a weeklong vacation in Atlantic City and Gregg and I get to spend the week over at our brother Rick's. Rick is married now, and we have a good time with him and his wife, Sue. We rent movies, go to the arcade and eat a lot of good pizza from Bob's in Nashua.

Unfortunately, while we are all gone, the house in Londonderry is robbed, and all of our Christmas presents are taken—even the new motocross dirt bike Mom and Dad had bought for Gregg. "It just doesn't seem right to steal a family's Christmas presents," Mom keeps repeating over and over.

A week or so later the police recover Gregg's motor-cycle from Robinson Pond. It's wrecked and, unlike his car, it can't be fixed. Gregg tells Mom and Dad not to worry about buying him another one because he probably won't have that much time for riding it anyway.

Chapter 7

Crossroads and Circled Stones

Dad has hung an old speed bag from his boxing days in the utility room downstairs, and I spend a lot of time hitting it. He's hoping I can strengthen my left arm. I'm slowly catching the rhythm of the speed bag and growing quicker. I want some music, so I grab a little cassette-deck radio. I plug it in and listen to an old tape that Aunt Carrie gave me. I swing away at the speed bag and listen to Grandmaster Flash and the Furious Five and the Sugarhill Gang. Over and over again, I hit the speed bag while the beat plays on. I like the new electric music; it's funky. I keep hitting the half-deflated speed bag, to the beat. I hit it every night after dinner and after my homework's done. I still can't hit it smoothly, like liquid, as Dad does. He taps it gently, but rough enough so that it bounces back to him in perfect time. First lefts, then rights, back and forth, he is a smooth stream as he hits the speed bag. He says, "Keep practicing, son, you'll get it."

There is a stuffed pheasant listening to Grandmaster Flash's "The Message" with me. It is another one of Gregg's trophies. It's been mounted on a carved and polished piece of oak, as if it's flying. One wing extended, the other is tucked behind its body, pressed to the wood. It's beginning to rot, in the musty dank of the utility room. On top of old cardboard boxes, it's been thrown, covered in dust, its fake marble eye, translucent black, staring at me, while I gain my timing on the speed bag.

Grampy and Grammy Smart come from Maine for a visit; they stay at the Howard Johnson's hotel in Nashua. It's got an indoor in-ground pool, surrounded by a huge glass greenhouse. The restaurant attached has good waffles for breakfast.

We swim in the middle of winter, as if we are on vacation. The greenhouse and water are warm. I watch Mom in her one-piece black bathing suit. She goes to the concrete steps at the shallow end. She steps down on the first step, reaches her hand into the water and splashes it on her wrists, each hand wetting the other. She splashes it a second later onto each of her legs and the top of her body. Wrapped in a thick white towel, I sit on a reclining sun chair, and the plastic strips on the bottom of the chair press itchy red stripes into the underside of my legs. I watch as Mom splashes the water up around the back of her neck.

Down another step into the water goes Mom. She pauses and re-splashes like a little bird preening itself proudly in a concrete birdbath. Sunlight diffused through winter sky comes through the foggy greenhouse window and lights up the tiny flashes of water on Mom's freckled skin. The room is silent. Mom is ready to swim. Smoothly leaning over, she slides into the water, barely making a ripple. It is a sight to see, my mother swimming. She's like a gold medal, Olympic synchronized swimmer. Her hairdo moves as a smooth swan across a pond. It's as if she is floating through space effortlessly. Her hair doesn't get wet, and it's as Dad says, "Your mother is the only woman I've ever known to swim and not get her hair wet and to wake up in the morning without a single hair out of place." Her hands flow through the water, gliding her across the top of the pool. She breathes smoothly, inhaling and exhaling in perfect rhythm with the strokes of her arms. She makes a graceful turn at the end of the pool, rests her hands on the concrete edge and sighs out a deep breath.

She looks up at me. "This is nice, huh, pumpkin."

"Yeah, Mom, I love swimming, this is great." She smiles and slides away backward from the concrete edge. She is just as smooth swimming backward, heading to where she started.

"Come on," she says to me, "let's have a swim." I walk to the edge; she swims a bit away from it and I sit down and dangle my feet in the water. She glides back across the pool and grabs my ankles, then floats in front of me, her feet kicking gently behind her. Instantly, I'm taken back to the memory of Mom and me swimming years ago, as I was learning. We were outside on a sunny day at some public pool, and I had held her ankles as she now holds mine.

"Come on in and swim." She says, again. I've been swimming all afternoon and my fingers are like raisins. As I wiggle my way toward the water, Mom reaches up for me as she used to do when I was a kid. I feel her hands lift me up from under my shoulders—something I haven't felt in years. She slides me into the water smoothly, and turns me around to face the length of the pool. She pushes me away softly, and I swim smoothly across the water away from her. I turn around and smile at her while she watches me, grinning.

I strut up the road, a pair of my crazy swimming shorts in my backpack. I like to swim in crazy shorts, the type with wacky floral designs in the Hawaiian or Japanese style. When I swim, it is vacation party time. I don a thick white towel, draped around my neck, as I swagger down Adam's Road. *This is cool,* I think. The two new cute sisters who just moved up the road have invited me over to swim in their pool. *I'm heading for my swim with the babes,* I think. *Yeah, I must be cool.*

Suddenly the sky darkens and I get nervous and stop walking. *What if they laugh at me when I take off my shirt? What if they make fun of my scrawny chest and arms?* I think about what Gregg would do. *Gregg would never turn down a chance to go swimming with the chicks.* I start walking again, gaining back my confidence. I say to myself, "I'm going swimming with the babes, it'll be all right."

When I get there one of "the babes" walks me back to a sunroom where they have been watching *Tom and Jerry* cartoons on an old TV. I take a look at the pool and the slide out of the window and it looks nice. The older sister says to me, "You can change down here in the bathroom; we'll change into our swimsuits upstairs."

"All right," I say. I walk into the bathroom near the kitchen, and shut and lock the door behind me. Suddenly, as I stand there getting my shorts out of my backpack, I feel sort of strange and excited. I think to myself, *There are two pretty girls, just above me, taking their clothes off.* I imagine them, in slow motion, sliding their tight jeans off and standing there in white panties.

Three knocks bounce off the bathroom door. "Almost ready," I shout too loud toward the door. I check myself one last time in the mirror, and I'm ready to go.

The pool is warm as I jump in with my white tee shirt still on. The three of us swim and play Marco Polo for a while. Then the little sister leaves and I'm cornered in the shallow end with the older one and she presses on me. Instantly I feel myself getting excited, and even though I wouldn't mind kissing her, I quickly jump out of the pool. "I'm getting cold," I say to her, standing on the edge of the pool, "let's, umm, play basketball, all right?"

She gives me a puzzled look. "Okay, I guess, but I've got to change first. There's a ball in the garage."

I go to the garage and search around for a basketball. I find one and start shooting nervously for the basket. As I run to the hoop for a basket, I slip on a circle of oily pavement. My feet come out from under me and I fall, like I'm going to land on my ass, but I land instead on the hand I've reached out behind me to soften the fall. Instantly, I feel my arm snap, right along the same spot where I broke it before. "Damn!" I scream. I'm in excruciating pain as I look down at my left arm, which is now twisted like an image in a warped circus mirror. On the inside of my arm, between my elbow and my wrist, the bone is pressing through the skin of my forearm. My left hand is bent backward and won't move, no matter how many times I try. *Call home*, I think to myself.

I start walking back down Adam's Road in a daze. I can't look at my arm—and I can't not look at it. I cover it with my sweatshirt but keep pulling it off to take another look. It's fucked. *My left arm is gone*, I think to myself. Dad picks me up halfway home and drives me to the hospital in

Derry. "Cover it up, buddy. It will be okay, just keep smiling," he says.

We get to the hospital and the doctor x-rays it and looks at me weird. He says he has to set it and it may take a while. I say okay as the throbbing pain in it seems to have gone numb, from the shot he gave me. He takes hold of my arm and places it on the bed in the room we are in. He places a flat plastic board under it. He adjusts and readjusts my arm on the board, looks at me and says, "This is going to hurt, a lot. Can you do it?"

"I can do it." He presses on it, pushing the bone that sticks up, down.

"Ahh!" I scream. The doctor twists my wrist back to a somewhat normal position. There are crunching and scraping noises, and I start to see little white sparkling dots everywhere.

"Let's have a look. Off to x-ray," the doctor says.

Five minutes later, he stares at the x-rays and says, "Nope, not yet, one more time." He sets my throbbing arm again. Fifteen times he sets and x-rays until he thinks he's got it. Finally, I am re-casted and the doctor says, "It needs to stay on for at least six months."

On the ride home Dad picks up some pizzas for us. My arm feels every little bump our wagon bounces over, and I can't help but think, *I'm starting over, healing from another break.*

At dinner Dad and I tell Mom and Gregg about what happened. I tell them my arm was bent really weird, like Rubber Man's arm and everybody laughs. Dad says he couldn't believe that I didn't pass out. He sounds proud of me.

That night I get to bed early but am awakened a short while later by a nightmare. I'm at the hospital and the doctor that set my arm has an anvil and big mallet-type hammer. He keeps placing my broken arm on the anvil and smacking it with the hammer over and over again. Each time he hits it the bone seems to go back in place, but then a second later the bone pops out again and he has to re-hit it. "Almost done," he keeps saying, but he is never done.

Behind our house to the left of the swamp, a stone wall crisscrosses across the forest. I am walking on it, knocking loose mossy granite onto the ground. In a ravine, with two hills on the left and right, I see something that doesn't look like the rest of the wall. A shelter of rock veers off from the wall, in a circle. *What can it be?* I wonder. *Did someone live here? Sleep here?* I picture someone watching the woods from inside the circle of stones, under the storms. If they faced the opening in the circle of rocks, this had to be the door that overlooked the hill that slanted down to the pond and swamp. The wall isn't that tall—maybe three feet. Maybe it was covered with broken branches and hemlock bows, like an Indian wigwam or rock teepee of some sort. Maybe it was built by early colonists, or maybe even before that.

I start digging around inside the circle of rocks, hoping to find an ancient relic or anything that will confirm my theory. I rake away leaves and pine needles with my hand. I find a few rusty old beer cans and lots of toppled rocks that have fallen from the wall. I start placing them back on top in places where they won't wiggle. I keep one downed rock inside the circle to sit on, a wide flat one that seems too big for the top of the wall. I wonder if this was their sitting stone. I slide it over toward the opening in the wall. I sit Indian style facing the swamp, listening to the forest, so full of noise and amazingly quiet. When the wind stops, I can hear the far-off echo of the concrete waterfall by the orchard.

I keep digging and don't find anything. But I do replace a bunch of the stones that have fallen. I walk on top of the rocks, trying to settle them into place. I go around the circle over and over again, jumping across the opening that faces the swamp. I search for a walking stick to help me balance on top of the rocks. I end up wandering back close to the house where I find a decent piece of oak, embellished with nice ant tracks. I take it back to the rock house. I stick it into the soft wet ground near the door.

Maybe it's a grave, I suddenly think to myself. Something creepy draws me to it like a magnet. There is a different feel to the air inside of it—something off center, a disorienting vibration. The light moves in an alternating pattern, slowed and twisted. The trees grow crooked near the rock circle. It feels like the heart of the woods, centered, yet off balance.

I sit on the rock wall and stare at the rock circle. I ask myself, "Why is it here?" I imagine a person crouched on the sitting stone, staring at the swamp and not seeing me. In a tattered black hood they are faceless. There are dark rocks in the person's hand. Hanging bones on sticks and clanging cans. The snow flies sideways. *What happened here? What changes the light, right here?* I start to scare myself, snap out of it and walk away from the stone circle. I can't help but think that the figure I imagined in the rocks was a forgotten shadow, from long ago.

I visit the circle over and over again, but I never stay for long. I wear a path between the rock circle and the concrete waterfall. Back and forth I go nearly every day walking between the serene world of the concrete waterfall and the altered realm of the stone circle.

I buy my first rap record at the Mall of New Hampshire in Manchester. It's a song called "Planet Rock" by Afrika Bambaataa and the Soulsonic Force, a twelve-inch vinyl record, the same size of an album, but with just one song on each side. I play it over and over again in my bedroom up in the pine.

I see on TV one Saturday morning on *Soul Train* kids from New York dancing like robots to "Planet Rock" and its electro beat. Some of the dancers spin on the floor on their backs. Others sort of fake fight each other while dancing, dipping and diving, and throwing kicks and pretend punches at each other. The other people on the dance floor stop dancing and make a big circle and watch. I am fascinated with the song and the crazy dances. I decide instantly that this is my music. It's new like rock and roll used to be.

I search around for books about break dancing at a bookstore at the mall in Manchester. I find one, and I immediately begin reading it. I learn about "the robot" and practice every chance I get. Gregg catches me doing it to "Planet Rock" in the utility room and he really likes it. "Wow, you're pretty good at that, little buddy," he says. "You would like where I go roller skating. There is a group of kids who dance like that in the middle of the rink." He starts bobbing his head to the beat, his long hair moving to the new electric music. He tries to do the robot as he walks out, laughing. "Keep practicing," he says.

I love the new sound and start searching for more music and books about "hip-hop." I find a big fat book about graffiti art in New York, at the mall in Manchester. The paintings on subways and buildings are incredible. They crash against the brick and concrete walls of the city, spray painted so bright and colorful in such drab surroundings, like a flower growing from the bottom of a rusted trash can. I start drawing my name in bubble letters. Over and over again, DEAN in bubble letters, better and better each time. I draw at the desk at the end of the little hallway to nowhere.

The summer I graduate from junior high everything changes. Grammy and Grampy Smart and Aunt Carrie sell their farm in Maine and move into a condo in North Londonderry. *I'll miss the old farm,* I say to myself, carrying some of the small boxes into their new condo, but Gregg is happy. He and Carrie have always gotten along and now she'll be closer. As we help them move in, I assume that I'll be seeing Gregg less and less as Carrie ends up going to Londonderry High with him. The separation begins right away after we are done moving in, as Gregg and Carrie ride off together in his orange Volkswagen Beetle.

Grammy Bellevue moves into the small apartment in the downstairs of our house. My parents tell Gregg and me that they need to keep an eye on her, as she hasn't been well since Grampy died. But, she is often mean to us and constantly tells us to be quiet, even when we are not really loud. She screams up from the apartment door in the foyer to Gregg and me every time we have music on. "Turn that music down," she says, her skinny head poking into the hallway. "Be quiet, up there!" She particularly dislikes my "jigaboo" rap music as she calls it. Other than that, she is mostly quiet and on occasion happy and nice. She eats caramel-colored popcorn called Poppycock in front of the TV a lot, watching Lawrence Welk and his orchestra or *Hee Haw*. If you say something to her that she doesn't agree with, she says, "That's poppycock." She says it to my dad all the time and he always looks like he's pissed after, but he never says anything. My mom seems to be always calming him down after Grammy joins us for Sunday dinners.

One Saturday we head to Manchester to meet my Uncle Jimmie's new wife and her son, my new cousin. "His name is Tommy," Dad says as we pull into the driveway, "and he's about your age." Tommy meets us at the door. Dad introduces us and we shake hands. He looks like he's about the same size as me. He has curly hair and freckles and a bit of a stutter when he speaks.

"I've been wait, wait, waiting for you," he says to me. "Do you want to go, go, go for a swim?"

"Oh yeah," I answer, "I love swimming." I wrap my cast in a plastic trash bag and we jump in the pool. Tommy likes fake wrestling, too, and we have a match against each other. He body slams me into the water and I do the same to him. We swim into the night.

As we pull out of my uncle's driveway, I see Tommy waving goodbye from behind the living room picture window. I think to myself, *We will end up being best friends.*

Gregg and I drive to Nashua for a Thanksgiving dinner, and as we get past Robinson Pond in Hudson, I say, "Hey, let's drive by the old neighborhood first."

"All right, good," he says, "that will give us a chance to smoke before we get there." He pulls out a joint and lights it, then hands it to me. "Kenny told me you smoke with him," he says, "it's cool, Dean, here." We finish it just as we drive past Memorial Field, the field Gregg won all his trophies on.

"Remember playing there?" I ask him, pointing at the field.

"Oh, yeah," he answers, "I made a few plays on that field."

"I know, I remember watching you when I was little. I was always standing behind the chain-link fence. I remember a catch you made along the third-base foul line, like it was yesterday. That was a wicked catch."

"Yeah, it was nice," he says, trying to downplay it.

"I remember when you had the game-winning hit in the same playoff game too, nice hit, it was a rocket."

"Yeah," he says, "but I struck out like ten times before that, you know."

"You did? I don't remember that." I look at him, astonished.

"See, you can't win them all," he says to me, "but you got to keep driving."

He steers the orange Beetle down Merrill Street, and we drive right over the spot where he beat up Carl, the bully who was harassing me in elementary school. We pull up to our old house, which has been painted a dark brown almost black color. We both look at each other in shock. All that is left of my weeping willow is a sawed stump and one little mint-green sprout shooting out the side of the trunk. Even the moss that grew underneath it has died. "Aw, man,

83

nothing ever stays the same, does it?" I ask him as we both stare at the empty lawn.

"Everything changes, Dean—there is no stopping it," he says, and he looks me in the eyes. I flash back to us as kids; he looks so much older to me now, compared to when we lived here. I see in his expression that he is feeling the same thing about me. "It goes quick, buddy—life, it goes fast. You just have to keep smiling, like Dad says, just enjoy yourself, that's what I do." Gregg slaps me on the back and gives me a half-hug across the front seat of the Beetle. "It's all right, Dean, everything is going to be all right." He looks up into the rear-view mirror, and I do, too. He looks forward and puts the car in drive.

Chapter 8

Atlantic City Breakers

The ride through New York pulls me back and forth from one end of the car to the other as if I'm watching a Ping-Pong match. Through the rolled-down window, I see groups of kids underneath the tall buildings playing basketball behind chain-link fences. *They're just like me,* I think, *trapped beneath the brick and concrete.* Some of the kids play hoop and some of them dance off to the side with a big radio. I imagine, *They must listen to their music over and over, again, like me.*

All around the basketball court and throughout the city are huge graffiti murals made up of squared and bubbled letters. I recognize one of the names from my book CRASH. But, most of the pieces in the book I own are outdated, compared to these bright, complicated murals. The artists seem like they are all trying to outdo each other. Some of the lettering can't even be read, as the letters look like they have been sliced and twisted into an incomprehensible scramble. These artists add arrows, lightning bolts and bubbles to their letters and at the end of the words or names are little cartoon characters making cool karate poses with jeans, sneakers, crazy hats and sunglasses on. The pieces of graffiti are so bright as they slide by on drab buildings and old subway trains, that I can't stop looking out the window. "Hey, Dean, I think they're break dancing." Tommy says as he points in the direction of yet another basketball court.

Dad tries to find a radio station as we drive over the long and high Tappan Zee Bridge. As he tunes through the dial, I hear some static-covered rap music and tell him to stop. We listen to a few songs I've never heard before, and I notice the rap music on the radio sounds newer, crisper and more electronic than the songs on my old tape in the utility room. I think to myself, *I've got to get some new records and catch up with the changing times.* There are a few broken-down cars abandoned on the bridge that have been stripped of almost all of their parts. New York City disappears in the back window of the wagon, and I wonder to myself, *What would it be like to live there amidst the brick and concrete, instead of the pine, maple and apple trees of Londonderry?*

After a long drive down the New Jersey State Parkway, Dad pays a toll and tells us we are getting close. We ride down the Atlantic City Expressway, a long flat freeway surrounded by practically nothing, just bogs, swampland and a bunch of giant billboards. The billboards are huge, and as we make our way down the expressway, they seem to be multiplying. "Billy," my mother says excitedly, "Tom Jones is playing here—we have to get tickets!"

"They will be very expensive, Judith." Dad says. "Besides, the dates for the show have already passed—look at the billboard, honey."

Mom sighs and reads the billboards as Tommy and I do the same thing. "Caesars Palace." "Bally's Park Place." "Golden Nugget."

"Look, Tommy," I say, "there's one for the wax museum."

"They look creepy," he says, as he studies the wax figures on the sign.

Dad says, "Hey guys, look straight ahead, there it is." I peer over his shoulder, and out the windshield, at the skyline of Atlantic City. In a haze across the swamp and far beyond the diminishing highway, there are a few very tall buildings all lined up in a row. There are a bunch of cranes and some skyscrapers being built. As we drive closer, the city seems even bigger and I can start making out the flashing signs on top of some of the buildings. From the highway it looks like Las Vegas.

"This is going to be wicked cool," I say to Tommy. "You're going to freaking love it."

We pass by Atlantic City and make our way to the beach house Mom and Dad rented a few towns over in Ocean City. The town we drive through is unbelievably nice, with beautiful old houses all lined up and down a main boulevard. Some of them remind me of the Moonie Manor except they are bigger and nicer. Most of them have really nice landscaping and fountains in the center of rounded driveways. We pass by a giant hotel shaped like an elephant. Tommy can't believe it. It's got two tiny windows for eyes. It's about three or four stories high. The sign says "Lucy" in turn-of-the-century-type letters that swirl around with style. On top of the "elephant's" back is a big red saddle with a gazebo built on top of it. As Tommy and I look back at it through the rear window, we see that right where its butt is there is another window half obscured by the "elephant's" tail. We both see it at the same time and start chuckling. *So weird,* I think to myself, looking out the back window of the wagon.

We cross a small bridge and enter Ocean City. After a few minutes of driving, we pull into the driveway of the beach house. The house is huge and has a big fountain that squirts water into a big basin below it in the front yard, just like the fancy houses we passed on our way in. There are four huge columns in the front like the ones in the front of The White House. The columns go up a full three stories. Tommy has a look on his face as if he's never seen anything like it. I can't believe it either.

"Wow, Dad, this is unreal—even nicer than I remember," I say. "I feel like a millionaire."

"Son," Dad says, "we didn't rent the whole thing, just the very top floor, like last time. We are up in the converted attic."

"Who cares—this is awesome, check it out, look at this place!" I answer.

I turn to Tommy and say, "The beach is just a few blocks behind the house."

"There is a boardwalk and amusement park too, Tommy, you guys will have fun," Dad says, "but first get unpacked."

Tommy and I unpack our clothes quickly, stuff them into the white wicker dressers and stare out the back window of the attic apartment toward the beach. A few blocks away beyond the nice houses that crowd and grid the streets is the Atlantic Ocean. It stretches before us along a smooth beach. There is a lifeguard hut painted white and a big white rowboat sitting in the sand next to it. In bold capital letters painted in navy blue, the rowboat reads OCEAN CITY N.J. I open the old wooden window and a gust of fresh salty air hits us both in the face. I hear the soft waves as they gently wash ashore. We stare at the people running and lying on the beach.

"I don't ever want to leave, man, this place is great." I say to Tommy, as we look out the window. Mom comes walking out after about an hour and she is all dressed up. She looks like she's ready to star in a movie or something. She has on a white cashmere sweater, and her hair is sprayed to perfection into a giant unmovable globe. Around her neck she wears a golden Egyptian goddess symbol of Cleopatra that looks like a hieroglyph, hung low on a shimmering chain. Her earrings even match the little Egyptian.

"How do I look, sunshine?" She asks me.

"Like the grand queen of New England, Mom, great." I answer.

"All right, guys, let's go," Dad says, "I'm feeling lucky tonight." He flips on his light-grey Members Only jacket and grabs his keys with a clang. He slides on his Clint Eastwood sunglasses and heads toward the door. He flashes a grin and says, "What are you waiting for—Christmas? Get a move on."

The lights at the top of the big buildings are starting to shine brighter it seems, as the sky begins to slowly darken. We pull into the city and drive down the main street, staring at the lights. Mom and Dad talk about which hotel to go to. But Tommy and I are struck with awe at the glitz of the hotels and casinos. "Let's go to the Golden Nugget," I say. "It's cool!"

Dad cuts off a fat guy in a black Cadillac with New York plates and pulls into the grand entranceway of the Golden Nugget. When he stops in front, a little old man in a tuxedo comes over to the car and opens the door for my mother. Mom steps out in slow motion and I picture in my mind flashbulbs going off, as she steps elegantly from the wagon. The guy in the tux takes her hand and escorts her from the vinyl bench seat of our family wagon. By the way she smiles as she steps out, I can tell she is in heaven. Dad steps out of the wagon and hands the guy in the tux the car keys. He struts around the hood of the car and grabs Mom by the elbow and hooks her arm. Dad pulls his wallet out and gives the tux guy a dollar. The tux guy then blows on his gold whistle and a young kid in a red vest runs across the entranceway. He makes a perfect catch as tux guy throws him the keys with a gentle toss. The valet hands Dad a ticket and says something about validation. I see a flashbulb go off as we walk under the bright lights.

We walk across the entranceway and step into a rotating door adorned in brass and gold. It spins as we go through, and when we come out on the other side we can't believe what we see. Inside the incredible lobby is a gigantic golden birdcage. We all step toward it. It must be three stories high. Inside it is a bunch of "animatronic" birds singing a song and swinging from solid gold perches arranged at different heights. A huge multicolored parrot leads them. We watch the birds sing another song, and as they move and swing I can hear puffs of air and the clicks of their mechanisms behind the music.

"Meet me right back here at the golden birdcage in two hours, son," Dad says as the birds stop singing. "Stay on the boardwalk and don't go too far from the hotel—okay, guys? Two hours, right here." Dad hands me a twenty.

"All right, Dad, see you in two hours."

Tommy and I are off. He follows me up the escalator past the bells, buzzes, cheering and moaning of the casino. Blinking and flashing electric multicolored lights are everywhere. When we get to the rear of the casino, I push open a door and we're in a world of a different kind. Stretched before us are miles of boardwalk, forty feet wide and disappearing into the horizon. *We're free.*

We stare out at the sandy beach and the ocean ahead of us. "We're way down at the end of the boardwalk." I tell Tommy. "Toward the middle there's more stuff and people. Where do you want to go first?"

"I, I don't know, Dean," he answers. "Let's just walk on the boardwalk, that way." He points toward the sparkling lights of a distant pier shaped like a cruise ship.

We walk along the boardwalk. Everything we pass is either very old like from the nineteen tens or extremely new like from this year or last. On the boardwalk everything is electric and flashing and ringing, but on the other side it's quiet—sand, ocean and windy sky. Gift shops, arcades, hot dog stands, saltwater taffy shops, hotels, casinos and psychic readers, all line up facing the ocean—flashing their blinking neon toward the sand, the seagulls and the sky.

The piers are the only things that stretch out beyond the beach as they stand on posts above the dark Atlantic. Most of the piers are old, very old—turn of the century old—and their lettering style and monikers are still left scattered along the boards, in the ancient must-filled places. I take Tommy into a big gift shop near the cruise-ship pier. They have everything Atlantic City: little slot machines and sweatshirts, shells, shot glasses, snow globes, bathing suits, cameras, dice and batteries, and postcards on a spinning wire rack.

I spin it and look at some of the older ones. Carrie and I had done the same thing right here at the same gift shop, so I show Tommy the postcards I like and remember. The diving horse jumping into the ocean. Houdini jumping shackled into the Atlantic at the end of one of the piers we are next to. The long shot of an old pier with an advertisement for Chesterfield cigarettes with fancy letters that I like, sort of similar to the graffiti in New York with a 3-D look. An old hotel with a courtyard garden fountain and pointy shrubs, and people relaxing all around it. The white wicker three-wheeled rolling carts that roll tourists down the boardwalk like it's nineteen ten.

I walk Tommy into the brand-new mall, just built over the old Million Dollar Pier, the same place that Houdini jumped from, I think. We pass the stores and walk to the end of the ocean liner. I want to wow him with another great view. We go up a set of escalators, walk past the fast-food restaurants and step out of the glass doorways at the end. We walk across a long concrete porch and stand above the Atlantic, behind rounded metal railings just like real cruise ships have. I look down on the forming breakers; a few gently foam to a point and settle back into the water as it reflects the sky back up to us. I see Tommy and me in the shimmer of the undulating water, our heads hanging over the railing, and it seems strange, to stand floating above the water and not be wet.

We walk away from the pier and head back through the mall; we step out onto the boardwalk directly across from Caesars Palace. One step inside, and my mind is instantly flooded with memories from my earlier trips. One trip Gregg and I spent so much time in the little arcade near the escalators above the casino. Dad always met us right here at the top of the moving stairs and gave us more money to play in the arcade while he and Mom gambled down below. I can't help but wonder what Gregg is up to at home alone on this summery Friday night near the apple trees in Londonderry. Tommy and I burn through the twenty bucks Dad gave me, and I check my watch, "We've got to meet my dad in about a half an hour, Tommy. Let's walk back up to the Golden Nugget."

We make it back early and sit on the metal railings on the beach side of the boardwalk, watching people walk by while the sea air hits our backs. I watch one of the rolling chair attendants lifting his cart up and spinning the wheels around in a circle while he tries to attract customers. First, he spins the wheel itself, then he spins the rotating mount the wheel is on. He moves back while still holding up the cart and stands there while it's doing a wheelie and its wheel spins and rotates.

I stare down a dark street between buildings on the city side of the boards, behind where the rolling cart guy spins his wheels. I hear rap music in the distance and see walking up the dark street, from behind the wicker cart guy, a group of kids coming up the street, toward the boardwalk. It looks like there are seven or eight of them, and the one in front has a huge boom-box radio over his shoulder. Another kid carries what looks like a rolled-up rug on his shoulder and another has under his arm a big piece of folded and flattened cardboard. As the radio gets closer, I whisper to Tommy, "What are they up to?" He doesn't answer.

The group of guys gets to a ramp that rises up from the street to the boardwalk, and the kid with the radio puts it down on the wooden ramp. He turns to the rest of them and says something that I can't make out, then walks up the ramp onto the boardwalk alone, as the others wait in the shadows. He looks to the left for a second, then to the right, then turns around and motions for the others to join him. They move quickly coming up the ramp. They are all dressed the same: blue jeans, white sneakers, red sweatshirts with hoods, and matching red Philadelphia Phillies baseball hats. The sweatshirts have iron-on Old English-type lettering on them, but I can't make out what the lettering says as they rush up the ramp. The kid with the cardboard unfolds it and slaps it down on the boardwalk. The guy, with what I thought was a rug, lays a piece of linoleum flooring over the cardboard. Another one places the radio right next to the cardboard covered in linoleum. Now I see it: on the front of their red sweatshirts, it reads "Atlantic City Breakers."

A few tourists are beginning to gather. They stop in front of the linoleum and look at the radio and the kids standing behind it. "Wow," I say to Tommy, "check this out, they're going to break."

Suddenly, the music comes thumping through the giant radio. The crew jumps into action. Two of the older kids step forward right after an electric drumroll tumbles out of the speakers. The others kneel down in frozen poses and watch the two that step forward. I know the song: it's "Owner of a Lonely Heart" by Yes, a progressive rock group, and it's not really what I figured these kids would be breaking to. I look at Tommy, amazed that it's not a rap song. He looks back at me, puzzled. "Yes," I say.

"Yes," he replies. "It's Yes." *Wow.* A solo rhythm guitar riff funnels through the boom box repeating itself several times, as the two breakers strut around each other in a large circle around the edges of the linoleum. They look at each other as if they might fight. They stop near the radio and face the small crowd that has formed in front of them. For a split second, they don't move as the rhythm guitar riff continues to play.

Then the beat drops, and the same guitar riff gets supported by an incredible electronic drumbeat. As soon as the first kick drum hits the speakers, the two kids fly forward and flip in the air, then do a synchronized landing on the boardwalk, coming to rest like they are sliding into third base. They push up on their hands as if on a pommel horse. Then they start breaking, moving in circles on the floor, hands, arms and legs flying through the air as they do their synchronized footwork. Their timing is nearly perfect.

The crowd grows and Tommy and I jump off the metal railing to move closer. We stand near the corner of the linoleum as the lyrics come out of the speaker: "Move yourself — you always lived your life — never thinking about the future." The dancers jump to their feet and freeze. An older heavy lady in the gathering crowd gasps. People start clapping wildly.

They flip to the floor again, and really start showing off. Both of them are doing their own moves, now; the synchronization is gone as they each fight for the crowd's attention. The lyrics of the second verse come through the speakers, and I look back and forth at the breakers, trying to study their moves. The lyrics flow through the radio at us, "Prove yourself — you are you and that's the only way."

I turn around and see that behind us the crowd has gotten huge. The chorus breaks as the smallest and youngest kid steps up and out to the crowd. He is tiny and must be, at the most, twelve or thirteen. He has long black hair that flips in the breeze from under his Phillies cap. He is the stopper, the show ender, and he knows it. He struts out like he owns the city. He starts off with a jumping sort of karate dance, as he throws punches and kicks into the air, while his body pops up and down. The crowd is instantly in love with his enthusiasm. He does it all: ground breaking, a big fancy spin and even some waves through his body. As I watch the crowd's reaction, I think to myself, *Man, I'm small – maybe they would love me, too.*

As the second chorus approaches, I look to see what the kid's finishing move will be. I realize he is going into the infamous windmill move I have seen on TV. His body starts spinning and rotating on the linoleum, his feet circling the air above him and never touching the ground. He goes around like seven times; then, to my amazement, he pushes his arms to the boards and his body rises up and he spins on the top of his head with his feet in the air. He rotates around three more times, and falls flat to the floor, landing miraculously with his sneakers in his hands. The crowd freaks out; they clap and scream so loud I can't believe it.

The rest of the dancers join him on the dance floor and take a bit of a bow, as the music still plays behind them. They send the little one to the edge of the crowd with his upside-down baseball cap in his hands. He smiles and nods every time someone drops cash and coins in it. He is racking it up, too; I see several tens and fives and tons of ones, and one guy in a nice suit tosses in a crisp twenty. The kid empties the hat a few times and keeps filling it. Then they shut the music off and roll up the linoleum, as the crowd starts to disperse. They grab the cardboard and make an exit down the dark street beyond the boardwalk where they came from.

"Un-fucking-real," I say to Tommy, "they must have made at least a hundred bucks, huh?" I watch them walk away slowly and I still can't believe what I have just seen. "The Atlantic City Breakers," I say to Tommy, "they were un-fucking-real."

My mind is in motion as we walk through the Golden Nugget to meet Dad and Mom. Still stunned, I keep saying to Tommy, "We've got to practice breaking, we've got to keep practicing! We need linoleum and cardboard and sweatshirts. Let's go to Hampton Beach, Tommy, and make some money."

"I barely slept last night." I say to Tommy, as Mom and Dad walk us down to the beach in the morning. I carry lawn chairs, the big ones that fold out into three rusty aluminum sections lined with plastic tube stripes to sit on. Three or floor blocks I carry the chair down the concrete sidewalk; my arm hurts by the time my feet hit the hot sand. We wait for Mom to pick her spot and it takes a while, as usual.

Tommy and I walk to the ocean and step into the tiny waves that break right near our feet. We walk out a few more steps. I look around and notice that, even though the beach is packed with people lying in the sun, there are only a few swimmers besides us. I look down in the water and see something translucent floating. *A little plastic sandwich bag*, I think to myself. Tommy stands beside me and next to him I see another little sandwich bag floating slowly toward us. "What the hell," I say to him, "what's with the little sandwich bags?"

"What sandwich bags?" he asks, but I don't get the chance to answer as something rubs up against my stomach. I look down at my waist in the water. It's not a plastic sandwich bag: it's a little jellyfish! I jump back as the fist-size jellyfish floats by and rubs on my stomach. I look at Tommy and then we both stare down at the water just as the sun breaks away from a cloud. It lights up the water and all around us are little jellyfish, floating shallow and deep and riding the surface of the calm waves, as the tide rolls in.

"I'm getting out!" I say. "These things sting, I think, and they're poisonous!"

We run to the shore, and I feel them hit my legs as my feet splash the ocean water in the air. "No wonder no one is swimming!" I say to Tommy.

I bring Mom and Dad back to show them the little jellyfish. I poke one of them that washed up on the beach with a piece of driftwood as Mom and Dad watch. As I poke it, it seems to shine an eerie glow. "Did you see that?" I say to everyone. "Did you see it, it's electric, it glimmered a weird flicker of light when I poked it. Watch—I'll do it again." I tap it again and it lightly flashes, shimmering on the sand in the hot sun, folded over onto itself and emitting a tiny magical spark. No one else sees it; they all look at me as if I'm crazy.

Tommy and I head to the outdoor shower on the side of the building. I get in and soap up behind the high wooden fence. I remember that the water is always hot at first, but it runs cold, every time, so I try to soap up real fast. I notice as the water starts to get a bit cooler that my stomach feels itchy. I scratch at it with the green bar of Irish Spring in my hand. As the soap runs down my stomach, I feel a few itchy spots on my legs. *What the hell*, I say to myself, as I continue to soap up. Then my shoulders and back and chest and sides start to itch. *This is insane; are there bugs in here or something?* I look down on the ground and don't see any bugs or anything. I look up to the sky above the fencing and don't see anything. I look at my soapy stomach and legs and don't see anything. The water grows cooler and the itching gets worse.

I rinse the soap off, look at my skin and notice that it's irritated, pink and prickly, in all of the itchy spots.

"The jellyfish!" I scream through the fence.

The next day Tommy and I take a little white tram bus to the boardwalk in Ocean City. We try to break dance but we have a hard time attracting a crowd. Our radio isn't big enough or loud enough and people just walk by, while it plays. We listen to the radio station that doesn't come in great and they only play hip-hop or rap songs every once in a while. Most of the time Tommy and I just stand there waiting for a song and we sort of practice dance. An old couple stops to watch us for a second, but then they walk away. "Wait for a good song." I keep saying to Tommy. "Then we'll really go for it." A good song finally comes on the radio and we dance, but there's still no one watching and no crowd gathers.

After a few minutes we give up. We're sweaty and our jellyfish stings are itchy as hell. "We've got to keep practicing until we're really good. Breaking could be our thing, you know? We're going to be fucking fresh, Tommy, I'm just telling you." I repeat this to Tommy over and over again, as we walk home on the boardwalk with the sun on our backs.

Chapter 9

The Kenwood

I lean on the wall in Grammy Dot's empty apartment, staring at the spot where Grammy had hung her little porcelain fisherman head. The fisherman head was one of those things that Grammy Dot always had. It was about the size of a fist. The head, which was an antique carving of a white-bearded man in a yellow rain cap, smoking a pipe with a strange grimace-like smile on his face, hung on the wall above Grammy's couch. She would sit there forever, chain-smoking her extra-long Benson & Hedges and eating her Poppycock. I stare at the smoke stain that surrounds the outline of the fisherman head and wonder if Grammy might haunt the apartment.

Tommy spins, on his head, on a square of baby blue linoleum laid in the center of Grammy Dot's empty living room. Tommy's head spins smoothly, his hands tapping his spin along, his feet revolving him and keeping the momentum. My radio is off to one side, painted in baby blue, white and gold graffiti. Bubble letters and B-boys. *We've been spinning through the seasons,* I think to myself. *Damn, Tommy's got the fresh head spin.* He lands, he freezes, positioned in a back bridge stretched above the linoleum.

"Fresh, Tommy." I say. "Nice, you're getting so fucking good. You're ready, right—you're ready for tonight, man?"

"Yeah," he replies, "but I need some pliers again for my hat."

"All right," I head to the utility room past Grammy's kitchen. I come back with the pliers. He takes them from me and pulls the little metal tab off the top of his baseball hat, so it won't leave a bruise on his head or rip his hair out, when he spins on it. "Let's get going," I say.

We walk up the stairway in the foyer to get ready for the night. Our white hooded sweatshirts match, with Old English iron-on letters we bought from the tee shirt shop at the Mall of New Hampshire. On the back, the hooded sweatshirts read "Battle Zone Crew." Down the right arm my sweatshirt reads "Hexster"—my new breaking name. I put on my belt buckle, the one I bought in Atlantic City months ago when my breaking name was Dizzy Dee. The belt buckle reads "Dee," in silver plated letters on a thick white leather band. "If the kids at school could see me now," I say to Tommy as I buckle the belt. I throw on my graffiti-covered jean jacket, "BZC" in huge colorful letters along the back of my shoulders. "They make fun of me because I wear my hat backward. How fucked up is that, but they ain't cool, man. I don't let them get to me—fuck them—they don't know shit, man."

"Let's get going." Tommy says, throwing on his jean jacket that's painted just like mine.

"Wait, I'm going to use Gregg's ski goggles." I open the door to the closet and reach up to the top shelf and grab Gregg's Rossignol goggles.

Just as I pull them down from the top shelf, Gregg walks into the bedroom and says, "Guys, wait until you see the stereo I just bought at Tweeter at the mall."

Tommy asks, "Where is it?"

"I'll get it in a couple weeks. It cost so much I have to make a few payments on it." Gregg flops down on the couch bed and looks up at me, as I pull his ski goggles up my left arm and strap them on my shoulder. "What are you doing with my goggles, junior?" He says to me. "You're not taking those breaking with you, no way, buddy."

"Yeah I am," I answer back quickly, hoping he won't stand up and tag me on the shoulder like he always does. I make a quick run for the door and, sure enough, Gregg jumps up and chases after me and we both start laughing, as he grabs the back collar of my jean jacket just as I try to turn the doorknob and escape. From his grip on the back of my jacket, he spins me around to face him, and he points his finger of death at me and drives it into my collarbone right next to the ski glasses on my shoulder. The three of us start laughing as Gregg pokes his finger into my shoulder, forcing me to drop to one knee.

"You'll be break dancing all over my goggles, you'll break, then my goggles will break, then you'll get really fucking broken," he says, laughing, then he lets me go and I stand up and place my hand over the goggles, hoping he won't snag them.

"I won't bust them, Gregg, come on, and let me wear them?"

"All right, man," he says, "but if you break them, you're dead, got it?"

"Yeah, thanks brother," I say, as I walk out of the room, surprised he's letting me.

At the mall Tommy and I lean against the big antique clock next to the food court. Matt shows up first. I see him walking toward us as he passes by Spencer's. He's got his matching sweatshirt on and an old Red Sox hat covering his curly hair that sticks out from the strap of the hat that rests in his forehead. Matt is tough, and the kids in Manchester know not to mess with him. He dresses like a burnout rocker kid and does not look like a break dancer, but he can dance and we practice a lot at his mom's dance studio in front of huge mirrors that let us watch ourselves. Matt shakes my hand, then Tommy's. "We got to fucking win tonight, guys," he says.

"We know, man." I answer.

"We will." Tommy says.

Froggy shows up with one of his wild outfits on, plastic parachute pants and a bright red and black double sweatshirt thing he got at the ultramodern clothes shop. We call him Froggy because, well, he looks like that kid from *The Little Rascals* that they called Froggy. He looks like one of the kids out of a Norman Rockwell painting, freckle faced with wild hair and a big goofy smile. But, he can pop, almost as good as me, and he takes the brunt of our jokes and always seems to keep smiling. We give him the crew handshake and hug and he says the same thing Matt did, "We got to fucking win tonight, guys." The three of us laugh at him.

I say, "That's exactly what Matt said."

Tyler shows up last; he's the only other kid in the crew from Londonderry, like me. He's also the smallest member, a real little guy, but he is quick and nimble and has great footwork when he breaks on the ground, and he's a quick spinner with the best and longest backspin in the crew. He shakes our hands and the five of us start our walk through the mall.

This is what I live for, I think to myself, as we strut down the hallway of the mall. When some of the other kids see us coming down the hall, they switch sides or walk by us, trying not to bump into us. We don't move out of anybody's way when we walk as a crew. *We look too cool,* I think to myself. *We are the freshest kids in town, Battle Zone Crew in the motherfucking house.*

We head out the glass doors near Lechmere to the outdoor covered hallway where we hang out. I place the radio on the brick flooring and hit play, while the crew stands around lighting their cigarettes. We stand, smoke and listen to the music coming out of the box while old people walk by and stare at us. Froggy looks at himself in the reflection of the glass doors as he practices popping to the music. Tommy and Matt lean against the wall with Tyler who is practicing his top rock a bit in front of them. I stand next to the trash can, watching people walk by. Old ladies walk as far away from us as they can, and they are usually holding on to their purses tightly, like we might mug them. *We must look like city punks.* I think to myself.

We get to the skating rink and the place is packed. It seems like every teenager in Manchester is there. For the first half of the night I watch everybody skate in circles around the rink, waiting until the dancing starts. I lean on the rail on the outside of the rink and start looking for little Jess. She glides by all smiles and electricity like sparkles in the dust as I spot her, and I watch her go around the circle over and over again. I watch her every week; everyone knows I like her, but I'm not sure she likes me. *She must see me staring at her,* I think to myself. *This week I'm going for it.*

A while later she skates right up to the railing in front of me. "Hey Jess," I say to her.

"What's up, Dean," she says. "Not skating this week either?" She asks.

"I never skate." I answer abruptly, trying to be cool. There is a weird silence as she looks at me. I stupidly ask, "Are you going to slow dance with me, baby?"

"I doubt it," she says, as she smiles at me and skates away, her curly hair aglow in tiny sparks of light. *Damn it!* I say to myself. *That was a stupid thing to say.* But then, as I watch her skate away, she turns back at me and smiles.

The night flies by, and before I get to talk to her again, the battle is on. A circle forms in the middle of the rink as the DJ plays Grandmaster Flash. Our crew stands on one side of the circle and we face a new crew we haven't seen before, although we've heard they're good. They send out their first breaker, and I notice Jess watching on the side of the circle. Matt takes out their first dancer and the crowd cheers him on after a nice windmill and freeze. They send out the next kid who is actually really good, but Tyler tops him with a great backspin. Then they send out a kid who's even better than the last dancer. He's popping like crazy, and Froggy heads to the center of the circle and barely outpops him.

Tommy looks nervous as they send out their next dancer—a skinny kid. "Don't worry," I tell him, "the crowd is with us." The kid tries a head spin but he doesn't last long. Tommy heads out and busts the best head spin and freeze I have ever seen him do better and the crowd goes nuts. The other crew sends out the popper again but I know

I can beat him. I glide out into the circle where I show off my new Mr. Wave move where I pop all the way down to the floor. The crowd cheers like crazy after I'm done and we start celebrating with our hands in the air as if we just won the World Series, and the crowd moves into the circle to celebrate with us. We start shouting "BZC" in unison and the crowd joins in. I see Jess off to the side smiling at me while we shout, but before I know it the lights in the rink are on and the night is over.

Outside in the rain I see Jess standing near the door. I walk over to her and say, half-joking, "Hey, baby, come give me a kiss good night." I turn around after I say it and walk toward the corner of the building, hoping she will follow me, even though I have a feeling that she won't. The rain starts to soak my hair and jacket, but I try to look cool. I lean on the wall and pull out my last bent Winston and light it up. Raindrops hit my glasses, and I can't believe it when I see her come walking around the corner. She steps right up to me, smiling, and puts her arms around me. I drop my cigarette onto the rain-soaked ground. I look down at her through the rain on my glasses; she presses her body tight against mine and I stiffen up and get nervous. Then she kisses me softly a few times and we start to make out. *Damn, this is good,* I think. The rain is soaking us. She pulls her lips away and lets out a gentle sigh, then says to me softly, "You kiss good."

"You do, too." She comes in for another one, and while we kiss I look up through raindrops that cover my glasses into the city lights. The rain glazed on my glasses makes the lights look like tiny blurred fireworks. I'm looking through wet diamonds. She lets go. I watch her through the sparkles of light and it seems like I can't move; I am stuck like a magnet to the aluminum siding on the side of the roller rink, staring at the shimmer of city lights.

I walk into our bedroom after school and Gregg is crouched in the corner with a big glass-covered stereo rack in front of him.

"It's here, you got it!" I shout.

"Yup, wait until you hear THE fucking Kenwood." He says.

"How long is it going to take to set it up?"

"It's almost done. I just have to get the wires in," he says as he stands up in front of the glass-fronted rack. He steps away, toward a bunch of opened cardboard boxes, and I catch a glimpse of it.

The phone rings.

"Is it for me?" I ask, as he grabs it with the wires still in his hand. He ignores me and starts his low cool talk on the phone.

"Is it Jess?" I ask a bit louder. He gives me a look and shakes his head a short no. *Fuck*, I think to myself, *why doesn't she call?*

I watch Gregg plug the wires in, as he keeps talking on the phone. *He talks quietly and is always grinning when he is talking to a girl,* I think to myself. Gregg moves the phone away from his shoulder. "Can you go get the Phillips head screwdriver for me, Dean?" He asks.

"I'll call you, baby" he says softly into the phone. I walk out of the room, trying to copy his little smile.

I grab the old Phillips head screwdriver out of the kitchen junk drawer. I open the fridge, find a soda and when I shut the fridge I'm staring at Gregg's phone messages, all girls' names and phone numbers. "I'll call you, baby," I murmur to myself, practicing my brother's soft voice and slight smile.

Gregg finally gets the wires in and spins the rack around and positions it under the window. I watch him fiddle with the big speakers. He plugs the Kenwood into the outlet and hides the speaker wires behind the rack. He steps away to see if it's centered and I see the system, sleek and black, shining behind the glass and flanked by its large black speakers. "Wicked nice, Gregg," I say, staring.

"It cranks," he says, "grab a record."

I flip through my record crate. I pull out "Planet Rock," my favorite breaking song. I walk over to the Kenwood, open up the glass case that fronts the components, and slide the record out of its case. I lift up the glass top that covers the turntable.

"Oh no, junior," Gregg says, "the Van Halen album first. It's my Kenwood; I get the first pick."

"All right, go ahead then." I say.

"I'll keep the sound down until I adjust the equalizers," he says, as he turns on the components in procession from the top to the bottom. Each section lights up with tiny red and green lights. He puts the record on and adjusts the volume knob. As he turns the knob a digital display counts down the volume he sets at twelve. The music comes through the speakers quietly. He sits down Indian style in front of the rack and adjusts the dual band graphic equalizers. Each side of the equalizer has about twenty little sliders for each frequency, but he figures it out and sets each side like the crescent of a wave—the highs and lows lifted and the middles down. He listens as he adjusts and he turns the volume knob up to twenty and the sound thickens a bit.

"I think that sounds good, huh, what do you think?"

"Yeah, sounds good, turn it up," I say.

"It's loud, you know. Mom and Dad are going to freak out," he says. He starts to turn the volume knob slowly on the display from twenty to thirty, and the music doubles in volume. "That's nothing," he says, "wait." He turns the knob up slowly, until it gets to forty.

"Wow," I say, "it sounds really good, how high does it go?"

"It goes all the way to one hundred," he says, smiling up at me.

I stand in front of one of the speakers and can feel a little gust of wind coming out of the speaker and hitting my tee shirt. I put my hand out into the speaker wind and with every low note a tiny burst of air hits my hand. "Feel that," I say to Gregg. He sticks his hand up to the speaker.

"Cool," he says. "Wait until I crank it."

He turns the volume up to fifty-five and the stereo is thumping. He looks at me smiling; I smile back. I say, "Wow," and he can't hear me. He turns it up to seventy; the window behind the stereo starts to shake in its sill and the floor seems to be vibrating. I look down at Gregg, sitting in front of the rack, and see the left and right sides of his long blond hair are being pushed by the wind from the speakers.

"Your hair is moving, look!" I yell to him. He looks down at his hair rustling in the wind. He positions his head closer toward the speaker to make his hair move even more and we start laughing. "It's just like that commercial." I say to him.

"Yeah, I know, it's unreal, huh?" he says.

"Is it live, or is it Memorex?" I say. "No, it's the fucking Kenwood."

He starts to laugh again. He turns it up to eighty-five and the floor is really shaking. The song ends and he lifts the needle off the record. "My turn," I say. I grab my record and put it on the turntable. "Let me control the volume, Gregg," I say. He shakes his head yes and I put the needle to the record. The turntable arm feels heavy compared to the one on my little stereo. I grab the volume knob and start to turn it down because I want to build up to the loudness again, like he did. As I turn the knob, it clicks precisely as the numbers on the display count down. "Whoa, that's cool, the way it clicks, so smoothly, huh," I say. He shakes his head yes again. I let the record go, and at the beginning of it where they say *party people*, I stop the record from spinning and get ready to scratch it like the deejays do.

"No scratching." Gregg says.

"It won't hurt it." I say.

"No scratching on the Kenwood, Dean, or you can't play it."

"All right, all right, no scratching." I let the record play. The beat comes through the speakers and I crank the volume all the way back up. Gregg starts his fake break-dancing moves and bops around the bedroom to the music. He does this sort of King Tut Egyptian move, and I start laughing at him.

"It's fresh, man." He says, smiling and laughing.

"Fucking Kenwood is fresh, Gregg," I say. The phone rings, he answers it. I turn the stereo down. "Is it for me?" I ask. He shakes his head no and starts his cool low talk, smiling on the phone with a girl—maybe the same girl, I don't know.

A half hour later, he's off on his date and I'm alone with the Kenwood. I spend the night practicing scratching. "I'll call you, baby," I say to myself over and over again. I'm trying to get it just right, trying to make Gregg's little smile come through on my face.

Chapter 10

Last Days in Londonderry

Carrie opens the front door with a cardboard box filled with bottles, clangs the box down on the second stair. Gregg and I walk up to the foyer, she smiles and yells up to us with her hands in the air, "Oh yeah! We're going to paarrtyy, tonight!" We both smile back at her. "Come help me with the rest." She says to us. We rush down the stairs and follow her out into the driveway.

"Looks like your fake ID works." Gregg says to her.

"Like a charm. I got a bunch of beer, too." Carrie says.

"Guess where I spent my week at school?" I interrupt her at the trunk of the car.

"Where?" She asks.

"In detention in the pink room."

"Oh no, me and Gregg spent a lot of time there, Dean — well, me more than Gregg, I guess. What did you do?"

"Got in a fight with one of my old friends when we were coming off the bus. We used to be friends but now he's a big jock and thinks he's cool, and he ran his mouth on the bus ride to school the whole way, saying he was going to kick my ass when we got off, so when we got off, he throws a punch at me and misses, so I hit him with three lefts and nailed him in the jaw with a right, just like Dad taught me. I was wicked nervous. Then the principal broke it up. He said he was surprised I won the fight because the other kid was much bigger than me. Then he gave me five days in the pink room, man, it sucks in there."

"Yeah it does," Gregg says. "Is everything still painted pink?"

"Oh yeah, all pink; it drives you fucking mental after a while."

We walk up the stairs and start taking the bottles and beer out of the cardboard cases in the kitchen. We line all the bottles of booze along the countertops. The light from the window and the sliding glass door reflects off the green and brown bottles and the kitchen looks like the back of a pub. We stuff the refrigerator full of beer. On our last trip out to the car to get the rest of the liquor and beer that Carrie bought, we see one of my friends from the neighborhood trying to push a full-size arcade game up our snow-covered driveway.

Carrie and Gregg break out laughing and look at me as if I'm nuts. "What?" I say. "He just moved in down the road and he's got a video game, so I told him to bring it for the party." They laugh at me, as I run down the slope of the driveway and help him push the game, strapped to a rolling dolly, up the drive.

In the downstairs TV room, the new kid from up the road and I plug in the game and place it next to the fireplace—*Tempest*, it's called. I've played it; it's a good game. You are an alien on top of a three-dimensional spiral. You shoot at enemies as they slide up the spiral and defend your ship by blasting them away. Gregg walks by just as the game boots up and says, "Unreal, Dean, this is going to be a crazy fucking party."

I have a sort of ritual that I do at parties: I grab a beer and sip it slowly all night so I don't get too drunk. I'm sipping my beer, watching the crowd grow. Girls start showing up, very sexy girls who are friends with Gregg and the older guys Gregg has started hanging out with. The upstairs living room with the Kenwood and round couch is getting packed with partiers. I ask Gregg, "Do you think too many people might show up?"

"It'll be all right, Dean," he answers.

The party starts to take off. Jocks from Londonderry and cheerleaders from Derry arrive. The house is completely packed. The smoke and crowd are overwhelming and my first Heineken is gone and there's still no sign of Jess. I'm beginning to wonder if she'll show.

Gregg's biker buddies start to arrive. He hangs with bikers on the weekend sometimes; they party in a sandpit in Derry, near the flea markets. He says they have a bonfire and drink and party all night and that he likes hanging out with them. My break-dancing friends start to show up too and a bunch of Gregg's longhaired heavy-metal headbanging friends.

I sit on the couch and watch Gregg. As usual, he's surrounded. There's a group of smiling girls sitting close to him on the round palm-tree couch. He talks softly and sweetly to them with that slight grin on. They love it, they love him, and it seems like he's not even trying. I watch as a tall thin girl grabs him by the hand and leads him down the foyer hallway toward our bedroom. They are both smiling as she drags him into the room.

The music pounds out of the Kenwood. The party is fucking crazy packed. I can't even walk to the kitchen to get a beer; it takes a long time to get back to the couch. I push through the crowd with my head down. I walk to the window behind the couch and look out. The whole road is packed with cars on both sides. I look around for Gregg in the crowd and can't find him. I suddenly feel alone and a bit scared. There are too many people; it's too much at once. I spot Carrie and she sees that I am worried.

"It's okay, Dean, just go with it," she says.

I look out the window and see cars parked in the driveway and all the way up the hills on both sides of Adam's Road. Jess and a few of her friends from Manchester are walking up the driveway. I think to myself, *I should run downstairs and open the door to greet her,* but then I think to myself, *I have never seen Gregg go chasing after a girl,* so I just sit back down on the couch and wait for her to come upstairs into the living room and find me. It doesn't take her long.

She gives me a little smile and slides next to me on the couch. "Wow, Dean, the party is packed," she says in my ear, trying to make herself heard over the music. She kisses me softly on the side of my neck.

"Yeah, it's wicked packed." I say. "Want a beer or a drink?"

"I'll have a beer," she answers and I grab a Heineken for her, to match mine.

I look over and notice Gregg is back on the couch, sitting next to a pretty blonde cheerleader. She is twirling his long curly hair and sitting closer and closer to him as I watch. She talks with a fake valley-girl accent. Her cheerleader top is red and white and reads "Astros" with a little rocket ship on it. Every other word out of her mouth is "like." She doesn't stop talking, "like totally awesome," "like gag me," "like the party is to the max," "like definitely."

I whisper to Jess in my best valley-girl speak. "Like yeah, she like looks like, like totally an Astro!" I say to Jess, and she starts to laugh.

"Yeah, she does," she says.

"Well, gag me with a Twinkie," I say to Jess, making fun of the cheerleader. Jess laughs and turns a bit red, as if she might spray beer out of her mouth.

When I look back in Gregg's direction, there is yet another girl hanging on his shoulder, this one with short dark hair. She is looking up at him, glossy eyed, with a smile on her face. He looks over at me and asks, "Is that your girl, Dean?"

"Yeah," I answer. I'm afraid to introduce my little Jess to him because I'm afraid she will fall in love with him and leave me. "Gregg, this is Jess. Jess, that's my brother Gregg."

Jess smiles at him and says, "Hi."

"Gregg, can I put on some of my music now?" I ask. I figure I better dance and divert her attention.

He smiles at me and says, "Yeah, go for it, Dean." I put on "Planet Rock" and it is blasting through the speakers. I step out from behind the couch and everybody begs me to dance. I start by gliding out in front of the glass coffee table. Everyone on the couch and everyone standing around it start to watch me. I pop and give them all my new moves, and at the end they clap and I feel great.

"Man, you are getting really good, Dean," Gregg says. "You are an unbelievable dancer, man." He looks at me and I can tell he's pretty buzzed. He shakes my hand and says,

"I love you, little brother." He gets very love-y when he's drinking.

I say, "I love you, too, man." I almost feel cool.

One girl starts to dance on the odd little landing that's directly above the front door. It's two feet wide but long enough that three or four people can stand on it. Another girl steps over the half wall and onto the landing to join her. I watch as the crowd continues to grow—on the stairs and along the half walls near the living room and along the hallway to the bedrooms and bathroom.

Eddie Money slams out of the Kenwood speakers and the girls are shaking and dancing. The "Astro" cheerleader climbs over the railing and joins the girls dancing and the crowd grows and gets louder. I look over at Gregg who watches from the hallway. I shake my head in amazement and he does the same back to me. We both smile and he rolls his eyes at me as if he is saying *What the fuck?* and I laugh a bit.

The song changes and Van Halen comes through the speakers, and the girls really start getting into it. The crowd gets very loud and I feel like the stairs might collapse because there are so many people on them. The girls take off their shirts and dance in their bras, and the guys go wild. We start chanting, "Take it off, take it off." To my amazement, the girls start stripping. Jeans fly through the air right past me and land in the living room, and I can't—fucking—believe it. *This is the greatest fucking party in the history of New Hampshire.* I watch the girls dance and look around at the partiers cheering them on and realize that this is probably the greatest night of my life so far. I can't stop smiling; it's unreal. The bras come off; the girls shake their asses to the crowd. Everyone cheers.

In the midst of all the excitement, the front door opens right below where the girls are dancing, and my older brother, Rick, and his wife, Sue, walk into the foyer. Rick just stares at the crowd as if he can't believe his eyes and Sue looks stunned. As they stand in the entry, they both start to smile as if they're the ones being cheered. Rick takes a bit of a bow, and Sue slaps him on the shoulder. I watch Rick's eye search the crowd for Gregg, then spot him at the railing near the top of the stairs. Rick yells something like "Why are you cheering us?" and he looks at Gregg who laughs and points to the girls who are still dancing on the landing above the door. Rick and Sue turn around and I watch their heads look up at the half-naked girls dancing above them. Rick is wide-eyed, but a smile grows on his lips, as he gives Gregg a silent thumbs-up.

"You guys are so busted!" Rick says to Gregg, trying to sound serious. "Gregg, there are cars all the way to the end of the street. It took us ten minutes to get here from where we parked. Mom and Dad are going to kill you guys — but get me a beer — this looks like a great fucking party!"

Gregg clears the couch in the living room of partiers, and we sit down across from Rick and Sue in front of the table covered with empty glasses and beer bottles. The glass ashtray on the center of the table has seven or eight joints laying in it. Sue looks at me as if she can't believe it, then grins and shakes her head. The girls keep dancing on the landing in the foyer. *Rick and Sue are having fun*, I realize. I watch as they look around in amazement at the mayhem of the most unbelievable party Londonderry has ever seen.

I wake up and the sun is shining through the bedroom window. I stare at the pine tops for a while and I can hear that Carrie is up; I can hear her in the living room cleaning. Gregg is snoring in his bed and looks beat when I glance over at him. I walk out into the living room and smell the Windex and Comet. Carrie is wiping down the glass coffee table with a paper towel. Next to the stairs there are three big black trash bags filled with bottles, cans and red plastic cups. "The evidence must be gathered," I mumble to myself.

Carrie asks me, "Dean, can you get all the empties downstairs, huh?"

"No problem, what a party, huh, I don't think we will ever top that one." I grab an empty trash bag from the kitchen.

"Definitely not." Carrie says.

I head downstairs and start gathering the bottles and cans and red plastic cups and drop them into the trash bag that I carry around with me. The beer bottles and cans clang off each other as I drop them in. When I come back upstairs, Gregg is out of bed and helping Carrie finish in the kitchen. The three of us walk through the house, opening up the windows to let the winter wind whip the house clean.

Gregg looks at me seriously and says, "Dean, this will probably be the last party we have here in Londonderry, now that we're moving."

"I know, brother, but it was the best party ever; I'll never forget it," I say, thinking about what lies ahead at Pinkerton, the new school I'll be attending in Derry.

"Me neither," Carrie says. "I think a lot of people will remember."

"Definitely," Gregg says, with his little smile.

We're upstairs in our bedroom and Gregg is walking by the packing boxes and suddenly says, "Hey, Dean, let's go for a walk to the orchard, like we used to when we got apples for Mom. I'll roll a number and grab a few beers, all right?" I'm surprised and look at him sort of funny. I think to myself, *Maybe he feels bad that he is not around much lately and we're moving.*

"All right, Gregg, let's go, cool." He rolls up a joint on top of the emptied black lacquered dresser and grabs a couple of beer bottles from the refrigerator. We walk out the front door together and down the driveway and the spring wind gently pushes his hair back, the bottles clang and the air feels good on my face. "Wicked nice out today, huh?" I say to him. He just looks up at me and nods his head. We walk down the driveway across the street and head to the hut in the orchard. We sit in the hut and open our beers and smoke. The sky grows pink over the maples and pines that line the edge of the orchard, and the sun starts to set behind the crooked old apple trees.

A calm quietness settles between us. As we watch the apple flowers, they seem to glow and light up the night. We can't believe it but neither one of us says it. We sit there staring at the trees. We watch the white flowers that look like they glow and look like they might light the branches and the trunks and the ground around the trees. We are caught within the glow of the apple flowers that light the whole orchard like a miracle. *Amazing, it's mesmerizing,* I think to myself. *I've never seen anything like it.* I stare up at the old "pick your own" sign hanging on the hut. I swish a sip of my beer back. Gregg does the same and we watch the flowers glow in the dusk.

I get up, step over to the closest branch and grab a tiny blossom off a twisted twig. I walk it back to Gregg in the little brown wooden hut. I cup it between my hands and look into the crack between my thumbs to see if it glows in the dark, and when I look, it does, shining the light off itself for me to see.

Gregg looks over, "Is it really glowing?" he asks.

"It is, it's crazy, look," I say to him. I put my cupped hands up to his face; he closes one of his blue eyes and peers in at the tiny white blossom with the other.

"It is," he says.

"It's crazy, huh?" I say to him.

"Yeah, I've never seen anything like it. The whole orchard is glowing."

A few fireflies sparkle green in the orchard, and before we realize it the night is on us, the glow gone.

"I don't want to go, Dean. I wish we weren't moving," Gregg says to me, as we walk away from the orchard.

"Me, too, Gregg. But like you said the last time, everything changes, right? We can't stop it."

"Yeah," he says, and as we walk up the railroad-tie stairs filled with little white pebbles, he turns, punches me on the shoulder, then grabs me and gives me a hug. When he frees me, I see a silver tear slide down his cheek. He opens up the door, looks back at me and says, "It'll be all right, Dean." I follow behind him, through the screen door.

121

Part Three

The View from the Skylight

Chapter 11

Skylights and Screen Doors

I drive down old Route 1 in Rye heading north toward the bunkers. Neil, my best friend from Derry, sits next to me in the passenger seat of my white Camaro. Nick, one of Gregg's friends, sits in the backseat with Tommy. I follow behind Gregg and a carful of his friends as they drive in Dad's sweet brown Jaguar. The Jag glistens in the summer sun and I watch the chrome of the back bumper slide down the road as I follow. I think to myself, *It's good to have parents who vacation a lot and leave the Jag keys. Vegas, Atlantic City — this is great.* I can see Gregg's long curly blond hair flying up into the Jag's open sunroof. The wind coming in from the Camaro's open T-top whips across my face, and I watch the huge mansions blur by us. "Damn," I say to Neil, "it would be unreal to live in one of those. Look at that one, I think it has a pool on the top."

Nick yells from the backseat for the tenth time, "Turn the fucking rap music down!" We ignore him and keep driving through the salt-scented beach air. Tourists walk along the man-made rock wall on the beach side and their parked cars line the road. I follow Gregg in the gleaming Jaguar as we drive down the winding road toward the bunkers.

"Chill out, Nick, we're almost there," I say.

We pull into the graveled parking lot past the wood-carved sign that reads "Odiorne Point State Park." Gregg steps out of the Jaguar, stretches a bit and looks out over the swamp marshland and then heads to the trunk of the car. He pulls out a case of beer and hands a few flashlights to his buddies. We get out of the Camaro and I point over toward the woods on the other side of the marsh and say, "The bunkers are that way, off of the trail, come on." They follow me into the woods.

As we get closer to the bunkers, I start to hear the faint sound of the ocean. The wooded path opens up toward a clearing that overlooks the beach. As the bunkers come into sight, everyone stops walking and looks up at a huge man-made hill with a concrete gun turret in the middle of it. The giant concrete pillbox, built into the hill, rises at a sharp angle about forty feet into the air on the left. On the right a rocky beach faces the Atlantic in front of the bunker.

"The opening is over there in the corner," I shout to everyone, pointing to the little cave that has been broken through the concrete on the side of the bunker.

I'm the second to last to enter. As I start to crawl through the narrow opening on my belly, I can hear the others inside, their voices echoing back through the opening. The tunnel narrows even more before it breaks to the left and opens into a large hallway inside the bunker. Nick is behind me, bouncing the case of beer that he's pushing, through the hole, against my brand-new sneakers. He laughs every time he does it. "Shouldn't have worn your break-dancin' shoes on this mission, rap master, huh?" he says, as Gregg helps me up into the opening of the hall.

125

"Pretty cool, huh?" I say to Gregg, looking for his approval.

"Yeah," Gregg replies, "I didn't think it would be this big inside."

"You can't see it all from here, but this is a huge hallway and there are a couple of rooms off the right side."

Nick gives his approval as he emerges from the crevice with the case of beer. "Good call, Rap Master Dean, this is pretty cool," he says. Gregg and his friends are waiting for me to show them the procedure.

"All right, get the flashlights and candles going, but we can't head down the hall until we do the traditional chant," I say.

"Oh, no—no more rap—we had enough on the hour-long ride here, rap master." Nick says, as he gives me one of his looks. I really enjoyed torturing him and the rest of the heavy-metal rock heads with my rap music on the ride to the bunkers.

"It's not a rap, it's a chant, bonehead, you know, like monks do. It sounds great in here, wait till you hear the reverb and echo," I try to explain. "Now, everybody repeat after me, it goes oooooh weee ooooh ohhhh owww." The group follows my lead and the seven of us chant it repeatedly, as everyone follows me down the hall of the underground bunker.

After a few minutes, the chant gets too loud so we stop because we don't want to get busted. "This is the room me and my friends usually hang in. It's the farthest one from the opening, so we don't have to worry about being too loud," I say, as Gregg and his friends follow me into the second room off the hall. Gregg and Nick smile as they see the giant red devil spray painted on the room's concrete wall.

"This place is wicked cool, Dean, how did you find it?" Gregg asks.

"My buddy Matt, from Manchester, knew about it before I did. We used to come here with our friends on Saturdays to hang out before the club opened," I answer.

We start popping open beers and sitting down in a circle in the center of the room.

"So, how is it going at the club, Dean? I heard you and Neil practicing in the basement the other night, it sounded great. I thought it was a record," Gregg says.

"We were working on our new song for the lip-synching contest at the club," I say. "The prize is, like, two hundred fifty dollars," I say. "But Joe, the manager of the club, says if we win he won't pay us, because he already pays me for DJing."

"So you guys are going to try to win by fake singing someone else's rap record?" Nick adds.

"No, pinhead, that's what everybody else that enters the contest does, they lip-synch, like Madonna or U2, you know. Me and Neil are lip-synching our new song—the one Gregg heard in the basement," I try to explain, but Nick isn't listening. He still insists it's a fake performance.

"Still sounds freaking fake to me, rap master. Why don't you just do your song for real instead of faking it?" he adds.

"Because, it's a lip-synching contest, not a battle of bands," I say, as I try to clarify the point.

Nick is growing belligerent and is ahead of us by several beers, like he always is. He loves to harass me every time he can.

"Don't be a fucking dink, Nick, just because we don't like Dean's type of music. It's still pretty cool that he does it on his own," Gregg says, standing up for me. "Anyway, one of these days he might get up and smack you. He's tougher than he looks, you know, and they say the best dancers make the best fighters."

"Yeah right, I would never get smacked by a little rap-master wannabe," Nick adds, as most of Gregg's friends laugh at him like they always do. We go back and forth arguing, over everything from the sampling technique rap music uses to the fact that most heavy-metal bands dress like girls. The conversation ends with Nick and I screaming insults at each other, both of us severely buzzed. Gregg doesn't intervene, so I know I'm on my own. Our screams turn into pushes, our pushes turn into slaps, and our slaps turn into punches. Gregg's friends yell, "Fight! Fight! Fight!"

We both hit each other in the face a couple of times. Then, after a few misses, I land a right. I hit Nick's nose and he goes down. I think to myself, as I watch him fall, *The speed bag in the basement and Dad's "golden gloves" lessons have really paid off.* I'm surprised and so are Gregg and his friends. At first, I think maybe he might have gone down on purpose because he didn't want to beat up his best friend's little brother. But, when I help him up and see his nose split and bleeding, I know I must have tagged him pretty good.

Gregg looks over at me, smiles, raises his eyebrows and shakes his head yes. "Good job, Dean, someone had to shut his big mouth," he says, as he shakes my hand. Nick and I make up, and he doesn't talk shit so much after the fight. After a few more beers, we crawl back through the hole and emerge from the bunker, squinting in the summer sunshine after being underground for so long. Gregg slaps me proudly on the shoulder and dust flies into the air and away in the sunshine.

Five beers later, the Kenwood blares from the living room in our new townhouse condo in Derry. I'm out on the porch, talking and smoking. I finish the last sip of my beer, turn around real quick to get another one and I step through the slider door, or try to anyway, as I rip right through the screen and the frame of the door comes off the track and trips me in front of everybody. *Nice move, Dean. You're such an idiot, walking through the screen door.* I fall to the ground and the frame of the screen door falls on top of me. Everyone starts laughing at me. Even I do. My nose hurts. I step up and stand on part of the ripped screen.

"What the fuck!" I yell, "Have that removed!" I wipe my nose, look down at my hand and see a spot of blood. "It's the story of my life," I say, shaking my head. "I win a fight in the afternoon, and that night I get my ass kicked by a screen door!" Everyone laughs and I grab myself another beer.

I sit on the round palm tree–printed couch in the living room. Gregg and his new girl, Pam, the blonde "Astro" cheerleader from our big party, are across the couch from me. I clank my beer on the round glass-topped table. Pam is twirling Gregg's long hair with her finger. I sigh to myself and sip my beer. *New place, same old story,* I think.

Neil and I race down the highway to Boston in the Jaguar. "Another Friday," I say to him, "and we're skipping again. I'm going to have to stay back this year, I think."

"Me too," he says, "but so what? Another year at Pinkerton won't be that bad, right."

"Guess not," I say to him.

"Where are your parents this time?"

"In AC again, but this time they flew, so they left us the Jag again. Fucking fresh, Neil, it's going to be a good night at the club, man."

"Definitely."

We park the Jaguar on the top floor of the parking garage next to Quincy Market and Faneuil Hall. We look over the concrete railing of the garage down at the city and we have a smoke. The fog we drove through is lifting and floating away above us.

We walk to the middle of Faneuil Hall across from the big stairs that lead to Government Center. We roll out our piece of linoleum. I hit play on the graffiti boom box and the music thumps through the speakers. I start popping and a crowd gathers. We dance out one song, taking turns, and I head out to the edge of the crowd with my baseball hat upside down in my hand. People drop change and dollar bills into it for us. A few fives even lay in the hat. We break dance for a couple of hours, like we always do, until we are worn out, and then we roll up the linoleum and walk back to the car.

I drive the Jaguar into the parking lot of Club 777 on South Willow Street in Manchester, and I feel like a superstar parking it all by itself at the end of the parking lot. Just as I'm about to turn the Jag off, Neil says to me, "Wait till the chicks see what we're driving tonight. Let's just drive up past the entrance a few times, so everyone sees us." So I cruise by the entrance and a few of the clubbers that are in line see us.

"It's too early." I say to him.

"Yeah, I guess so."

"Let's just park and go in."

I park the car closer so that we can be seen coming out of it. We walk in and Joe, the balding club owner, looks over at me and says, "Late as usual, Smart, get in there."

"All right, all right, sorry — traffic." I say to the owner. He shakes his head and looks at me like he doesn't believe me. I squint my eyes, as they adjust to the darkness inside. I look into the club, and even though it's early, the big room — where the DJ from Kiss 108 plays R&B and dance pop — is already filling up. The hip-hop room is still empty except for a few of our friends from Manchester. When they see Neil and I walk in, they get up, walk over to us, shake our hands and give us hugs.

I can't stop smiling, as I step up the three little stairs that rise into the elevated disc-jockey booth. *I did it!* I think to myself. *Fuck, I really did it. I'm seventeen years old and I'm a DJ at the biggest club around. I'm the first B-boy in New Hampshire; I can't believe it.* I think about the kids from Londonderry and Pinkerton who have given me a hard time. *They are probably sitting in their houses right now talking to their friends on the phone or watching TV, while I'm about to start another Friday night at Club 777.* I hit the power switch in the booth. The equipment lights up. I hit the lights for the dance floor and it glows and flashes.

In our new loft bedroom at the townhouse condo there is a skylight. The skylight is mounted in the roof that starts a few feet above the floor in the bedroom. On the side of the loft where the skylight is you can't stand up or your head will hit the roof, so we put my bed against the sidewall where the roof comes low. Gregg and I wait until my parents go to sleep, after they have finished watching TV in the room below the loft, and we stand in the skylight window. We pop the screen off the frame and we open the skylight as high as it will go. We both stand up in the skylight, and our legs are in the house and the rest of our bodies are outside in the night air.

Standing there in the skylight feels almost like flying or standing on the edge of a huge cliff. The roofline and shingles are at our elbows and I look down four floors, out over the golf course across the street. We smoke a joint in the skylight. I wonder if people driving by on the street can see the smoke that billows over the roofline. I stare down at the giant weeping willow on the golf course and remember back to my old willow in the front yard of our house in Hudson so many years ago. I look up into the night sky and stare at the stars and the moon and a few clouds that float away into the darkness. I look over at Gregg, as he exhales into the night air, and the smoke rises around his face and weaves through his long curly golden hair with the wind. He smiles at me, his blue eyes bright in the darkness. "Remember the willow?" I ask him.

"Oh yeah," he answers, "you used to sit under that tree, hiding in the branches all the time when you were little."

"Yeah, I did, I loved it under there. Under the weeping willow it was peaceful, quiet."

"Just like the skylight, this is cool, huh, brother? It's peaceful up here."

"Yeah, I like it. It's nice looking out the skylight before bed every night."

"Yeah, it is probably the coolest thing about this place, but who are you going to smoke with when I'm gone, when I move out?"

"I don't know, Gregg. I'll just smoke by myself, I guess, but I'll miss you."

He looks over at me in the night sky and taps me on the shoulder. "Good night, little brother, see you tomorrow."

"Night, Gregg, see you tomorrow, brother. I love you."

"I love you, too."

He steps out of the skylight and gets into bed. I pop my head back inside, put the joint out and get into bed. I look over at Gregg and he is already asleep.

Neil and I are sitting on his screened-in porch. He has just gotten back from vacationing in Florida with his parents, and I sit staring out the screens in the windows sipping my beer and wondering how I'm going to tell him. I stare out the black screen so long my eyes go fuzzy, like I'm in sort of a trance or like the whiteout of a snowstorm or like looking through a fog or mist. I think to myself, *Fuck it, just tell him, you have to.* I turn away from the window screen and my eyes refocus.

"Neil, I've got to tell you something." I say to him, as I sit back down on the chair on his porch.

"What?" He asks and he sits forward a bit, interested.

"You're going to be fucking pissed, but just stay cool, all right?"

"All right, just fucking tell me. What, man?"

"Last weekend when you were in Florida, your girlfriend was at the Sevens and, umm, she was hanging all over another guy and she was making out with him at the end of the night, and I'm pretty sure she left with him both nights, too."

"What!" he screams. "What the fuck? She's such a cheating little bitch — who was she with?"

"Well, that's the fucked-up thing, buddy — it was your friend Paul."

"Wow, fucked up, that's fucked up." His head drops and he sighs. I reach over and tap him on the shoulder a few times. He sighs again and starts shaking his head no.

"Fucked up, man, how could they do that?" He asks.

"I don't know, man, it's just crazy fucked up. It wasn't easy trying to tell you, my man."

"Crazy, man, she is all done!" He jumps up, grabs the telephone and calls her, asks her if he can come by and see her. He hangs up, grabs his car keys and tells me he'll call me and let me know what's up.

Really early the next morning the phone rings and I answer it, still lying in bed. It's Neil. "Why are you calling so early?" I ask him.

"You are not going to believe what happened," he says to me, sounding nervous.

"What?"

"Well, I went over to Terry's house that night after you told me what she did — and I screamed at her for a while and then I broke up with her and I just left—thinking fuck her, right."

"Yeah, I figured you would break up with her."

"Well, Dean, that's not it. I guess when I left, she went into the garage and . . . umm . . . killed herself."

"No fucking way, you're kidding, right, tell me you're fucking kidding, Neil."

"No, I ain't kidding, Dean. I just got off the phone with her parents and then the Derry police called me, too."

"No way, fucked up, are you serious?"

"I'm totally serious, Dean, for real." As he says it, I start to feel sick. *It's my fault, I should have never told him what happened while he was in Florida.*

"Holy shit, Neil. It's my fucking fault. I shouldn't have told you. Shit."

"Yes, you should have, you have to tell your friends shit like that—it's not your fault. Anyhow, she had a lot of other problems besides me breaking up with her." I feel the stress in Neil's voice coming through the phone line. He sounds like he's about to cry. I think to myself, *I can't believe it. If I hadn't said anything, she would still be alive.* I don't know what else to say to Neil and we both just sit there silent on the phone.

"How did she do it?" I ask stupidly.

"She did it with the car, you know, the exhaust in the garage, but the worst part is—" I hear him start sniffling and sighing and crying through the phone, "she tried to change her mind, I guess."

"What do you mean?"

135

"Well, they found her on the stairs like she was trying to get inside but it must have been too late, man. It's just crazy. What the fuck do I say to her parents and the police?"

"Just tell them what happened — you know, the truth. It'll be okay, buddy."

"Can you come over and have a drink with me?"

"All right, buddy, stay cool, I'll be right over." I hang up the phone, get dressed and drive over to his house, and we both sit on the porch, drinking beers and staring out the porch screens. I just keep telling him over and over it's not his fault and I keep telling him that I'm sorry, like people do on TV when someone dies. He cries a few times and I keep hugging him and telling him it's going to be all right.

A few days later, Neil and I sit together in the back row inside the small funeral home off a side street in Derry. We both fidget uncomfortably in our shirts, ties and suits. When Terry's parents come in, we both hug them and say the usual, that we are sorry for their loss. But I think that Neil and I are both a little sorrier than some of the other kids in attendance. We sit back down in the last row and watch the mourners come and go from the casket. Neil breaks down and starts crying, so I put my hand on his shoulder and tell him again, "It's going to be all right."

Neil and I stand on the side of the stage in the big room at Club 777. The place is jam-packed with people for the final round of the big lip-synching contest that has gone on for a month or so. The Red Sox are playing the Mets in the World Series and the Sox are one game away from winning it.

The intro to the song Neil and I recorded in the basement of my condo begins to blare through the speakers. Neil and I jump onto the stage as the crowd goes nuts, and we strut back and forth onstage dropping our own pre-recorded rhymes and lip-synching the lyrics. The song ends sort of suddenly and the crowd starts cheering. We step off stage and the crowd is chanting, "Cold Noize, Cold Noize." The DJ calls all the participants back onstage to ask the crowd to pick a winner through applause. We win hands down and get the loudest cheers of all. We stand onstage, and when they announce that we have won, we raise our hands in victory and we hug each other and walk off the stage.

The DJ says through the speakers, "The Red Sox are one out away from winning the World Series!" and everyone cheers. The game plays on a big projection screen on the stage. The DJ shuts the music off, the crowd stops dancing and everyone watches the game. The crowd groans as the Mets get a couple of hits with two outs in the ninth inning. Then they start cheering on the Sox pitcher, hoping he can get the final out. Mookie Wilson bats for New York; the Mets are down by a run with two runners on. Wilson hits a grounder toward first and the crowd holds its breath because it looks like an easy out. Unbelievably, the ball rolls right through the feet of Sox first-baseman Bill Buckner and dribbles into right field. Buckner turns around and watches it roll into the outfield, as the two runners for the Mets cross the plate and celebrate their comeback win in the ninth by raising their arms in victory and hugging. The crowd goes silent and the people start to boo and hiss.

I head to the DJ booth and take up my position. *Better spin some records.* Joe, the club owner, comes walking over to the DJ booth in the rap room and stands next to the stairs as I pull out a record. I turn around and he says to me, "Smart, I can't pay you the five hundred bucks for winning the lip-synching contest—'cause, well, you know, you work for me."

I was expecting this, but I still look at him, pissed off. "What the fuck, that sucks, Joe, wow." I shake my head at him in disappointment. "Do you at least have a trophy for us—or a plaque—anything?"

"No, sorry," he says and he walks away.

"Shit," I say to myself. *No prize money and no trophy, and the Sox blow the Series.* I turn back around in the DJ booth and I spin records, and the music keeps pumping and the lights keep flashing and the dancers keep dancing, and I keep smiling, standing up in the DJ booth, looking down into the crowd.

Chapter 12

Highways and Haircuts

Dad pilots the brown Jaguar north on Route 95 in southern New Jersey, and I watch the cars go by from the backseat window. Mom and Dad talk about stopping in Atlantic City for the night, after such a long drive coming home from Florida. "Just one night, right, Mom?" I say, leaning into the front seat. "Because, I've got to work at the club this weekend."

"Yeah, monkey face," she says, "just one night."

"Mom, don't call me monkey face, okay? I'm not a kid anymore."

"All right, honey, I'll try not to," she says.

I lean back in the seat and look out the window, watching the cars go by. We pass a big old Firebird that looks just like Neil's car. As we pull ahead of it, I look into the passenger seat and see the silhouette of someone with a high-top fade haircut, just like Neil's. I call it the eraser-head — the hairdo made famous by the rap group Kid 'n Play. Dad slows down and the Firebird catches up to us. I look at the driver and it looks just like Neil's dad, Jack. I stare at him and look again to the eraser-head sitting next to him, and I swear to God it's Neil. "No way!" I shout.

"What?" Dad says back to me.

"It's Neil, driving right next to us!"

Dad beeps a few times and Jack and Neil look over at us driving next to them. They both look shocked and start to laugh. Dad signals them to pull over and we follow them into the breakdown lane. I lean to the front seat. "Maybe they can come to AC with us, huh, Dad?" I ask.

"Sure, if they want to," he says back to me.

I step out of the Jaguar and Neil steps out of the Fire-bird, and as we walk toward each other, we are both smiling like we can't believe it. I shake his hand and we hug, "How crazy is this?" I ask him.

"I know, it's unreal." He says.

"The odds of something like this happening have to be like a million to one or something, huh?"

"Yeah, wow, unbelievable."

"Hey, you think your dad will let you come with us to Atlantic City for the night?"

"I'll ask him—maybe he'll think it's a good idea."

Neil walks over to the car and leans into the window. His dad must like the idea because Neil smiles and turns to give me a thumbs-up. "We'll follow you," he calls out.

Neil and I sit on the top of the metal railing on the beach side of the boardwalk in front of Caesars Palace. We watch the tourists go by the electric lights of Atlantic City. The sea breeze hits our backs and I still can't get over the fact that we ran into each other on the highway. "We haven't been down here in a while," I say to Neil, "huh?"

"Yeah," he says, "it's been awhile."

"Where are the breakers?" I ask him. "Looks like they aren't around anymore."

"I guess not," he says back to me. "What were you doing in Florida?"

"Oh, we were down at Gregg's apartment—well, not Gregg's apartment, his girlfriend Pam's apartment—I mean, his *fiancée* Pam's apartment," I say, emphasizing the word I've been having trouble with.

"What? He's getting married to her?"

"Yep, he is. I know, it's crazy, I never thought he would get married, especially to a college girl like Pam."

"No, why not?"

"I don't know, she's like fake with all that valley-girl popularity shit and she's weird. We were at dinner with her in Florida and she drank like fifteen Diet Pepsis at dinner and then she started talking real fast and every other word is like, like, like. She kind of talks like a robot and her voice just annoys me, for some reason. She has the fakest smile sometimes; I mean her smile is so fake I wouldn't be surprised if she had false teeth." Neil laughs. "She just doesn't seem to be his type, you know what I mean?"

"No, she doesn't."

"Oh, but listen to this, we're at the restaurant where she drank all the Pepsi and listen to what Gregg does—this is funny."

"What?" Neil asks.

"It's a Mexican restaurant with the menu like in Spanish or whatever and Gregg, I guess, couldn't pronounce what he wanted to the waitress so when it's time to order he says, 'I'll have the chicken vaginas.' He pronounced the chicken fajitas like chicken *vaginas*, we fucking died laughing and so did the waitress—it was wicked funny."

141

Neil can't stop laughing. He looks over at me, red faced, and says, "I'll have the chicken vaginas, too."

"Yeah, I'll have an order of chicken vaginas, as well." I repeat back at him.

"I think Gregg did it on purpose just to make us laugh. Man, I'll never forget it."

"When is he getting married?"

"When she graduates, and then, they're moving back. She wants to be a reporter up here, I guess. Gregg's going to work with my dad selling insurance, he says. Oh, she's a DJ at the college where she goes. I guess she plays metal all night and they call her the maiden of metal."

"Really, they call her the maiden of metal, huh?"

"Yeah. I just can't understand why Gregg likes her so much. He could have any girl he wants."

"Yeah, probably."

"That's how it goes, I guess. Let's just walk down to the Golden Nugget and see if the breakers are down there."

"All right," he says.

We step off the railing together and we walk down the boardwalk. It seems like every kid we walk by has his baseball hat on backward and has sneakers on with fat laces in them. There are graffiti tags everywhere on the board-walk: on the trash cans, on the lampposts, on the sides of the buildings. Rap music comes out of the arcades and the beats float in the sea air across the boardwalk. Hip-hop is everywhere and they are still selling the tee shirts that read "Fresh" on the front in every tee shirt shop. We sit on the railing across from the Golden Nugget and we stare at the spot where we used to dance. There is no crowd, no boom box, no linoleum and the Atlantic City Breakers are gone.

I walk down the wooden dock that stretches across the water on the shore of Lake Winnipesaukee. I see Gregg sitting on the back of Dad's pride and joy, a brand-new thirty-two-foot Carver yacht. Dad just traded in his old twenty-five-foot boat for the Carver. It glimmers in the sun, as I walk toward it. The back of the yacht reads "Bill Me Later, Derry NH." I think to myself, *This is Dad's trophy.* Gregg sits on the back of the boat and sips a Corona with his blue Vuarnet sunglasses on and he looks like an ultra-rich rock star. The yacht looks huge as I walk up to it and open the little hatch door to the spot where Gregg sits. "What's up, Gregg?" I say. "Have you seen the inside?"

"Oh yeah, it's incredible." He sips his beer in the sun.

"It has it all inside, huh, a little living room, a kitchen, a bathroom with a shower and a bedroom in the stern. It's like a floating apartment; you could easily live in it."

"Yeah, it's almost bigger than the apartment Pam and I lived in, in Florida."

Pam comes walking through the sliding glass door that goes down to the galley and the living room. She steps up the stairs with a video camera in her hand and sits down next to us. "Hi, Dean," she says.

"Hey Pam, what's up," I say.

"Nothing, we're just waiting for my parents to get here, so we can start planning the wedding."

I walk down into the galley and hug Mom who is making a snack tray with cheese and crackers. "How is it going?" I ask her.

"Lousy," she answers with an aggravated look. "We keep disagreeing with Pam's parents on a lot of the wedding plans."

Dad looks over at her and says, "Calm down, Judy, don't let Pam hear you."

"Don't worry, Mom," I say to her. "Before you know it, the wedding will be here and it will all be over, so just try to enjoy it."

"I'll try," she answers back. "Honey, can you bring the cheese and crackers onto the deck for me?"

"Sure, Mom, no problem," I answer, and I take the tray from her hand and walk over to the slider. I see Pam's parents step onto the back of the boat. "They're here," I call back to Mom and Dad. I hear my mom sigh as I open the slider.

I step out onto the deck, and as I turn around to slide the door shut, I hear what sound like gunshots going off right on the boat. I jump and drop some of the crackers and turn around. I see Pam's father laughing, as he looks down at a pack of firecrackers popping off on the dock. *He must have lit them and thrown them,* I think to myself, as I catch sight of Gregg and Pam, laughing.

Dad comes up the stairs and out onto the deck. "What the hell is going on out here," he laughs. "You're going to give me a fucking heart attack."

Pam's father looks at him and laughs, "Just firecrackers, Billy, that's all."

Gregg is videotaping us on the deck of the boat. He turns the camera toward Pam as she comes walking up the stairs, through the sliding glass door. She stops on the top step and slides the door back and forth. "Look, I'm in the slammer," she says. She does it again and everyone looks at her and laughs.

I look over at Gregg who looks a bit embarrassed by the whole thing. He shakes his head at me and says, "I don't know, she's crazy, I guess."

My girlfriend from Pinkerton sits across from me at the kitchen table so pregnant she looks like she might burst. I slide a glass of ice water across the table to her. Mom and Dad have offered to watch the baby for us at first, just until we can figure things out. *We're lucky*, I think to myself. *Damn lucky.*

Mom looks over at me from the rattan chair and says, "I can't wait to see Gregg."

"Why?" I ask her, as I sit down.

"He's getting it cut today before he starts officially working with your father."

"No way he's going to cut his hair off! I bet he sits in the chair at the barbershop and then jumps up and runs away."

"I hope he does, he'll look good, I bet."

"I don't think he's going to do it." I repeat.

The front door opens downstairs and we hear them coming up the condo stairs. Dad moves out of the way as if he is presenting Gregg to us. I stare at my brother. His long hair is gone and he has just a normal short businessman haircut. He is wearing a really nice grey suit and a shirt and tie. Mom jumps up out of her seat with a great cry of happiness. She walks over and hugs him, a huge smile on her face, "Oh, honey," she says, "it looks so good, you look great, and you'll look great for the wedding."

Gregg smiles at us. "Thanks, love you, Mom."

Mom turns her head and says in his ear, "I love you, too, Gregg, I'm so happy."

"What's Pam going to say about the haircut?" I say.

"Oh, she is not going to be happy. She just keeps saying, 'Don't cut it, put it in a ponytail for work.'"

"Oh, you are dead, she's going to kill you."

"Well, what's she going to do? It's not like she's going to leave me because I got my hair cut, right?"

"Well, if she did, it might not be so bad, right?" I say to him, trying to get him to laugh. "You could just cancel the whole wedding—it's probably a good idea anyway." He looks over at me and smirks and I continue to taunt him. "Besides, have you checked to see if she really is a robot?" Gregg starts laughing and punches me on the shoulder. I stand up and do a robot move, turn to Gregg and pretend I'm Pam. I talk like a valley-girl robot and say slowly, "Like-where-is-your-hair-Gregg-like-I-told-you-to-put-it-in-like-a-pony-tail-like-you-are-dead-I-am-like-a-mad-robot-beep-beep." I punch him on his shoulder, as he keeps on laughing, Dad and Mom joining in. "Just cancel it, come on, we'll party like we used to," I say, giving it one more shot.

"That would be great, Dean, but it's a little late for that," he says. He looks so different in his suit and tie and with his hair now cut. *Where's Gregg?* I think to myself. *Where did Gregg go?*

Gregg and I, along with the rest of the groomsmen, step into the long white limousine. I sit down on the leather seat and my starchy tuxedo shirt is scratching my skin like crazy. I think the suit jacket is just a bit too small and it's making the uncomfortable shirt and tie worse. "Damn jacket—this thing is fucking horrible," I say to everyone. "Pour me a fucking drink."

Gregg gets in and sits down next to me in the backseat. Rick is on the other side of me, fidgeting in his tux, too. Gregg tells the chauffeur to come on, we're running late. The chauffeur rolls the glass divider up and Gregg says, "Open the champagne, let's get this over with."

We quickly go through a few bottles and the champagne goes down a bit too easy for me. I feel a bit lightheaded. I start to stare at the bubbles rising in the champagne flute. Rick looks over at me, and starts giggling. "I think Dean's buzzed already, Gregg." We laugh.

Gregg smiles and takes a sip. "I think I am, too," he says. He opens the dividing glass window and says to the driver, "We'll have to stop and get some more champagne." The driver shakes his head yes and the dividing glass rises.

The limo pulls into the parking lot of a little neighborhood market. Gregg jumps out of the car and says, "I'll be right back."

Rick looks over at me and can tell I'm buzzing. "Well, what do you think about this, Dean?" He asks.

"Well, Rick, you know I don't really dig Pam, right?" I say quietly to him, so the groomsmen won't hear me. He looks at me with a questioning look.

"Yeah," he says.

"Well, I don't think the marriage will last a year." I say stupidly because I'm buzzed.

"I can't believe you're having a kid," Rick says to me, changing the subject, "and I can't believe Gregg's getting married."

"I know. It's crazy how fast it all goes, isn't it?"

"Yeah, it goes fast, and my little brothers are all grown up. I think I'm going to cry," he says and he slaps me on the shoulder, laughing.

Gregg jumps back in the limo with a bottle of champagne in each hand. He raises them into the air. "Let's party!" he shouts, and we all start cheering and yelling. The limo drives off, as one of Gregg's groomsmen pops open another bottle.

I stand in the church with my back to the pews and stare at the altar. *I can't breathe*, I think to myself, *I'm getting dizzy.* The rest of the wedding party is coming down the aisle, hand in hand, and they are walking so slowly it seems like everything I see is in slow motion. *Come on! Get down the aisle!* I'm starting to sweat. I look down at my shirt and can see a few spots of perspiration coming through the rough fabric. I look down the aisle again and they're still walking in slow motion. *Come on, get down here!* I let out a huge sigh.

Rick, on my left, looks at me and squints like he's worried. He whispers to me, "You all right, Dean?"

"Yeah, I'm just hot." I say back to him and I wipe the sweat off my forehead.

He whispers very slowly, "It's the champagne."

I try to catch my breath and look back to the aisle. It's empty; they finally made it down. Sweat drips down my face and I'm burning up, and I feel like I'm wobbling a bit and like everyone in the church is staring at the back of my head.

The wedding march begins to play. Gregg walks down the aisle, smiling. I feel like my knees are going to give out. I look down at my shirt and it is drenched and the sweat keeps dripping down my face. I look back up the aisle just as Pam steps up to the altar and takes her place next to Gregg. A flower arrangement that has been resting on the altar topples to the ground. Someone from the front row of pews steps over to the flowers and puts them back up and then hurriedly sits back down.

Time stops and I start to see little white dots growing in my eyeballs. Rick looks over at me—my knees shake—I start to wobble even more. I turn to him and say, "I'm going . . . down . . . Ricky." He catches me with his hands on my back and stops me from dropping to the floor. When he does, I sort of wake up a bit and I start to catch my breath. He holds his arm behind my back and holds me up while Gregg and Pam finish their vows. It's over. Everyone cheers and I look down at my shirt and it is soaked as if I just took a shower with it on.

Rick turns to me and says, "You made it, Dean. Too much champagne for you."

"I didn't think I was going to make it." I say to him.

I sit in a small sunroom off the side of the hospital staring at the trees coming into leaf in the distance. I like it in the sunroom; I can feel the sun warm against my skin. I watch the wind blow through the new yellow leaves of the trees outside and wonder how all of this will work out. How will I pay for everything the baby is going to need? I just graduated; I have no money, no real job. I scratch my head and stare back out the glass wall of the sunroom. *How will I take care of my girlfriend?*

I hear my dad's voice come through my head saying, "Marry her, son, it's the right thing to do." I look back out the sunroom glass, but all I see is my worried reflection.

Mom walks in the sunroom with my new daughter all bundled up in a pink blanket in her arms. She is so happy; she is glowing. I don't think I have ever seen my mother happier. She sits down next to me and says, "She's perfect, look at her, son, she's wonderful." *She's right; Ashley is beautiful.*

"I know she is, Mom, she's awesome."

Mom smiles at me and stares down at the baby and smiles as if she might want to cry, she is so happy. "Who is my little sweetheart?" she says to Ashley. "Yes, who is Nanny's little sweetheart?" She smiles and shakes her head yes, "It's Ashley, she's my little sweetheart." Her baby talk reminds me of when I was a kid. "Here, hold her, son," she says to me, then she hands my daughter to me.

I take Ashley in my arms and she is so tiny and her eyes stare up at me. Mom says to me, "Everything is going to work out just fine, don't you worry, monkey face."

Gregg comes walking up the stairs into the kitchen of the condo while Mom, Dad and I are having dinner. He gets to the top of the stairs and stands there with his hands behind his back, in a dark suit and tie. He's got his sunglasses still on and he says to us, "Guess what?"

I look over at him, jealous of his nice suit. "What?"

"Guess what I am?" he asks.

"I don't know, what are you?"

"I am Metropolitan Life's—Rookie of the Year!" He smiles and pulls his hands from behind his back and he is holding a trophy. He raises it above his head and says, "Let's party!" I stare up at it, as he holds it above his head. It's a plaque with a golden emblem. I smile up at him and think it's unbelievable he has done it again. Just like way back in Hudson at the playoff game, he wins it in the end every time, he's unbelievable.

Dad and Mom stand up and hug him. Dad says to Gregg, "I'm so proud of you, son."

Mom says, "You're doing so great, son, I love you."

I get up and shake his hand, and as I walk back to the table, I say, "Maybe I'll win Rookie of the Year next year, huh."

I look at the plaque in his hand and he places it on the glass-topped kitchen table and sits down in the rattan chair. "When are you going to start?" Gregg asks me because he knows that I have just passed the insurance exam and am about to start training.

"Soon, brother, soon, and then you're in trouble," I say, joking, trying to challenge him. "It'll be fun working together."

"Yeah it will, buddy," he says as he looks over at Ashley sitting on her Nanny's lap and says, "Now where is my little princess Ashley?"

He leans over toward Mom, and Nanny hands Ashley over to Gregg. He picks her up into the air and flips her around and puts her stomach on his shoulder while she faces forward, and he grabs her little arms and flies her through the air. He flies Ashley all around the condo past the palm-printed round couch and around the modern glass coffee table and back into the kitchen and around the rattan chairs and the kitchen table and past the sliding door, and he makes airplane flying noises and Ashley laughs and laughs, and he flies her all around the condo, and we can't stop laughing at them.

Neil and I are recording in the basement at the condo in Derry; we are recording lyrics over one of our beats. We stand in front of the wall that we have spray painted with a big mural that reads "System Def," our new name. Pam walks in and stands at the doorway and looks at me while Neil raps on the microphone and I record him. I look over at her like she is interrupting us, and I raise my head at her like *What's up?*

Neil stops halfway through his part and pulls the headphones off and looks at me.

I stop the beat on the equipment and I look over at Pam standing in the doorway to the basement.

"What's up, Pam?" I ask her.

"Nothing," she says. "You guys sound really good."

"Thanks, so what's up?" I wonder why she is down here trying to talk to me. She never does that.

"Well," she says, "you know I'm working at the high school in Winnacunnet, right? I'm the media coordinator and some of my students are making a video for a contest."

"Yeah, and —"

"Well, I was wondering if you guys would make a rap song for us, for our video."

"What's the video for?" I ask her.

"It's for Florida orange juice." She says and then she looks at me kind of strangely and she twirls her hair on her finger and gives me a fake little flirty smile. I look over at Neil like *Did you see that?* He shakes his head with a small yeah.

"What's it for?" I ask her again.

"It's for orange juice," she says to me.

"Fucking orange juice?" I say to her. "I'm supposed to rap for fucking orange juice? I don't know, Pam, I don't really rap for, umm, citrus fruits, you know—we rap for rap—you know what I mean?"

"Oh," she says.

"Well," I say to her, "we could just give you one of our beats we aren't using; you could use it for background music in the video, maybe."

"Okay," she says and she walks out of the basement door.

"That was fucked up." I say to Neil. "She was kind of flirting with me—did you see that?"

"Yeah, she was. I saw it," he says.

"I ain't fucking rapping for *orange juice*."

"Yeah, neither am I."

"That was just fucking really weird, fucked up, right?"

I walk up the stairs of the condo heading to my bedroom and Gregg is sitting on the tweed couch in the TV room below my bedroom loft. He's hunched over and has a necklace made of beads in his hand. I'm surprised to see him, because he's not here much anymore after getting married and moving up the block to his new condo. I stop at the top of the stairway and say, "Hey, brother, what are you doing here?"

"I'm waiting to head over to Sun Ho, the Chinese restaurant I like to go to on Fridays."

"You going to get a scorpion bowl like you always do?"

"Yeah, I've been asking the waiter for months to bring me a scorpion bowl for eight, and last week he finally brought a huge one over to the table. It was funny, you should have been there."

"What's with the beads?"

"I don't know, I just like to feel them in my hand," he says and he looks up at me as if he's worried about something.

"What's up, brother? Is everything all right, man? What's going on, bro?"

"When do you start working with Dad and me?" He asks.

"In a couple weeks, I start, when I'm finished training."

"You want to come to Sun Ho tonight, brother?"

"No, I can't. I'm going dancing with Neil and everyone, but I'll come when I start working with you, all right?" He looks back down at the beaded necklace in his hands, as I walk up the stairs to the loft.

"I'm jetting." He says to me.

"Oh, talking like a B-boy now, you're jetting, huh, all right, later—*homey*." I say to him, laughing from the loft above him.

"Later, homey." He says up to the loft at me. He raises his hand up above his head in a fist and then he points at me with it and smiles. "Later, homey," he repeats and pumps his fist at me again and then he points at me one last time.

Chapter 13

The First Day and
The Night of Division

I step into the lobby entrance at the offices of Metropolitan Life Insurance and catch a glimpse of myself in the glass door. I hardly recognize myself and it catches me off guard. I stop and stand there, staring at the reflection. I can't believe it; I look really professional in my suit and tie. In one hand, I have Dad's old brown leather briefcase; in the other, a cup of coffee. "You look like you're going to trade stocks on Wall Street," I say to my reflection. "Wow, looking good, Dean." I smile in the glass and I walk toward the door of the office where I'm about to begin my first official day.

I swing open the glass door and walk into the offices my dad has worked in for years. I walk by the two computer terminals that are near the door and recognize his office, behind the glass walls. Dad has the first of the three nice offices on the floor. I head in the opposite direction and I walk down a few steps where the cubicles are.

I drop Dad's old brown leather briefcase on the floor near the side of my new desk. I sit down in the chair, sigh, and loosen my tie a bit. I grab the briefcase, open it and grab my planner. I open it up to this week and stare at my appointment schedule. I stare at the plastic storage thingy on my desktop. *Cool, it spins.* I spin it and it rattles a bit. "Cool," I say out loud. I open my skinny desk drawer and reach for the cold-call cards. I stare down at them. "Okay, Dean, let's give it a try."

I grab the top card off the stack, pick up the phone and dial the number on the card. The phone rings and rings, again and again. I hang up and mark the card N.A. for no answer and date it May 1.

I grab the next card and dial the number; it rings twice and someone answers. "Hello," I say, "this is Dean Smart calling from Metropolitan Life Insurance Company. Did I catch you at a conven—?" I hear the phone click on the other end of the line and then a dial tone. I mark the card H.U. for hang up and date it May 1.

I sip my coffee and sigh. I grab the next card and dial; it's an N.A. The next is B for busy. I bounce the eraser and spin the spinner. I put my feet on the desk and lean way back in the chair as if I'm the CEO. I take my feet off the desk. I think to myself, *I don't know how long I can take the excitement around here.*

I walk into Dad's big office with the glass walls. Gregg sits in the nice leather chair behind the desk. He's leaning way back in the chair talking on the phone with it propped on his shoulder. He looks over at me and raises his hand and puts up one of his fingers to say shhhh. I stand there and look at him. He looks completely official as he talks with his smooth quiet talk on the phone with his little smirk on, just like he used to do when he talked to girls. I shake my head and smile a bit.

I walk behind him to the big window in the back of the office. I sit on the window frame and watch Gregg spin in the chair away from the desk and look back at me. I stare at the wall where Dad has all his awards hung and there are like twenty-five of them; they read things like "Salesman of the Year" and "Leaders Conference." They are all mounted on stained wood and have gold emblems and embossed nameplates.

Gregg talks his talk and says things like "cash value" and "interest rate." He gently bounces himself in the leather chair as he talks. He looks at me and winks like he might have a sale. I look out the window and watch the Nashua River shimmer in the morning sun. I look back at Gregg. He says goodbye into the phone and hangs it up. He gets up from the big leather chair and walks out of the office and says, "Universal life — sell it."

"Who *was* that?" I ask myself, as I watch Gregg walk away through the glass wall.

I sit down in the leather chair behind Dad's desk and I lean back in it like Gregg and start bouncing myself gently. I spin around in the chair and look at the picture of Mom standing and waving on the back of the boat with our dog in her arms. I spin back toward the desk and stare at the little plastic figurine Dad has on his desk. It's a cartoonish chubby guy and his legs and hips are on backward and he is looking down at himself with a puzzled expression on his face. On the bottom of the figurine, it reads "Bass-ackwards." I smile and bounce in the chair. I say to myself, "Universal life — sell it."

The phone rings and I wonder to myself, *Should I answer it?* I let it keep ringing until it stops. A minute later, it rings again. *What if it's someone really important like the president and I'm answering my dad's phone?* I let it ring. It stops again and I sigh.

The secretary's voice comes through the intercom. "Billy, are you there?"

"He's not here," I say, nervously. "It's Dean."

"Dean, do you want to take a message for him?"

"I guess so. Is it all right if I do?"

"Yes, of course."

"All right, my first official phone call."

She laughs, and says, "Line three." I hear her hang up.

I stare down at the phone and the button marked 3; it flashes with a red light. I pick up the receiver and hit the flashing button. "Dean Smart, Met Life, can I help you?"

A lady on the other end says, "Oh, I thought I was getting Bill."

"No, it's Dean, his son, can I help you?"

"Yeah, I have an appointment with Bill tomorrow night and I have to cancel."

"What time was the appointment?"

"Eight o'clock."

"I'll let him know, and he'll call you to reschedule — thanks, and have a good day, goodbye." I hang up the phone and mumble to myself, "Well, that sucks, my first official call is a cancellation."

I stand behind Gregg at the computer terminal in the middle of the office near the door. Gregg is typing into the computer. I put my hand on his shoulder and ask him, "When you're done, will you show me how to get to the right screen?" He shakes his head yes and keeps typing.

Dad walks in through the lobby door and walks over to us. "What are you doing, boys?" He asks.

Gregg says, "I'm getting ready for my appointments."

"All right, good."

"Dean, will you do two proposals, one for one hundred thousand dollars and one for two hundred fifty thousand dollars, okay?"

"Yeah, okay, soon as Gregg is done. Oh, I took a message for you, Dad, earlier."

"Who was it?"

"It was our appointment for tomorrow night at eight."

"Yeah, and —"

"Well, that's what sucks, she cancelled."

Gregg looks over at Dad and says, "Yeah Dad, that *sucks*." And he laughs. Dad laughs and looks at me, shaking his head.

I smile at him and say, "Well, you know what I always say, don't you?"

"What, son?"

"I always say that—every success—begins with suck." We all start laughing, as my dad's partner comes walking in.

"What the—are you Smarts multiplying out here? It's like the firm of Smart, Smarter and Smartest!"

"Yeah, who's who? Who's Smartest?" Dad asks.

"Well," Dad's partner answers, "I can tell you from experience that Smartest has to be the new one!" Everyone laughs.

Gregg gets up from the computer and walks over to the printer. I sit down where he was sitting and I log in. He gently rips his proposal off the printer and puts it in his leather planner. He stands behind me at the computer; he points to the screen and shows me where to go. I feel his hand on my shoulder. He reaches into the pocket of his light-grey suit coat and places a paper clip on the table next to the computer where I sit. "Lucky," he says. He rubs it on the proposal and slides it back into his suit-coat pocket and starts walking toward the door. "Later, homey," he says, as I stare down at the keyboard.

I turn around and look up just in time to catch a glimpse of the back of his head, as he walks out the lobby door in his light-grey suit with his leather planner swinging in his hand. "Bye, Gregg." I say to myself.

I sit Indian style under the skylight in the loft. I play baseball on Nintendo as I do every night before bed. I blow a drag of my cigarette out of the skylight screen. I hear sirens off in the distance. Mom and Dad watch TV happily in the living room below me.

The phone rings. I answer it with my usual hello.

"Hello." The voice on the other end is unfamiliar and nervous. "Is this the Smart residence?" the woman asks.

I can hear the strain in her voice and I quickly respond, "Yes, who's calling?"

The voice stumbles a bit as it responds, "This is Gregg Smart's neighbor; are you related to Gregg?"

"Yes, he's my brother, why?"

The voice stumbles and stutters again, as she says, "I think you should come over here as soon as you can because your brother is . . . he's . . . he's sick."

I hang up the phone. I step into my muddy white sneakers as fast as I can. I run down the loft stairs. I stop at the bottom of the stairs. I push aside the window curtain. I look out the window. I look up the street. I see sirens coming from the circular driveway of Gregg's condo. "Crazy," I say to myself.

I scream at Mom and Dad, "Let's go, something's wrong over at Gregg's. Let's go, right now!" They turn and look at me, stunned. I yell again, "Emergency calls, sirens, come on, right now!" I run down the next set of stairs, as Dad and Mom jump up behind me. "Hurry up!" I yell back. I hear Dad's car keys clink in his hand, on the landing above me. "Forget the car, Dad," I yell back at him, "it'll take too long!"

I run down the last flight of steps and throw open the front door. Another police car is racing down the street. I run across the driveway and look back for a second. Dad is still standing in the doorway, looking up the street. His mouth is hanging open, and his eyes are wide. He looks to me and then down to his socks. "No time," I yell. "Run!" I dash across the road and run through the mist toward the flashing lights.

I sprint halfway up the small hill and look back once to see Dad running as fast as he can in his black socks and pajamas. Mom is running behind him, wearing her bathrobe and slippers, her hands flailing. I force myself to stop and breathe. I place my hands on my knees and put my head down. I take a big breath of the murky night air. I look up at a street sign; it reads Sundown Drive. I look up at the condo. The driveway is bathed in red and blue flashing lights. The sirens are blasting away. There are three police cars, an ambulance and a fire truck in the circular driveway.

I think to myself, *This doesn't look good.* I breathe in the fog, as I look back at Dad again. He's coming up the hill, behind me. He coughs and slows down a bit. Mom is still behind him, and I hear her screaming something into the night. She sounds completely panicked through the sirens. I breathe in deep again. I think to myself, *I got to quit smoking. When was the last time I ran like this? Must have been when I was a kid — when Gregg and I were kids.*

I sprint to the top of the hill, and as I turn the corner I look up at the street sign for Misty Morning Drive. I run by the two police cars, fire truck and ambulance. As I run through the mist toward the door, I think, *Oh, man, this doesn't look good!* A policeman sees me dashing for the door. He makes an attempt to stop me from climbing the three concrete steps in front of the screen door. I push, pull and wiggle myself past him and I get to the top stair. I see another cop standing inside the screen door. The cops are both yelling something at me, but I can't hear them through the sirens. I grab the handle and try to open the door, but the cop inside pushes it shut and holds it. I look past him into the entry hall of the condo. I see Gregg lying face down on the floor. The cop moves to the left to block me from looking in and he says something to me, but I don't hear him. I shift to the right and look through the screen again. I see Gregg's body stretched out on the tile in the entrance hallway. The cop says something else to me, but all I hear is a loud hum.

"Why aren't you doing anything?" I yell at him. He doesn't answer me or I don't hear him. He leans to the right and blocks my view again. I lean the other way, and look in. My eyes blur as I strain to see through the screen. I see Gregg's head and neck tilted to the right on the white living-room carpet. His hair looks wet and matted. There is something — a white pillow — a foot or so away from his head. I see his leather planner on the floor near his feet, one leg of suit pants rising above his sock. His left arm looks broken and sort of mangled. Lying next to it is a brass candleholder. His pen is on the floor.

"Why aren't you doing anything?" I scream again at the cop. He blocks my view again. His lips move, but I can't hear anything. I see Gregg's suit jacket, crumpled, riding up the back of his neck.

I hear the cop in the doorway ask me, "Who are you?"

I scream, "I'm Gregg's brother! Why aren't you doing anything?"

"Because he's already dead."

I'm stunned into silence. I look through the screen door and my eyes go fuzzy as I strain to see my brother's body. Slowly, I step backward down the concrete steps with one hand on the railing holding me up. I am outside of myself, rising out of my body and looking at the scene in the driveway from a few feet above. The cop at the bottom of the stairs says something to me and I just shake my head and take a few steps away from him. I stand on the edge of the grass, staring into the lights flashing in the driveway.

Dad runs right by me in his pajamas and black socks. I watch him rush up the concrete stairs to the screen door. *Oh, no,* I think. I watch him stand there for a second and the cop walks him off the stairs and over toward a police car. Another cop opens the back door of the police car and Dad sits down in it with the door open and his feet hanging out. The cop kneels in front of the open door and talks to my dad.

My mother stomps by me with her head high, like she's going to get to the bottom of this situation. I watch her strut up the stairs and stand at the door, proud. A fireman pulls her off the stairs and talks to her while I watch her nervously shake her head back and forth. Her face seems to go blank like she is lost for a second and then I see the fireman pull her into his arms. She lets him hug her for a second and then wildly flicks his arms off her, as she dashes toward the screen door, screaming, "I have to see him . . . my son . . . Greggory . . . I have to!" The fireman grabs her. She keeps screaming, "Please . . . please . . . I have to!" The fireman hugs her and she starts hitting him in the chest. She deflates in his arms and slides through his grip and falls to her knees on the pavement, screaming, "No . . . No . . . No . . . Greggory!"

Dad steps out from the backseat of the police car and runs over to Mom. Dad and the fireman lift her back to her feet. They hug, and from the edge of the driveway, I watch the tears stream down their faces—silver tears that shimmer red, blue and white in the mist. They hold each other, as I stand off by myself, silent and alone, on the edge of the grass.

The officers walk us into Gregg and Pam's neighbor's condo, and we sit down in their living room. Pam is sitting across from me in an armchair in front of a couple of windows. Mom and Dad sit on a couch along the wall, between Pam and me. The woman that owns the condo tells my dad that she was the one who called a minute ago with the news. Dad tries to answer her, but all that comes out of his mouth is a stuttering sort of mumble. His eyes are still wide.

The officer tells us what they know so far; they believe the cause of death was a blunt trauma to the head, possibly caused by a brass candlestick. *The bent candelabra, I think, I saw it through the screen.*

Mom cries out, "Oh, no!" and she starts crying again. Dad puts his head down in his hands and shakes his head. Pam's expression doesn't change.

The officer continues. "It looks like he might have walked into an attempted burglary."

From the armchair in front of the windows, Pam interrupts him, "Like, where is Halen," she says, "where is the dog? Can somebody get the dog?" She asks the officer. He looks at her. I look at her, too, and wonder why she is asking about the dog. *Fuck, man, Gregg is lying dead in the condo and you're asking about the fucking dog.*

The cop doesn't know how to answer her and he says, "The dog is okay. We will bring him in, in a while."

She asks again. "Where is Halen? I want the dog!" and I look at her and see that she isn't really crying and I think, *What the hell?*

Her blank gray eyes look over at me. The sirens are behind her, flashing red, blue and white through the windows. Her steel eyes keep looking at me as if they're searching for my approval—like she wants to know if I believe her. *Fuck, I do not believe any of this shit, including her.*

Right then, I know. *I know she has something to do with this.* I can't look at her or the flashing lights shining in through the windows.

Chapter 14

Morning, Noon and Night

I sit at the kitchen table with Mom and Dad. Dad makes calls to all the relatives and breaks the news. I watch him tell them that Gregg has died. Mom cries, recuperates and then cries again, over and over. With every phone call, Dad's new nervous stutter gets worse.

I'm in a daze and I'm shaky. *This is so fucked up,* I think to myself. I keep turning around and looking out the slider behind me, as if I'm being watched. I open the slider and the wind comes in, and I'm thankful the sirens have finally gone silent. I look back at my parents sitting at the glass-topped kitchen table. They look so different, suddenly. I don't say much of anything; I just sit at the table in front of the slider and watch it all go down.

Relatives start to show up in the middle of the night: Rick and Sue, Jimmy and Debbie, Jeff and Michele, my girlfriend, without our daughter Ashley, after I talk to her dad in the middle of the night and explain what happened. I don't know what to say to any of them. I just sit in front of the slider door, watching the hugs and tears. The whole thing is fucked up, and I can't help but think that nobody fucking robs a condo, and if they do, they don't kill the guy that lives there when he comes in and interrupts them — they run.

I look over at my dad sitting at the head spot at the table and wait for a lull in the conversation. I blurt out, "I think Pam had something to do with the murder—I think she is involved in it."

Mom says, "Don't be ridiculous, Dean!"

Dad just looks at me and shakes his head in disapproval.

"But, I'm telling you, no one would rob that condo; there are too many neighbors. And, besides, if someone interrupts a robbery, the robbers usually just run—they don't kill. They just want the loot."

Everyone looks at me a bit stunned, but a few look as if they might agree with me, so I keep talking. "Did you hear her ask for that fucking dog over and over again? What about Gregg—why didn't she ask about him? Come on, you know what I mean, guys, right?"

Dad looks thoughtful. "Yeah, that *was* a little weird Dean—right, Judy?" Mom just shakes her head yes.

I feel like they might be with me on this, so I keep going. "She wasn't showing much emotion, either. I mean if you really looked in her eyes, she looked like a robot. It all seemed canned, like she had practiced her responses or was lying about something. I'm telling you, I think she had something to do with it." No one answers, the kitchen falls silent and Dad stares at me.

Mom looks at me, her eyes tired and red. "That's enough, Dean. I don't want to hear it anymore. Got it?"

"Yep," I mumble.

Dad shakes his head in agreement with Mom and looks at me, his eyes squinting *listen to your mother.*

I sit down and say, "Sorry, guys, this whole thing is just crazy, but that's what I believe."

I finally try to go upstairs and get some sleep. I sit at the foot of my bed, under the skylight. All I can do is stare at Gregg's bed that he hasn't slept in for a long time, but when I look at it, I can't help but think, *He's never going to sleep in it again,* and I start to cry. I remember back to our old bedroom high up in the pines. I lie down in my bed, my feet stretched out where I usually lay my head, staring up at the skylight. "I'm sleeping like this from now on." I say to myself. But every time I close my eyes, all I can see is the view of Gregg's body through the screen door.

The misty morning sun shines white through the skylight. I open my eyes and think to myself, *Maybe the whole thing was just a nightmare,* but I can hear everybody talking downstairs in the kitchen, and I know it really happened. I look at the clock; it reads 5:23. I sit on the edge of my bed, sigh, and lie back down. I look out the skylight and wonder what really happened inside Gregg's condo. *Damn, they must have hit him hard with that candlestick, to kill him.* I feel lousy just thinking about it and I start to cry. *It's day one, the first day after,* I think to myself. I try to find the courage to walk down the stairs.

The glass table in the kitchen is packed; everyone is still sitting around it. Mom's eyes are red and I wonder to myself if she moved from her seat or has been there all night. Everyone hugs me and we all start crying again, especially Mom. I pour myself some coffee. I listen to them talking and hear the words but can't really focus on the details. *Obituary, funeral, detectives, reporters, murder.* The phone rings. Dad answers it. Everyone gets a bit quieter to hear what he says. *Pictures, obituaries, meet at the door, no comment.* I keep looking out the glass slider.

By noon, I'm tired of standing in the kitchen looking out the slider and taking messages on the phone for Dad from reporters. I decide to try and watch the news, so I head to the TV room. As I enter, there is a picture of Gregg in the corner of the screen and a reporter is talking about the murder. I see the photo change from a close-up of Gregg's face to a shot of him lying dead on the foyer floor through the screen door. When I see it, I cringe and it's as if I'm there all over again. I close my eyes and look away, but it's still there, burned into my mind.

Dad comes back from the store with a newspaper and drops it on the kitchen table. We all take turns reading it. He starts to cry as he tells us the police waved him down on the way home and told him that the cause of death wasn't the candelabra: it was a gunshot wound to the head. Mom can't take it. She screams at the top of her lungs. *Oh, no.* She is hysterical again and Dad attempts to calm her. After seeing the flash of Gregg's image on the news and now watching Mom break down again, I feel like this is never going to end. *This is so fucked up,* I think, *the same thing all over again.*

Mom and Dad leave for a while to go to the condo to meet the police and pick up one of Gregg's suits to bring to the funeral home. When they come back, Mom is even worse, sobbing crazily on Dad's shoulder. Dad has Gregg's dark suit folded over his arm and I take it from him and hang it up. Mom goes off again and this time she can't seem to stop.

That night I sit on the edge of my bed and look over at Gregg's, trying to imagine him lying there. I sigh and lie down backward, staring up at the skylight into the night.

Suddenly, I'm floating over Gregg's truck in front of his windshield, floating in the air, looking right at him as he drives the truck and his music blasts. I scream at him, "Don't go home, Gregg!" as loud as I can, but he can't hear me or even see me. I scream louder, "Don't go home!" My eyes open and I'm talking in my sleep. I look up at the skylight in the darkness, sit up and catch my breath. "What the fuck, man," I mumble to myself, "what the fuck." I look over at Gregg's bed. I lie back down and the sun rises through the skylight.

I stand in the funeral home. Mom sits behind me crying, as Dad and I look down at Gregg's body. They've tried to make him look good but to me he looks bad—bloated, beaten and dead. "The makeup doesn't look right," I say to Dad. "He doesn't look like himself." He agrees and then takes a red ruby ring off Gregg's finger and puts it on. I whisper to Gregg, "I love you," and touch his hand. I walk over and sit next to Mom. I hug her and we cry and then I move back toward the door.

I watch Mom at the casket with Dad next to her. I remember being here in the same building for the funeral of Neil's girlfriend, years ago. I watch as Mom is clinging to the casket and Dad tries to walk her away and she won't let go. She gets hysterical as he finally pulls her away. *It's a fucking crazy nightmare,* I think to myself, watching Mom and Dad cry and hold each other. *They look so tired and lost.*

The next morning I stand near the slider in the kitchen and the table is covered in newspapers again. I think, *Man, I guess it's going to be the same every day from now on.* Mom sits in her bathrobe, head down, reading an article. *At least she isn't crying.* The light from the slider shines through the newspapers on the table. Dad is on the phone and the others are talking with yet more new words: *forensics, leads, interviews, suspects.* Dad is having a heated dispute with someone on the other end of the phone. He keeps repeating that Gregg's casket is going to remain open for the whole funeral. After a few minutes, he hangs up and says to Mom, "That was Pam. She wants the casket closed. I just keep telling her no, but she is very persistent."

Mom clangs her coffee cup on the table, sighs and says, "He's our son and we want it open. She's going to have to deal with it."

I stare out the slider and then down at the newspapers. On the front page of the *Derry News* in bold headline it reads:

POLICE HUNT FOR MURDER CLUES

There is a picture of Gregg and Pam from their wedding; Pam has a weird smile on her face and Gregg has his little grin on. I stare, as the sunlight shines through the photo. *I'm never going to see that grin again.*

"Why does she want his casket closed, Dad?" I ask.

"I don't know, son, maybe she just doesn't want to see Gregg like that."

"Yeah, well, I tell you what, Dad, I have an idea why."

"Don't even start on that again, Dean, not today."

I look down at the glass-top kitchen table and scan the headlines again. One reads:

DERRY MURDER A PUZZLE TO POLICE

Another reads:

FAMILY AND FRIENDS PUZZLE OVER MURDER

I think to myself, *The police are clueless. I don't know if they will ever figure it out.* We watch the news and there is nothing new there, either. I shower before the funeral. In the waterfall of steam and mist, I try to erase the image of Gregg lying on the foyer floor. It's no use, and I cry, as I put my suit on, after Dad ties my tie for me.

Dad parks the Jaguar in the parking lot of the funeral home across the street from Londonderry High where Gregg and I went to school. We walk up the stairs, go through the door and sign the book at the entrance. I see Gregg's steel-grey casket at the front of the room. The casket is open and surrounded by flower arrangements. Family and friends hug me and give me their condolences, and I even see Mrs. Cavendish from the pink room at Londonderry High. I introduce her and her husband to my parents. We thank them for the nice comments they made in the paper about Gregg. "Such a terrible tragedy for such a nice young man, we are so sorry." Mrs. Cavendish says.

Mom sits down in the front row directly across from the casket on the Smart side of the room, because the chairs are separated with an aisle, one side for our family and the other for Pam's. After Mom sits, Dad and I head outside for a smoke, and I notice that Pam's side of the room is empty.

"Why is her side empty?" I ask.

"They're not here yet, I guess, Dean," he answers.

Dad and I stand away from the entrance stairs and smoke on the edge of the grass near the pavement. Pam shows up with her parents, wearing a purple dress. She comes over and hugs us, then walks away. I ask Dad, "Why isn't she wearing black? Aren't you supposed to wear black at a funeral?"

"Yes, you are," he says. "She's just being fashionable, I guess."

The parking lot is filling up quickly and the stairs are packed with people waiting to get inside. I watch Pam walk up the stairs arm and arm with her mom and dad. When she gets to the top of the stairs, I see her greet two shabbily dressed longhaired teenagers. I watch her hug one of them and smile for a second. Then she hugs the other teenage boy with long black hair; she seems to hold him and embrace him just a bit too long for my liking. I turn to Dad and say, "Hey, Dad, who the hell are they? I know all of Gregg's friends and I don't know those two guys."

"They must be people she works with," Dad says, but he doesn't look too happy about it either.

We start to walk back into the funeral hall. Ahead of us, Pam and her family and the two scruffy-looking boys walk in. I watch them sign in the book—all except for the two boys—then walk into a side room instead of sitting down on their designated side of the aisle.

"Where are they going?" I ask Dad.

"To the side room, son. I guess she's decided she doesn't want to see Gregg."

"Dad, those two boys didn't sign in. Weird, huh?"

"Yes, it is, son," he says. "But you've got to let it go for now, son. Remember what I said."

When it's time to go to the church in Derry, Mom is hysterical again and won't leave her seat in front of the casket. She clings to the chair frantically, as Dad and Rick try to pick her up to her feet. She finally stands up and they walk her out to the car. As they place the now-closed steel-grey casket into the back of the hearse, I watch as Pam throws a red rose on top. I think to myself, watching her cry, *I can't believe she didn't come out of the room. I can't believe she didn't say goodbye to him.*

On the way to Derry, I look out the back window of the Jaguar to the sound of Mom whimpering as Dad drives. It seems like there are more than a hundred cars in the funeral procession that stretches out behind us. We hold up traffic through Londonderry for a while and the drive seems like it's taking forever.

As I listen to the reverend give his speech, the whole time I am staring at the blue and yellow flower arrangement in front of me. I imagine the flowers falling as they did at Gregg's wedding, and I start feeling dizzy with all the people sitting behind me. The flowers don't fall over, and the pallbearers carry the casket down the aisle and out the big doors. Everyone follows behind, out the doors and down the granite steps. A group of photographers takes pictures. The flashbulbs spark in the reflection of Gregg's steel-grey casket.

Around the gravesite, everyone holds hands in a circle, taking turns placing red roses on Gregg's casket. I watch the mourners, one by one, drop a rose and say goodbye. I say goodbye, but it doesn't feel like goodbye. We walk back to the car, and I climb in to the backseat. I turn to look out the window and watch Pam and her parents drive out of the cemetery. *I know you're behind this, Pam. I just know.*

Chapter 15

Trophies and Trash Bags

Two days after we bury Gregg, Mom and Dad come home one afternoon, and as they come walking up the stairs, I see Dad carrying two big black trash bags. He walks into the kitchen and plops the bags down ón the floor next to the table. Mom walks in behind him whimpering and in her hand is a big golden trophy. She places it on the glass-top table. I look up from the newspaper articles that I am cutting out and I notice its Gregg's baseball trophy. "Where did you get Gregg's trophy, guys?" I ask.

"Pam left all this stuff at the front door with a note on it that said she doesn't have room for it at her new place in Hampton." Dad answers.

"It's all Gregg's stuff? You mean she didn't want to keep any of it to remember him by?"

"Guess not." Dad says.

I fold up the article I'm holding in my hand and place it in the shoebox with the other newspaper clippings. I look up at Gregg's trophy just as a ray of light from the slider shines on it. I nod at Dad, "Remember that—the day Gregg won the championship?"

"I remember," he says and then he stares out the slider and I watch a tear run down his face. "Judy, I think we should go through the bags another day, okay, honey? I'm just not ready for it yet."

"Neither am I," she agrees. I carry the bags down into the basement and hide them in the corner behind the old couch.

I come home late that night, and when I walk in the front door of the condo, Mom is sitting on the top stair. As I walk up the first few stairs, she says to me in the darkness, "Is that you, Gregg?" I stop on the stair, stunned. *Oh, no – this isn't good*, I think to myself. I wait a second and see her face shimmering with tears in the kitchen light. She asks again, with her head down, not looking at me. "Is that you, Gregg?" she asks again.

I sigh and answer quietly and softly, "No, Mom, it's me, Dean." I walk up to her and sit down on the top stair next to her while she starts to cry harder. I put my arm around her and she sighs. "Mom," I say, "it's late, you've got to get some rest, okay?"

"I know, Dean. I'm just waiting for him to come home, and he's late again."

"Mom, he's not coming home tonight, all right, it's time for bed, come on." I help her upstairs to bed and then head up to the loft. I stare out the skylight and have a smoke and try to sleep, but the nightmare is back again and I'm afraid it will never let me go.

Sunday after the funeral, Dad, Mom and I sit at the kitchen table and Pam comes walking up the stairs. Glittering in her hand is something large, round and wrapped in tinfoil. In her other hand she has a little notebook. She says hi and sits down across from my mom and dad. I sit in front of the sliding door and the afternoon sun warms my shoulders a bit until a cool breeze comes through the screen. I look at Pam's steel-grey eyes as she squints a bit in the sun. She drops her notebook on the glass table and pushes the round tinfoil item toward Mom. "What's this, Pam?" Mom asks.

"It's our wedding cake, and I want you guys to have it. I know how the Smarts love cake." She makes a grin toward my mom and then looks over at Dad. I look at Dad to check his reaction.

He smiles and says, "Are you sure you don't want it?"

"No, I don't really eat cake," she says.

"But aren't you supposed to eat it on your first anniversary, for good luck, you know?" Dad says.

"I can't, I just can't, you guys, please take it, okay?" She says as she makes a slight frown. "But I'm going on the news later, for the anniversary."

"Are you sure you want to do that so soon?" Dad asks. Pam doesn't answer; she just shakes her head yes.

"Are you sure you're ready?" Mom asks.

"Yeah, I have to — for our anniversary."

"Well, Pam, remember the police said not to mention anything about the burglary." Dad says.

"Yeah, I know," she says, "but I think it's important to say something." She pauses and pretends to sigh. "I really think it's time for me to get on with my life."

Dad raises his eyebrows for a split second and shoots a quick glance at me. He looks back at Pam, doesn't comment, and she continues.

"I can't believe I'm twenty-two and I'm a widow." She looks down into the glass-top table and sighs. "I not only lost my husband, but also my best friend. Not only did they rob Gregg of his life, they robbed us—the two of us—of our future." She starts to whimper.

Mom starts crying and Dad fidgets. I turn around and look out the slider. It's like I'm trapped in a bad soap opera.

"We didn't have any problems, we were very happy," she continues. "All I saw when I opened the door was him—and I got help immediately—I thought he was hurt—the house was robbed—burglarized—I'm convinced of it—things are missing—but I can't talk about it."

Dad interrupts her and says, "Pam, the police told us all not to mention that, because it might interfere with the investigation." He looks at her from over his reading glasses.

"I know, Billy," she says, "but the police aren't telling me anything that's going on in the case and I'm tired of it, so, I'll just mention it briefly, like I just did."

Dad sighs and looks at me, then looks back at Pam.

She goes on, "If this had happened to Gregg when he was sixteen, he wouldn't have had all the happiness he did have up to the time that he died." She pauses and looks up. "What would have happened if this had happened when he was thirty and we had three kids? Would it have made more sense then?" She looks back up at us, waiting for an answer. No one speaks and she sighs. "No," she says. She looks down at the glass table.

After Pam is gone, I say to Dad and Mom, "It's a little fucking early to be *getting on with your life*, isn't it?"

Dad looks at me and says, "Well, it isn't easy for her either, son."

"Yeah — well, I still think — "

He interrupts, "That's enough, Dean."

"All right, but I'm telling you."

I go out for beers with Neil and Matt from Manchester, and when I get home late Mom is sitting on the top stair of the first floor again.

"Gregg, is that you?" She asks.

"No, it's me, Mom, it's Dean."

"Gregg's late," she says.

"Come on, Mom, you've got to get some sleep. I don't think Gregg's coming home."

I help her to her bedroom and walk back across the hall to my own. I stand up in the skylight, the night wind on my face. I smoke and try to sleep, but I'm above Gregg's truck again, yelling for him not to go home. He doesn't hear me.

The next morning I walk downstairs and see the newspapers on the glass-topped kitchen table. *This is how it will always be,* I think. I say good morning to Dad who sits at his spot at the head of the table, sipping his coffee and smoking a Winston. I look down and read the headline of the *Derry News:*

FOR PAMELA SMART LIFE MUST GO ON

"Did you read it?" I ask Dad.

"Yeah," he answers. "She shouldn't have said the stuff about the burglary."

I pick up the paper off the table and read the article, and as I do, I realize it is the same exact thing she said to us yesterday, almost word for word. "Look at this, Dad, it's the same thing she said to us yesterday—the stuff about how she has to go on with her life—and the crazy shit about how if this would have happened to Gregg when he was sixteen, or when he was thirty with three kids. Damn, we were her practice—her *rehearsal*. She fucking tested it out on us! Can't you see it, Dad—she's full of shit!"

I slide the article back across the glass at him. There are two pictures—one of Gregg and one of Pam—next to the headline. The photo of Gregg isn't a good one; he looks angry. Pam's photo looks familiar and I realize it was taken at the funeral. It's a close-up of the same shot one of the papers ran a few days ago, and in this one I can see that even though she has her eyes closed and her head tilted as if she is upset, she has a bit of a smirk on her face.

I sigh and look at Dad as he takes a drag off his Winston and sips his coffee. He stares out the slider and doesn't say a word.

I sit in a small room in the Derry police station for questioning. They ask me all sorts of questions: Did Gregg owe anybody money? Did Gregg sell drugs? Are you a break dancer–rapper? Do you think the dancers and rappers you battle might have mistaken Gregg for you and tried to kill him?

"No." I answer to all of the questions.

"What about his friends, do you think they could be involved?"

"Nope, I doubt it." I answer.

Then they ask, "Well, who do you think did it?"

"Pam," I answer, and they look at me, but they keep going, and I feel like I'm the one being investigated.

"Did Gregg do drugs?" they ask.

"Yeah," I say, "he smoked some weed — we all did — what's the big deal?"

"What makes you think Pam did it?" they ask.

"Because when she talks I can tell she is full of shit. Man, listen, I'm telling you she had something to do with it. Have you guys checked out the kids that showed up at the funeral?"

"Yeah, we're looking into it," he says.

Good, I think. *About time.*

Chapter 16

Showdown

I open the door to Neil's screened-in porch and step inside. "It's Friday night, want a beer?" he asks. "They're in the fridge."

I pop the top on the beer, sip it and sit down next to him. "How's it going?" he asks.

"Same old shit. It's like every day has been repeating over and over again." I sigh and stare out the screened-in porch.

"What do you mean?" he asks.

"Well, ever since Gregg, all we do is watch the news and wait for something, anything, to happen. I try to convince my dad about Pam, but he doesn't want to hear it. Pam keeps practicing her news speeches on us and, fuck, I still can't sleep, it's been like a fucking month. A month of the same shit repeating over and over. I feel like I'm going fucking nutty—ha-ha-ha."

He laughs and says, "Well, you've always been nutty."

"Seriously, Neil, it's been a fucking nightmare. Everyone is paranoid like someone's going to come into our house next and kill us. I'm getting fucking sick of being paranoid all the time. And fucking Pam loves to be on the news. She gets all dolled up and practices on us and says the same thing every time—first to us, then to the news. You know, she always wanted to be a reporter, and—it's like she enjoys the attention. I'm telling you, she had something to do with it."

"I know, Dean, I think so too, she probably did, but what if they never bust anyone—man, that would suck."

"Fuck, I don't even want to think about that, man—wow, that would be crazy! I'm starting to think the police blew it, like they have nothing to go on or maybe they just don't know what the fuck they are doing." I sip my beer and look out the window. Neil looks at me as if he doesn't know what to say.

"You know what else is annoying, every fucking time I go anywhere with my dad, people recognize him from his interviews on the news and everybody comes over and says they are so sorry. It's nice, I know, but after a while it gets on my fucking nerves. I mean total strangers everywhere we go—the grocery store, restaurants and then all of our customers do the same thing. *I'm sorry*, they say. It gets annoying. I wish no one knew who we were. It's like we can't go anywhere anymore. I wish they all would just leave us the fuck alone. I mean, I don't want to be reminded of it every time I leave the house, every time we go somewhere. It just fucking sucks, it's a fucking crazy nightmare I'm trapped in, and the next time some fucking-ass stranger says to me they are sorry, they're going to be sorry, because I'm going to kick them in the fucking throat until they're sorry they said they were sorry." Neil starts laughing; he loves it when I go off on my angry rants, and I start laughing, too.

He looks at me with a sinister grin and says, "Well, holmes, I'm sorry to hear that!"

I jump up and start fake-attacking him, as we laugh. I punch him in the arms and gut a few times until he says, "All right, all right, enough."

I stare down at the newspaper on the glass-topped kitchen table. The sun shines through it. The headline reads:

3 JUVENILES ARRESTED IN DERRY DEATH

I look at Dad as he sits in his spot at the kitchen table, staring out the slider door.

"Someone finally busted!" I scream and I grab the paper from the table. I read it as fast as I can. "They're from Seabrook, Dad, Seabrook! That's right next to Hampton —"

"I know, Dean, but just wait until tomorrow. I'm sure there will be more to the story."

"I'm telling you, Pam's involved, Dad, I just know it!"

"You might be right, Dean," he says to me. "We have to stay calm, though. The police are looking into it, that's all."

"But I'm telling you, they know it's her —"

He looks at me sternly. "I talked to them, and we're going to see — what develops. Okay? So let's just stay calm and wait."

I come home that night, park the car and walk toward the front door of our condo. As I walk across the pavement of the parking lot, I can't help but look up the street toward Gregg's. I shake my head, as I remember running up the road that night. I close my eyes. I feel like I'm entering that foggy night again and I can almost hear the sirens and see the flashing lights.

I look up the street again. I haven't been there since that night; maybe it's time. *No, not yet.* I sigh, light a butt and feel like I don't want to go home, either. I have my key in the door, but I stare up into the darkness, again toward Gregg's. "Three kids from Seabrook," I mumble to myself into the night, "what the fuck did they do to him in there?"

I flick my cigarette onto the pavement, stomp it with my sneaker. I turn, sigh, open the door to our house and walk through. I flick the switch for the stairway light and look slowly up to the top step. She's not there, and I smile a bit.

I wake up and walk down into the kitchen. Dad's in his spot and Mom is in hers. I look down at the glass table, like I always do, and the paper's on top of it but it's upside down and directly in front of Dad. I reach for it. Dad covers it with his hand and says, "Dean, sit down for a second."

"What is it? What does it say?" I ask him, as I head to my chair in front of the sliding door.

"Just wait a second, son, before you read it."

"All right, but just tell me what's going on."

"Your mother and I—" he pauses and I wait. "Your mother and I think—that maybe, just maybe—you're right about Pam having something to do with it."

"Yes!" I raise my hands in victory. I jump out of my chair and head over to him. I shake his hand and give him a hug. I turn and give one to Mom. "Well, it took you guys long enough!"

"But, son," Dad says, as I walk back to my chair, "that doesn't mean we are sure that she did it—that she killed him. She might just be involved somehow."

"So, you're not all the way with me, you're not sure still—right? Fine with me—at least you're listening and considering it."

"Well, we will see what happens." He says, as he slides the paper across the table to me.

"So what happened?" I ask.

"Just read it. I don't want to tell you."

I grab the paper and flip it over to the front page. It's the lead story in big bold print under the paper's moniker. It reads:

THIRD TEEN ARRAIGNED IN MURDER

Right next to the headline there are four photographs lined up in a row. I see Gregg in the last of the pictures. The other three photos are the kids from Seabrook. The first one has a little grin on his face, and I recognize him right away. He's the one who I thought hugged Pam a little too long. "It's them," I shout, "the kids from the funeral!"

"Are you sure?"

I stare back down at the photos on the front page. "Yeah, I'm sure. I'm telling you, Dad, it's them."

"They go to the school where Pam teaches," he says in a monotone and looks at me as if he knows what I'm going to say next.

"I told you she had something to do with it!"

He doesn't answer; instead, he gestures for me to finish reading the article. I look back at it and reread the headline. Underneath, in smaller print, it reads:

Showdown

ANOTHER ARREST EXPECTED IN SHOOTING
OF GREGORY SMART

I immediately think to myself, *It's Pam, they're going to arrest her!* Then I say it aloud, "They're going to bust her, Dad, she's next!"

That night, we watch the news and a reporter goes up to Pam's door at her new condo in Hampton. She answers the door and she looks like she's been crying for hours.

"How do you feel about the arrests, Pam?" The reporter asks.

"I'm sickened and devastated," she says.

I yell at the screen, "Yeah and you're next!"

Dad puts his head down and sighs, and when I look over at Mom, she looks angrier than I've seen her for quite a while. Dad looks at me and says, "Why is she devastated?"

"Because, she knows she's next, Dad."

Mom doesn't say a word. She looks at me with sort of a lost look of amazement, a look that says, *You might be right after all.*

I'm up in the skylight looking over the golf course. I feel like I can breathe for the first time since Gregg died — since Gregg was murdered. I sip my beer and look down to the ground. I stare at the giant weeping willow and try to think myself back in time and it's as if I'm in the mist again. It's like staring too long into a window screen or staring into white drywall. It's a haze, a cloud that fills my mind's eye and then the fog rises and I see.

187

My back's to the bark again and I'm under the weeping willow in front of our old house. I hear Gregg playing in the woods, as the wind rustles the willow leaves. Now he's in the yard playing catch with Dad, wearing his golden hat and his smile, shimmering through the mist and through the willow leaves as they sway in the wind. I watch him, as he smiles and throws the ball at Dad, and he whips it good and it zings and snaps into Dad's mitt. The fog lowers again, blurring my vision. The mist is covering everything, and I watch as Gregg's face disappears in the heavy fog.

I search for Gregg in the mist, and the haze lifts and I'm at the Little League field standing against the chain-link fence. I'm watching him as he plays third base in the championship game on Memorial Field. He slides over the chalky foul line, snagging a line drive. The white foul-line chalk floats in the air all around him. Chalk and mist fill the scene and it fades away.

I close my eyes, and I see Gregg chasing me around the house in Hudson, tormenting me with the deer hoof in his hand. We're in the orchard and he cups an apple blossom in his hand, and he looks in to see if it glows. He smiles the first time he cranks the volume on the Kenwood and he bangs his head to the music. The girls are hanging all over him, as he sits on the round couch at the big party in Londonderry. He's hugging my mom in the kitchen and smiling with his new insurance haircut. He's running around the condo, flying Ashley on his shoulders, the two of them laughing. He's on the couch below me in the TV room, holding beads in his hand and looking at me, worried.

I try to go back again but the fog has come down, and all I see is Gregg lying in the foyer through the screen door. I suddenly think of his trophy stuffed in a trash bag in the basement. I step out of the skylight and walk down the stairs. I find the trash bag, grab the trophy, and carry it back up the stairs. I place it on the end of the bureau as close to the skylight as I can get it.

I stick my head back out the skylight. I remember the nights when Gregg stood here next to me, the both of us looking out into the night. I imagine to myself that he is standing here now, sipping a beer with me, then the scene fades and he's gone—and I want to crank that Kenwood so loud Gregg can hear it.

Part Four

The Trial

Chapter 17

Inside Information

"I just couldn't believe it, Bill — I mean, she did it over and over again, stepping on it, not once, not twice, a bunch of times — until someone put a towel over it and then — well, you won't believe it, but she stepped on it again! It's just ridiculous, her lack of respect."

It's a voice I don't recognize. I turn the corner at the bottom of the stairs to find Dad and Mom standing in the kitchen with two police detectives. The older one, the one who was speaking, is a big guy, barrel chested, like Grampy Smart. The younger detective looks like someone out of a crime novel, tough looking, dark haired and handsome, with a thick moustache. Both of them reach out and shake my hand, then hurry out the door after promising my parents they will keep in touch.

"What's going on, Pop?" I ask, sliding into my regular seat.

Dad pours himself a cup of coffee. "Oh, they were just filling us in on the latest news about the boys that got arrested." He joins me at the table. "Apparently, they are, or were, Pam's students from the high school where she works."

I jump up from the table. "You mean, she *knew* them?"

192

"That's what it says in today's paper."

I grab the newspaper and stare at the headline:

MRS. SMART HAS VISITED HOME

OF MURDER SUSPECT

"Holy shit, Dad, I told you!"

"I know, son, you were right." Mom has joined us at the table and lets out a deep sigh. "And there's another story right next to it about how the boys were spotted at the funeral—they were there, son, just like you said."

"Goddamn it!" I scream out loud. I start to get shaky and feel the anger rising inside me. "I can't believe it! You guys got to believe that she is definitely, totally involved in this shit."

I quickly turn back to the newspaper and read both articles straight through. When I finish, something is nagging at me. *Some piece of information. What is it?* Then it hits me. "Listen to this!" I shout. "The widow of murder victim Greggory Smart and one of the teens recently charged with the killing worked together on a video at the suspect's Seabrook Beach home on a number of occasions, according to the suspect's mother."

I look up from the paper. "You know, she asked me and Neil to make a rap for that stupid orange juice commercial, too, so I know that the part about the video is true. And there's more. Listen to this quote from one of the suspect's mothers: 'They spent time here on the weekends doing the video—I can't describe that relationship.'" I repeat the word. *"Relationship!"*

Dad is staring at me. "Where does it say that, Dean?" he asks, his voice rising. I point out the article and watch his face turn red as he reads.

"Son of a bitch." Suddenly, he jumps up and grabs his brown leather binder from the kitchen counter. He heads to the wall phone and starts dialing. "I'm going to get to the bottom of this right now!"

Mom looks up. Her face registers that she has been taking this all in. "Be careful, Billy," she cautions. "Remember what the police said." She gives me a quick look and turns away.

"What *did* they say, Mom?" I ask, but she just shushes me, pointing to the phone.

Pam must have picked up because I hear my dad starting in on her; he's shouting and talking so fast I only catch half of what he says. "Why the hell were you at his house? Why the hell do you even know these punks?"

I make out Pam's tinny robotic voice on the other end of the line. She is trying to explain to him about the video project.

"A video project, huh?" Dad shouts back at her. Pam is still talking and whatever she says causes him to soften a bit. "Well, I'm sorry, Pam—I got very upset after reading today's paper and finding out that you knew these kids."

They talk for a while. Dad's tone gets calmer, but the whole time he is jotting notes on his yellow legal pad. When he finally hangs up the phone, he looks exhausted. "She always wants to know if I've heard anything from the police," he says to himself. He finishes jotting a few more notes, then looks over at Mom.

"Judy, why don't you head upstairs and get some rest? You look tired." Mom nods her head, gives him a quick hug, then heads up the stairs in her bathrobe.

As soon as she is gone, Dad turns to me and points to the yellow legal pad. He gives me a little smile. "Well, son, you aren't going to believe it, but your mother and I have been asked to keep track of what Pam says and what she does. I've been keeping these notes for the police." He waves the pad.

"Wow! Dad, you mean you're like a detective, a spy?"

"Well, yes, but not a spy—I suppose they said we are 'agents of the state,' " he smiles at me smoothly and adds, "*special* agents of the state."

"Unreal, this whole thing couldn't get any stranger— now my dad is a special agent!"

"There's more, Dean," his smile turns serious. "The police detective gave us some other facts that are pretty upsetting. For one thing, remember when Pam went to the condo to gather up her things? Well, apparently, she kept stepping on Gregg's bloodstain in the foyer."

"Wow, that's un-fucking believable, Dad—just unreal!" I try to picture it: Pam walking back and forth over the dried blood.

"Yeah, and they gave us some other disturbing news about what went on inside the condo that night." He pauses for a moment. "Apparently, there was . . . umm . . . a scuffle . . . a fight . . . I guess Gregg put up a fight with the two boys." I see a tear slide down his cheek.

"What the fuck, Dad! *Two of them did it?*" I shout. "*There were two of them?*"

"Yes, son, it seems so. They fought with Gregg and obviously they won . . . then they put him on his knees . . . ," his words come out haltingly, his voice low, "they . . . put . . . a butcher's knife . . . to his neck."

My fists are clenched, my throat dry. "Oh my God, those fucking little bastards."

"They put a pillow to his head . . . to muffle the noise," Dad can barely get out the words. "Then they . . . shot him . . . in the back of the head . . . exe . . . cu . . . tion style." I watch as my father breaks down, sobbing, at the head of the table. He shakes his head back and forth in disbelief.

I'm trying to process what he has said—to make some sense of it—but I can feel the anger rising. I slam my fists on the glass table. "This is a crazy fucking nightmare—we're never going to get out of it, Dad. It's never going to end."

He hugs me and tries to calm me down. "Don't worry, son. They're going to get what's coming to them."

"They better try those little fucks as adults or, I swear on Gregg's grave, I'll kill them myself."

"Easy, son." He sits back down at the head of the table and starts writing again on his yellow legal pad. *At least he can do something.* I stare out the slider and think about Gregg. I think about how he felt when they put a knife to his neck. *Why didn't he fight back? He must have lost the fight. I should have been there to help him.*

I wake up in the middle of the night to the sound of something rustling around in the den, directly below my bedroom loft. Instantly, I think, *Someone has broken into the condo to kill us.* I lie perfectly still, wondering what or who it is. I force myself to sit up in bed and listen closely. I get up my nerve, walk over to the railing and look down. Mom is sitting on the couch, her face a ghostly blue in the light of the television.

I wonder whether to go to her. I watch for a while, as she stares back and forth from the floor to the muted television screen. She starts crying harder and I make up my mind. I walk down the stairs and sit next to her, she hugs me, sobbing in my arms, and even though I want to console her, my anger is still there, too. It's always there.

"What's wrong, Mom?" I ask, realizing what a stupid question it is.

"I just miss him so much, Dean," she manages to say, as she squeezes me in her arms.

"It's going to be all right, Mom."

"I don't think so, Dean. I don't think it's going to get any easier for any of us." She lets out a huge sigh and drops her head onto my shoulder. She won't let go, and we sit that way for several minutes. Finally, she lifts her head and looks up at me, wearily. "It's my fault, Dean. I named him Gregg after my brother. He died in a car crash when he was just twenty-three, just like Gregg, same age and everything—it's my fault, Dean—I cursed him with that name."

"No way, Ma, it's just a weird coincidence. You can't blame yourself for what happened." Her tears start up again, and I change the subject to make her stop crying. "Why are you up so late watching TV?"

She lets go from our hug and catches her breath. "I wanted to watch the news—to find out if those boys are going to be tried as adults."

"Let's hope so, Mom. If not, they will get out of jail when they turn eighteen, in only two years." I realize right away that this was the wrong thing to say, as she starts to cry again. I reach for another hug and rub my right hand in circles slowly across her back, just as she used to do to me when I was a kid, but I realize that nothing I can do for her is going to fix this.

I sit Indian style on the sun-warmed lawn in front of Gregg's gravestone. I swig down a sip of one of the beers from a six-pack I brought with me. There's a carved heart on the stone above the epitaph. I read the words over and over again:

> *A life that touches the hearts*
> *of others lives on forever.*

A black Volvo wagon drives by slowly and I see that the driver is staring at me. *Mind your own business,* I think to myself, *leave me the fuck alone.* I sip my beer and light the joint I brought to share with Gregg. I stare down at the big porcelain scorpion bowl someone has left there for him. I wonder if it is the exact one he and his friends used to drink from at the Chinese restaurant he loved. It looks like it might be the one. I imagine him ordering his "scorpion bowl for eight" and I can almost see the flames coming from the little volcano in the center of the bowl. "Man, I wish you were here, brother," I say out loud.

I stare up into the summer sky beyond the edge of the woods, wondering if he can hear me. I continue, "Well, holmes, you ain't gonna believe this, but I think—well, we think—that Pam did it—that she had you killed, buddy." I blow smoke into the wind and watch it float away into the horizon in front of the trees at the edge of the cemetery.

I finish off what's left in one can of beer and place it on the base of the gravestone. I pop open another and pour a bit of it into the ground in front of the stone. "That's for you, Gregg." I say. I let out a sigh and my head drops to my chest. "I think you know anyway, don't you, bro—that's why you looked so worried that day on the couch with your beads in your hands. Remember? I asked you what was wrong and you never answered. Yeah, I think you knew, didn't you?" I swig back more of the beer.

"What the fuck did they do to you that night?" I go on. It feels good to talk to him, even if he can't answer. I put the joint out on the ground and twist the roach until some remaining weed falls out, then I nudge it along the ground, toward the headstone. "There you go, homeboy." I sigh and start to cry. "Wish you were here." I watch the sun slip behind a grey cloud.

"Those motherfuckers!" I yell into the air. I swig back the final sip of my last beer, crush the can in my hands, and whip it at the gravestone. It bounces off and lands nearby, crumpled in the grass. "Later, holmes," I call back over my shoulder.

A week after their first visit, the two detectives are back again, sitting around the kitchen table with Mom and Dad. They seem to be right at home. I've learned the younger detective with the moustache is Detective Daniel Pelletier. He has his full policeman uniform on, and I can't help but stare through the glass-top table at his holstered gun. The black-textured pistol handle gleams in the sun. The captain, Loring Jackson, isn't in uniform today, and I'm surprised that he looks more like a businessman than a cop. He still carries his pistol, though. I can see it even from where I'm sitting, in a shoulder holster, underneath his grey sport coat.

Piles of paper are spread across the table and I listen as they talk about the case with all the usual words—*investigation, testimony, state's evidence.* I listen as closely as I can.

"I can't reiterate enough," Captain Jackson is saying, "that you guys have to be careful out there, be very observant to everything that goes on around you—especially in crowded places—and if you feel you're being followed, mark the license plate down and try to remember the car make, model and color, even if you're not sure. It's better to be safe than sorry, right?"

"Yes, we understand," Dad answers. "If we see anything unusual, we will certainly let you know right away. By the way, can you tell us how the wiretap is going?"

"We've encountered a few technical problems," the captain responds quickly.

My ears perk up—I don't know about any wiretap. "Sorry to interrupt, Captain, but what's this all about?" I blurt out.

The captain looks at Dad. "Bill, is it all right?"

"Yes, go ahead," Dad nods his head. "He should know."

Captain Jackson looks back at me with a serious look on his face. "Okay, but remember, this is all confidential. Absolutely no one can know of this except the people sitting around this table, understand?"

I sit up a little straighter and say, "Yes, sir, I understand completely." I look him in the eyes.

"We have wired one of Pam's students, Cecilia Pierce, and are taping their conversations—and as I was saying to your dad earlier, we hit a few technical snags, the transmission failed a few times. At least once or twice the microphone just went out because Pierce accidently unplugged it, but I think we got exactly what we needed."

"Wow, what did you get? Did Pam say anything incriminating?" I ask.

The captain says, "Well, let's just say that she just doesn't know how to keep her mouth shut, son."

Dad slides his yellow legal pad filled with notes across the table to the captain. "Nice job, Bill. Your help has been very valuable to us." He rips off the pages from the pad and stuffs them into a manila folder. "Also, you should know that the three boys are most likely going to turn state's evidence against her."

I look over at Mom and Dad and see the relief on their faces. I can't help but wonder how I'm going to keep all of this news to myself. *They're finally going to bust her! I can't fucking wait!*

"Just to let you know," the captain continues, "before we actually arrest her, we're going to leak the story to the media to see if she does something stupid, like flee or make some other mistake." He smiles. "Also, we'd like *all* of you guys to be waiting at the courthouse in Derry when we bring her in. We want her to know that you guys have been aware of what has been going on all along. You okay with this, Bill?"

"Oh yeah, sure, we'll be there." Dad smiles. "I can't wait to see the look on her face when she sees us."

"So when you gonna get her?" I ask, imagining Pam's look of surprise.

"Soon," Detective Pelletier says, smiling. "We plan to pick her up at her school."

"That's fucking fantastic, man!"

"Yeah," the detective continues, "and here's what I'm going to say to her: 'Well, Pamie, we got good news and bad news—what do you want first?' I know she'll ask for the good news first, and I'll say, 'Well, the good news is that we found the murderer,' and then she'll ask for the bad news— and I'll say, 'The bad news is—it's you! Put your hands up, you're under arrest for the murder of your husband!'"

We stare at him for a minute, taking in the full meaning of what he is saying, and then we all burst out laughing. I look down at the glass-topped table, and in the reflection, I see Mom and Dad laughing and smiling. *It's about time*, I think to myself. *It's about fucking time.*

Chapter 18

The Corolla and The Courthouse

After having a few beers at Neil's, I come home late to find my mom alone in the kitchen. She looks upset. "What's wrong, Mom — where's Dad?"

"He's outside, Dean. He's been outside for hours — and I don't know what to do."

"What do you mean outside — where, outside?"

"He's sitting in Gregg's old car at the end of the parking lot. I went out about an hour ago and pleaded with him to come in . . . but . . . but . . . he wouldn't." She looks frantic.

"Don't worry, Mom. I'll go out and get him — just give me a few minutes," I promise.

Once outside, I look to the end of the lot where Gregg's old blue Corolla has been parked for years. We haven't had the heart to move it. I can just barely make out Dad's silhouette in the driver's seat. I take a step forward into the night fog, but something pulls my eyes toward the street that leads to Gregg's condo. I'm transported back in time to that night and I swear I can see myself running up the street with my parents far behind me. Suddenly, I'm standing at the screen door, and I can see Gregg's body lying there. I close my eyes and try to block out the vision flashing in my mind. I turn back and make my way slowly toward the old Corolla.

Stopping a few feet from the car, I look through the rear window and see Dad sitting in the driver's seat with the dome light on and his head pressed against the steering wheel. I stand there for a minute, wondering what I'm going to say to get him to come back inside. He lifts his head off the steering wheel, and I see his shoulders rise as he takes in slow, deep breaths. I can't believe what I'm looking at: my father sitting in Gregg's old Corolla alone in the dead of night.

I walk around the side of the car and open the passenger door and look in. I sit down in the seat next to him and shut the door. "What's going on, Dad—are you all right?" I ask.

"No, Dean. I just can't seem to stop crying, son." His face is red and his eyes are swollen and bloodshot. His shirt is soaked with tears. "I just can't stop thinking about Gregg's last moments and what he must have been feeling."

"I know, Dad, me too." I see that he is nervously turning something over and over in his right hand.

"What's that you got, Dad?" I ask.

"It's Gregg's lucky paper clip—he used to take it on his sales calls and it worked most of the time." He breaks a bit of a smile.

"I remember it, Dad." I say. "That last day at work, he rubbed it across my proposal for good luck."

"I carry it with me everywhere . . . ," he trails off, looking at the paper clip, and I reach across the car and pat him on the back.

"Come on, Dad, let's go inside now. Mom's worried, and you can't just sit out here all night."

"All right, son." He agrees.

It's at least another five minutes before I coax him out of the car. We start to walk back to the condo, but about halfway there he stops and looks up the street toward Gregg's old place. "It's hard not to look up there—and think about what happened," he says, then begins to break down again.

"Yeah, Dad, I know. I did the same thing on my way out here." I put my hand on his back. "But remember what you used to always say to me? 'Man—you got to keep smiling.' Remember, Pop?"

He manages a slight grin and pats me on the back. I squeeze his shoulder and shake him playfully, like I always do, and we walk together toward the condo door.

Mom and Dad sit on the small tweed love seat directly in front of the TV and I'm on the couch next to them. We listen to the all-too-familiar theme music as the newscast begins. A few stories are reported, but there is no mention of the case.

"I wonder why nothing's happening yet," I say impatiently. "It's been a whole week!"

Just then, the reporter swivels in his chair and an image is flashed in the corner of the screen. It's the image I'm always dreading, always trying to get out of my head—the photo of Gregg, taken through the screen door. Gregg, lying dead in the foyer of his condo. I lean forward but instinctively close my eyes and look away. I hear the reporter's voice. "Coming up after the break, a new development in the Smart murder case." A commercial comes on and I open my eyes and stare at the screen. Somewhere a telephone is ringing, but none of us get up to answer it.

"Let it ring, Bill," my mother says, even though Dad hasn't budged. I sit forward on the couch.

It takes a long time for them to get to the story. *They always leave this stuff for last,* I think. I try to distract myself by looking out the window and staring into the night sky. I hear a siren going off somewhere in town. The voices from the TV fade away, my eyes blur, and I see myself running — running up the street toward Gregg's. I'm running and running, but I never get there, never see what's ahead. I shake my head and try to break out of the memory. The sound of the news theme music pulls me back and I turn to face the TV.

"A new development in the case of the Derry man found murdered in his condominium back in May. Derry police have three juveniles from Seabrook in custody. The office of the New Hampshire Attorney General is attempting to have them tried as adults for the murder of Greggory Smart — but authorities say a new arrest in the case is expected soon."

"A new arrest! Goddamn it! Finally, there it is!" Dad screams in triumph, jumping up from the love seat.

The phone is ringing again and Dad runs to the kitchen to answer it. For the next hour, Mom and I sit at the kitchen table while he answers call after call, explaining the situation to friends and relatives. We can't stop smiling.

Suddenly, after picking up yet another call, Dad's smile fades. He grabs his yellow legal pad and begins writing furiously. Mom and I shoot each other a look. *Pam,* we mouth silently to each other. Dad winks at us and smiles, and Mom and I lean in a little closer.

"Like, I don't understand," Pam is shouting, "I don't understand why they're not telling me anything! Like, why do I have to hear it from the news that they are going to arrest someone? It's not right, right? I mean, I'm his wife, right?"

"They aren't telling us anything either," Dad says slyly. "I don't know why." He rolls his eyes at Mom and me, and we sit, holding back our laughter, as Dad jots down notes on his legal pad, grinning.

I look out the rear window of the Jag and see several reporters and photographers lined up in front of the Derry courthouse. Mom starts to get out of the car, but Dad gently urges her to wait. "We want to see the look on her face, Judith," Dad says, "when she realizes that we knew — that we're waiting for her."

He looks back at me through the rear-view mirror and smiles. His jaw is clenched, his forehead tightened, and I can feel his stress in the air. A car pulls into the parking lot, but it's not the police. I stare out into the white overcast sky above the brick courthouse. "They must be running late," Dad says. I hear another car and turn to see a Derry police cruiser pull abruptly into a spot in front of the courthouse. Another cruiser follows close behind and parks alongside it. Someone is sitting in the back of the second cruiser, and even from the back, I can tell that it's Pam. "There they are," I say, my heart racing.

Dad looks out the driver-side window at the two police cars. "Don't move yet. We'll let them bring her in, before we get out of the car."

"But what if she doesn't see us, Dad—don't we want her to see us?"

He nods. "She will, son, she will."

The doors of the first cruiser swing open and two officers in white sport coats step out. As if on cue, they march to the front of the second cruiser where they stand and wait. It takes more than a few minutes, but finally the doors of the second cruiser open and Detective Pelletier steps out. He looks serious in his black suit and tie. He walks solemnly to the back door of the cruiser and opens it, and I see Pam's head emerge from the backseat.

"There she is!" I say excitedly, grabbing the door handle. I jump out of the Jag and slam the door shut as hard as I can, but she doesn't turn around. The detective is ushering her toward the courthouse doors, and I'm afraid she won't see us. She stops and lifts her head and looks straight at the reporters who are taking pictures of her. *No, I think to myself, that's just what she wants!* As if reading my thoughts, she suddenly turns in my direction and our eyes meet. For a split second, she seems startled to see me, but her expression quickly changes to one of disappointment. I stare at her, hoping to drop her to the ground. Instead, she turns her gaze to my dad and shakes her head a firm no at him, then turns back toward the detective who ushers her up the courthouse stairs.

We follow close behind, listening to the furious click of cameras, as the photographers snap picture after picture. The flashes are blinding, so I put my hands up to my face to shield my eyes. The reporters point microphones at us and shout questions as we walk by. At the top of the stairs, Dad turns toward them and says, "No comment." He opens the heavy doors and we head inside.

Mom and Dad sit at a small table in the waiting area drinking coffee, but I'm too anxious to sit down. I scan the waiting area and stare at the faux wood paneling that covers the walls. I think about Pam. *Where have they taken her? I wonder. Is she already in the courtroom?* I look over at the set of double doors, each one with a window and black painted capital letters that read COURT on one side and ROOM on the other. I can see from where I'm standing that the glass window has metal mesh glazed into it — probably to protect it from being broken. I wonder whether someone once tried to smash it in and suddenly I remember why I'm here. *My brother was murdered.*

"I'm going to look and see if she's in there." I say to Dad. He nods "okay." I walk over to the courtroom doors, but I'm afraid to open them. *What if she's in there and what if she looks at me again?* I want to see her because I want her to know how glad I am she's busted, but I also don't want to see her because I don't know how I'll react. *No wonder they use shatterproof glass.* I stand frozen with indecision and I start to panic, as I begin to feel the crowd staring at me — as if I've done something wrong.

Suddenly Mom and Dad are by my side and Dad is slapping me gently on the shoulder. "Let's head in, son, okay?" As soon as he says it, it's as if time stops, and I feel lightheaded as I watch his hand move toward the door handle, everything in slow motion. I see Gregg's ruby ring on his finger, glimmering in the light. Finally, Dad's hand reaches the handle, wraps around it, twists it and pulls it open. He steps through the doorway and Mom and I follow close behind him. The courtroom smells of must, and I think to myself, *We have entered the machine, there's no stopping it now.*

We seat ourselves at a long bench in the third row. I take a quick look behind us, but still no sign of her. I look toward the judge's bench and then glance over at Mom and Dad sitting next to me. Every few minutes one of them turns and looks back at the doors. "Oh man, I wish they would just get on with it." I say to them.

I hear the doors open behind us. I turn around and see that they are walking Pam in. She is looking straight in front of her, but when she reaches our row, she drops her head. *Can't look at us – can you, bitch?*

They sit her down at a long table in front of us. The judge enters the court and we all stand and sit obediently, and then just like that the lawyers start speaking in turn. There are four of them, two for each side, and I see their mouths moving, but I can't concentrate on anything they are saying. I just keep staring at the back of Pam's head – at the fake bow she has in her hair. The lawyers talk of setting dates for this and that and they bicker back and forth. I keep looking at the back of Pam's head, wondering to myself, *Why couldn't she have just divorced him? Why is she sitting there practically motionless, like she doesn't know what's happening? Why isn't she totally freaking out? If it were me,* I think to myself, *and I was innocent, I'd be making a scene, I'd be yelling, "I'm innocent!" But she just sits there, as if nothing matters. It's because she's guilty – guilty as shit.* I want to jump up and tell them this, to put an end to their endless talking. I can feel my heart pounding in my chest.

I watch her calmly take a sip of water. I think, *If it were me, and I was accused of murder, I wouldn't be calm. I'd whip that glass through the courtroom-door window and I'd jump on the table screaming my innocence.* But she just sits there, still and quiet, and it's driving me fucking nuts. *I want to yell over to her, "You suck!" But I can't. I want to yell, "Murderer!" and point at her, but I can't. I want to jump up and grab her, but I can't.* I hear the lawyers talking about sealed affidavits from the boy's best friend, and the secrets float above me like dust in the musty old courtroom. Pam doesn't react to any of it. I sigh and look over at Dad and Mom, as they listen intently to the lawyers. Dad turns toward me as if he feels me staring at him. Our eyes meet, and he gives me a slight grin like it's going to be all right. He taps me on the knee and looks back up at the proceedings.

The lawyers are talking about the boys, *the minors,* and about their testimony against Pam, and I start to wonder whether this means they might let her out on bail. I look over at Dad and he appears to be listening intently, but I wonder if he really is. Mom is staring at the back of Pam's head, and I can tell she is tense by the way she sits forward and fidgets nervously. It feels like I've been separated from everything and everyone in the room, as if I'm here but also like I'm not, like the proceedings are happening but I'm not part of them. It's as if I'm trapped in sort of an inner limbo between reality and my own crazy existence.

Suddenly, the judge bangs the gavel and it's over, just like that. They stand Pam to her feet and get ready to walk her from the courtroom back to the police cruiser. At that moment, the double doors swing open and someone rushes in, yelling, "I love you, Pam!" It's a girl I don't recognize, and the police have to move quickly to usher Pam past the girl and the gathering crowd. The girl hurries ahead, following and shouting, "I love you, Pam! This is wrong!" The crowd looks toward her with interest, but Pam barely looks up, as she ducks into the waiting police cruiser and is driven away.

I stare at the fleeing police car. *Is this how it's going to be?* I wonder. I had expected this to be a triumphant moment for us. I thought we would finally be able to relax, to go back to normal, to be happy. But, now I understand it's just the beginning. I look at Mom and Dad as they walk down the granite steps of the courthouse. I realize there's a long narrow highway still ahead of us and that we're going to have to drive down it alone.

Dad stops at the base of the stairs and calls out to one of the reporters in a calm but firm voice, "I'd like to make a comment." Quickly he is surrounded by half a dozen reporters and photographers and even a TV camera. He puts his sunglasses on, takes in a big breath of air, looks up into the white overcast sky, and says, as his voice shakes and quivers, "The murder was senseless. I stand before you as a father, with all my family members around me, except one. She has taken a loved one from us—and if, indeed, she is guilty, they should teach her a lesson. She should get the maximum sentence that the Lord and God above us would give her." He puts his head down, wraps his arm protectively around Mom and steps down onto the road.

Chapter 19

Winter Waiting

The papers are lined up along the kitchen table. *Time to relive yesterday,* I think to myself, as I pick up one of them. The headline is in bold print across the top of the front page:

POLICE SAY WIDOW HELPED TEEN
MURDER HER HUSBAND

Underneath is a photo of Pam leaving the courthouse. Her head is down as she descends the stairs, escorted by the two policemen. Next to it is a smaller photo of Dad talking to reporters. He looks kind of cool with his sunglasses on and a tough look on his face.

The paper is packed with stories about the case, and I read through each of them slowly, sipping my coffee. Between articles, I stare out the slider, watching the summer sun throw a kaleidoscope of patterns on the glass.

One article reveals how the neighbors at Gregg's condo aren't surprised that Pam has been arrested. Another compares Pam's behavior before and after her arrest. Another has the photos of the three boys from Seabrook all lined up next to a picture of Gregg that's the same size. *I hate it when they do that,* I think to myself, *it's like they want to put Gregg in the company of those murderers.*

The fourth article explains the contents of the mysterious sealed affidavits: How Pam was in love with Flynn, and asked him to kill Gregg, so she didn't lose the condo, the furniture and the dog. How she got mad when they lost a glove in the field after she told them not to wear gloves. How the boys admitted they killed Gregg to one of their friends. How Pam had spent a few weekends with Flynn, before the murder. *Unreal, man,* I think, *I still just can't believe it.* I slap the newspaper down on the glass table. The title of the article stares up at me:

LOVE IS A POSSIBLE MOTIVE

"Yeah, well, no doubt, it *is* the motive," I say to myself.

I get out of the shower and I look into my parents' bedroom. On Mom's side of the bed on the nightstand is a pad of paper and a pen. I walk across the bedroom wondering why the bed isn't made, because Mom always makes the bed. I look down at the pad of paper and see that it's filled with Mom's handwriting, her nearly perfect cursive. I can't help myself. I grab the pad of paper and begin reading:

It's September 4, 1990, and today is my son Gregg's 25th birthday. I'm just sitting here waiting for him to come in the front door and up the stairs, so his dad and I can wish him a Happy Birthday and give him a hug and a kiss. We usually celebrate our birthday together because tomorrow is my birthday, also. Gregg came over to visit every other day to say hello and to play with our granddaughter Ashley. He loves Ashley and comes to play with her as often as he can. But today is different, for deep down in my broken heart, I know he isn't coming today and never will again. Four months ago, Gregg was brutally murdered by some savages who never even knew him, but did know his wife. Gregg's life and wonderful future were taken from him by a single gunshot wound to the head. I cannot believe this has happened to my son and our family. Gregg was here the day he died and I'll never forget that wonderful smiling face as he ran back and forth in our living room with Ashley on his shoulders. After a while he said he had to go home because he had some things he had to do, so he said goodbye to us, and I gave him a kiss. As he left, Gregg said he'd see us later, but that night they murdered our son and he's been taken from us forever.

Gregg was a happy-go-lucky kid and enjoyed everything he did in his life, he made friends easily and everyone seemed to like him. He could make you smile. For as long as I live, I'll never understand the horrible circumstances that surround his death and why such a senseless and terrible thing had to be done to my son. The night Gregg died, I think I died with him. I have this hollow space in my heart and stomach. I'm praying that my husband and I and our family will be able to make it through this horrible, horrible nightmare. We hope these savages that killed our son will know what it is like to suffer so much, that at times you wish you were not on this earth any longer. She (Pam) will never know what it's like to lose a child. It's the most horrible thing a parent could ever experience, and the grief is so overwhelming that you don't know if you can possibly face another day. Gregg will be in our hearts and memories until the day we join him. We all miss you terribly.

> Happy Birthday, Gregg.
> We love you dearly,
> Mom

After I'm done reading, I close my eyes to hold back the tears, but I can't stop. I sit on the edge of the bed, sobbing, until a memory surfaces. I see Gregg, bouncing around the living room with Ashley on his shoulders and the sheer joy of it lifts my spirit. I drop the pad down on the rumpled bedspread, and wipe my eyes with the back of my hand. "They're flying," I whisper softly to myself, and smile.

I sit for a moment, letting the memories flood back. Then I put the letter back on the nightstand with the pen next to it and I walk away.

Dad and I are driving to work. I'm having my usual rant while Dad drives silently, listening to me go off. "I'm so fucking sick of it all, fuck her, it's fucking ridiculous, all this shit!" I look down at the newspaper on my lap and stare at the headline:

PAMELA SMART'S PARENTS PLEAD FOR HER RELEASE

In a Letter to Superior Court Judge,
They Express Concern That She Is 'Slipping Away'

"Unreal! I can't believe her parents actually expect the state to let her out! It's outrageous—they don't just free murderers before the trial starts!"

I look at Dad again, hoping for a reaction, but he's ignoring me, his hands on the wheel and eyes on the road. I go on with my rant. "It's like every other day, like every week, it's something else. First, they arraign her, then they indict her, then her fucking lawyers try to get her out on bail, and then it's denied. Then we wait and wait for the fucking kids from Seabrook to be certified as adults, and

216

there's still no answer on that one, even though we've been waiting forever. Then her lawyers say the tape is frivolous fucking hearsay. Un-fucking believable! I'm fucking sick of cutting out newspapers! I'm fucking sick of watching the news! It's like we're stuck in a fucking bad movie. It's a goddamn nightmare and we're never going to wake up!"

I finally have Dad's attention. He looks over at me sternly and says, "Now just relax, Dean. Don't get yourself all worked up."

"Relax, Dad? How the fuck am I supposed to relax? I haven't fucking been able to relax since the night we found him. That was in May, and it's the fucking end of October and they haven't even set a date for the goddamn trial! Relax, huh? Yeah Dad, I wish I could relax, but it ain't happening—sorry."

Dad's silence only encourages me. "I can't even go anywhere. Every time I'm anywhere there are people staring at me or coming up to me to say they're fucking sorry. *Sorry?* They don't have a clue—they don't know what fucking sorry is. And then there are the clients! All they want to talk about is Pam and when the trial is going to start, and they all just sign up for insurance, no questions asked, because they feel bad for me and feel bad for us. I hate selling fucking life insurance, and I don't want to do it anymore."

"It'll be easier when this whole thing is over, son, I promise." I watch him shake his head as if he doesn't even believe what he just said, and it gets me going again.

"And another thing—the fucking reporters never stop calling. I mean, do they think we have nothing better to do but answer the same damn questions they've been asking us for months? I mean, come on, what the hell is left to say?

Fuck, I'm surprised they're not following us again today in their fucking news van with the fucking satellite dish on top. I bet fifty bucks the phone at home is ringing off the hook right now, Dad. I bet they'll be at the office bugging us to comment. I bet they're knocking on the door at home right now bugging Mom." I pause to catch my breath and look down at the newspaper on my lap. Pam's face is pictured next to her parents. I show the headline to Dad and point to where it reads that she's "slipping away." He glances at it and rolls his eyes, and I whip the paper into the backseat of the car.

"What a shame—poor little Pamie doesn't feel good," I say, imitating a little baby. Dad finally starts laughing a bit and so do I. I continue with the baby talk, "Oh Pamie don't feel good, poor baby, we should let her out of jail, because poor little Pamie is depressed." I drop the baby voice and say, "Yeah, well, you should be depressed because you're a fucking murderer and you're going to rot in jail forever."

Dad pulls into the office parking lot and we both notice at the same time that a reporter is standing in front of the building. We give each other a quick look. "See, Dad? I told you, it's not going to stop."

"You never come out anymore, man," Neil says to me, as he sits on the edge of Gregg's old bed in the loft. He sips his beer and looks over at me. "I never see you, holmes."

"It's been a long fucked-up ride this winter, Neily. I mean, I know—I guess I just like chilling here, for now." I sip my beer and look over at him. "Sorry, man."

"The three kids from Seabrook pled guilty, huh?" He asks.

"Yeah, they did—they pled guilty a couple weeks ago." I answer. "As soon as they were certified to go on trial as adults, they admitted it." I shake my head and laugh a little. "Soon as they find out they're not getting off, because they're fifteen years old, they turn and admit it for a lighter sentence." I laugh again. "The whole thing's just unreal."

He looks over at me with a slight frown. "I don't know how you fucking deal with all this shit, Dean."

"Yeah, and that ain't the end of it. After waiting six months, now Pam's lawyers want to exclude all of the teens' testimony, as if to say it doesn't count. So now we wait for an answer on that, too. It's always fucking something."

"Wow, man, fucking crazy," Neil says.

I stand and turn up the music and swig back the rest of my beer. I grab another and sit back down on the end of my bed. "Roll that number up now, all right, Neily?"

"All right, man—so what else you been up to?"

"Oh yeah, well, check this out—now they're fucking making a movie about the whole thing."

"What, no way! They're making a movie?" he asks. "See, this is why I'm afraid to come over—because every time I do, the story gets crazier!" We both laugh.

"Yeah, they're going to make a fucking movie," I say, shaking my head. "You know the student that taped Pam, right? Well, she's the one who sold her story to the movie company."

"What the fuck!" He looks at me, stunned. He spins the joint and drops it on the blue and brown bedspread, and I have a sudden flash of Gregg and me, sitting on the same bed in our bedroom in Londonderry. *So long ago, like another lifetime.*

"See, that's the problem, man." I blurt out to Neil. "Everything reminds me—of Gregg. I look at the bureau, it reminds me of Gregg. I see his trophy," I point to it, "it reminds me of Gregg. It doesn't stop, man." He looks over at me, worried. I wash back a big gulp of beer.

"Time to smoke," he says, trying to change the subject. He tosses the number at me and I catch it. He smiles at me and says, "Spark it."

I put it in my lips and let it hang there. I grab the lighter and say, "But I guess I'm lucky, man."

"How in the hell do you figure you're lucky, Dean?" he asks.

I stand up and pop open the screen to the skylight. "I'm lucky because I haven't gone crazy like everybody else around here."

"Well, that's because you had the natural advantage of already being fucking crazy, before this whole thing happened." He starts laughing.

"Yeah," I say, laughing, "you're probably right." I reach under the skylight screen, grab the handle and click it open, just a few inches.

I sit back down on the edge of the bed and light the joint. I take a hit, hold my breath and blow it out toward the open skylight. Some of the smoke wisps away, then swirls in front of me in circles. A warm breeze spins it back into the room like water around rocks. I stare up at it and can feel the whiteness pulling me in. I close my eyes and take another hit, hold it, then let it go. "Everything reminds me, Neily, even the smoke." I pass the joint to him.

"One hundred thousand dollars," I say to him.

He exhales and the smoke swirls around him. "What, one hundred thousand dollars?" he asks.

"That's how much the wiretap girl is getting for the movie," I answer.

"No way, dude—so she's getting rich from it. That's unbelievable, man."

I watch the smoke move under the skylight and another warm breeze floats into the loft. "You feel that, man? Summer's coming."

He shakes his head yes, as I take a sip of beer. "Trial's coming in a few weeks, man, and I want to just get the fuck out of here after that—it's been the longest winter ever—I'm thinking like California, where it's warm all the time." I pause and look up at the fog filling the loft. "I don't know, maybe New York City."

"Yeah, but what if she gets off?" He glances over at me, and I know he feels bad for saying it. I let his words linger and then imagine them drifting off like so much smoke out of the skylight and into the darkening white of the sky.

Chapter 20

Memory and The Machine

I sit in the back of the old Jag, staring down at my tie. I straighten it. Dad drives and Mom sits and fidgets in the passenger seat. We're heading toward Rockingham County Courthouse, about an hour away, where the trial has been set. "How long do you think this whole thing is going to take, Dad?" I ask.

He shrugs his shoulders. "It depends, son — you never know what could happen at a trial — a couple months maybe. I don't know — it all depends."

I lean toward the door and start fiddling with the little reading lamp that's on the roof above the side window. The light is molded into a socket and I pull it out, snap it back in and then pop it out again. I rotate the small flashlight-like lamp, and it pivots and shines a cone of light wherever I direct it. I turn it on and off and spin it in circles, watching the ray of light as it darts around the backseat. I snap the reading light back into its socket.

I lean over to look out the front windshield and watch as the staggered yellow lines flash by. We're heading due east, toward the beach and the courthouse, and the sun has just risen ahead of us. It shines and sparkles off every little nick in the windshield. *It seems blinding after such a dim winter,* I think to myself. I squint and stare ahead. *Shame to be heading toward the beach – and not be going.* I feel the sun warming my face through the windows and it seems like spring might actually be around the corner. "So nice today, Dad. Can you crack the windows open?" I ask. Dad nods and the windows slide down a few inches.

A warm breeze rushes in and I watch it rustle the wisps of grey hair on the back of Dad's head. Suddenly my mind flashes back to Gregg and I can see his long mane of hair before he cut it, *before all of this happened.* I'm driving behind him, following him to the bunkers. His long blond hair is flying up toward the sunroof, his blue Vuarnet sunglasses glimmering in the sun. I sigh, squeeze my eyes shut and shake my head, trying to block out the vision. I manage to snap out of it and stare out the windshield again at the horizon above the shore.

The whiteout comes back. Now I'm standing and watching with our friends as Gregg crawls out of the bunker, rising from his knees and emerging from the cave. He squints in the sun and his lips move, but I can't hear anything, just a dull wind-like noise. He slaps his knees and shoulders, swatting sand and dust up into the air. The dust floats and fills the air all around him. He stops brushing himself and looks at me, smiling wide, and he speaks again, but I hear nothing, then he punches me on the shoulder, laughing. The dust, the cloud of powder, swirls around him and he fades away.

I stare out the windshield up toward the sun. I smile, thinking of Gregg, and then I change my expression back to the blank sort of angry face that I've been practicing in the mirror for the trial. I look over at my reflection in the side window and I look pale and exhausted. *No sadness, not today,*

I think to myself. *You're not allowed.* I make my angry-concerned face at the window. *Pretty good,* I nod to myself in approval, as the trees on the side of the highway glide by.

Beyond my reflection, I see an outcropping of rocks covered in ice. The bedrock outcropping has been blasted out to make way for the highway, and it's like a cross section of half a hill. Out of the bedrock grow tiny stunted trees and I wonder how they survive, clinging to nothing but a rock face. Seeping from the outcropping are big globular ice chunks. The ice is not the everyday ordinary ice you might find, say, in a driveway or clinging to a tree branch. The ice is almost like sculpture—a waterfall frozen in time. The large rounded chunks seem to flow and move in spite of their frozenness. This ice is clear as glass, not the faded type with snow mixed in and not the dirty ice that's non-transparent; this ice is clear as crystal, and when the sun hits it, it glows a magical pale blue from its center. The blue is mesmerizing, naturally electric, trapping my eyes. *Spectacular,* I think to myself.

As I stare at the ice formations, my thoughts drift to the trial and the day that lies ahead. I'm thinking about Pam, about how she'll act in the courtroom. "Hey, Dad," I ask, "how do you think this is going to go?"

"I wish I knew, son, but let's all try to pay attention to everyone and everything, all right?" *Why does he always seem to read my thoughts?*

"Sure, Dad." I answer.

He looks back at me through the rear-view mirror and flashes me a serious look. I lean back and watch the ice through the window, as the sun rises on the horizon ahead of us. I can't stop myself from thinking about the trial and Pam, and if she'll finally get what's coming to her.

The Rockingham County Courthouse is bigger than I expected. It's an imposing structure, built almost entirely of stone, except for two brick wings that jut out on either side. The taller middle section features six square pillars that rise from the ground to the roofline. Stone steps lead up to a huge set of glass double doors at the building's entrance. Above it in bold brass letters is a sign that reads COUNTY OF ROCKINGHAM.

We pull up the large driveway bordered by a patch of grass that separates the building from the parking lot. I look out and notice tripods mounted with cameras littering the lawn. A cluster of people is already milling around, some of them scattered about on the grass, others on the courthouse stairs. Several of them have cameras slung from their chests. There's a line of people, only a few, standing near and inside the glass doors at the entrance. Dad looks over at Mom and I know what he's thinking. *Here we go again.* He looks back at me. "Ready, buddy?" he asks.

"No, but we have no choice, so let's go!" I answer. Dad pushes open the door and steps out, and Mom and I follow.

I'm amazed by Dad's composure. He walks with confidence and determination, his dark suit rustling slightly with every strut. He quickens his pace as he makes his way closer to the cameras and reporters, and we do the same. As we get close to the cluster of reporters at the front door, they catch sight of us and immediately head in our direction. "Mr. Smart?" they yell, trying to capture his attention. "Mr. Smart, Mr. Smart?"

Dad shakes his head no, without losing his stride. "Not now," he calls out, "not now, no comment—please." He picks up the pace and we hurry past them and up the courthouse stairs.

At the top of the stairs, the photographers start taking pictures of us, and we have to turn our heads to avoid the repeating flashes of light. Dad puts his hands up to cover his eyes and says again, kindly but firmly, "Please—not now, no comment."

The reporters seem not to hear, they keep yelling, "Mr. Smart, Mr. Smart, do you think she's guilty?" "How do feel about the teenage boys, Mr. Smart?" "Mr. Smart, do you think she did it?" Dad starts to lose his patience. He shakes his head one more time, then pulls open the glass door and ushers us inside. The door slams shut behind us.

It takes a minute or two for our eyes to adjust, and when they do, we find ourselves standing in a line, in front of a large metal detector. There's a wooden table set up next to it, a uniformed security guard manning the machine. I watch as the guard lets people through, one at a time. After signing his name on a list, Dad retrieves his car keys from his pocket, then drops them into a plastic basket and walks through. Mom does the same, but when it's my turn, I set off the detector and the guard makes me come back and take my belt off and go through all over again. I feel everyone's eyes on me, as I retrieve my belt from the basket and put it back on.

My embarrassment wears off as I look around the lobby of the courthouse and take it in. The room is enormous, with high ceilings and walls made of thousands of tiny white tiles mixed in with randomly placed tiles of different colors. The walls shimmer white as the light reflects off them, and as I look at them, I begin to stare off, until Dad snaps me out of it and says, "Come on, son, let's go."

I follow my parents down a hallway covered in wood paneling. A trail of multicolored electrical wire runs crisscrossed along the wall and stops at a door up ahead. There is a sign on the door that reads COURTROOM ONE.

A voice behind us says, "Mr. Smart?" We turn and it's Sandi, the pretty, blonde victim-and-witness advocate from the state who is supposed to guide us and help us through the trial. She smiles at us kindly and reaches out to give Mom a quick hug, then ushers us away from the courtroom door to let others head in before us. I peer around the line to get my first glimpse of the courtroom. It's bigger than the one in Derry, and it's already packed full of people. I look at the rows of wooden benches and wonder if we'll get a seat.

Finally, everyone has filed past, and Sandi leads us inside. As we pass the rows of seats on each side of the aisle, I can feel everyone's eyes on us. With each bench we pass, the feeling gets stronger. Sandi leads us right to the front row on the left side of the aisle, and as Mom and Dad take their seats, I notice a sign taped to the end of the bench that reads "This row reserved for the Smart family." A sense of pride rushes over me, but it spirals quickly into a sickened feeling, as I take my seat.

A hushed silence fills the courtroom and everyone turns at once toward the double doors. The bailiffs are bringing Pam in. From my front-row seat, I try to make out her expression but the large bailiff in front of her blocks my view. After her walk down the aisle, she is seated at a long table in the front of the courtroom next to her lawyers whose faces I recall from the arraignment. I watch as she whispers something to one of them. All I can see of her is the back of her head. The chatter in the courtroom resumes until the bailiff's voice booms from the front of the room, "All rise for the Honorable Judge Douglas Gray."

The judge enters and takes his seat in a high-backed leather chair. He leans his head forward slightly and stares down at the court, his eyes piercing over the rims of his glasses. I look at the brass eagle that tops the flagstaff next to him. *He is perched to attack,* I think to myself. *Goddamn if he doesn't look tough as shit, like a weatherworn cowboy, squinting in the sun.* I recall Sandi telling us about this judge: how he's tough, but fair, and how most of the lawyers know not to anger him, and that not a single one of his decisions has ever been overturned. I instantly like him, in all of his official but wild-seeming strength.

The lawyers from both sides rise and gather in the front of the courtroom before the judge's bench. I find that I can't take my eyes off Pam's lawyers, Mark Sisti and Paul Twomey. I stare back and forth between them, watching as they exchange words. I recall reading in the papers that they are the best defense attorneys in the state. I watch as Sisti, the shorter and stouter of the two, pleads with Judge Gray over some point. He appears to be an effective debater, as Judge Gray nods his head yes to him several times. I remember that Sisti and Twomey have worked together for years and have won several important trials. I start to worry that they will get Pam off, and she'll be freed.

The prosecuting team also has two attorneys, but as I look at them argue before the judge, I can't help but wonder if they're tough enough to defeat the smooth and confident team of Sisti and Twomey. Diane Nicolosi, the state's prosecuting attorney, is tall, with long dark hair and a soft smile. Paul Maggiotto, a prosecutor with a strong reputation, has been brought all the way from Brooklyn to strengthen the team, but with his short black tightly curled hair and wire-frame glasses, he looks quiet and reserved — nothing like what I'd imagined. I figured he would be flashier, a smooth-talking New Yorker dressed to the hilt in an expensive suit. I look up at them and hope that they're tougher than they appear.

Twomey suddenly steps away from the judge's bench and makes his way toward the defense table where Pam sits, motionless. His dark hair is parted to the side, and as he struts confidently across the courtroom, he looks smooth, calm and comfortable. He grabs a manila file from the table, whispers something to Pam, and walks back toward the judge's bench. He points to something in the manila folder as he places it in front of Judge Gray. This riles Maggiotto, who is shaking his head angrily, causing the judge to motion him to calm down. Suddenly, all four lawyers head back to their tables at the front of the courtroom.

The bailiff steps up to make an announcement: "The court is in recess until tomorrow morning when opening arguments will begin. The jury will go on a tour of the crime scene, followed by a visit to the defendant's office in Hampton."

"What just happened?" I turn to Mom and ask. I wonder if I missed something.

"I'm not sure," she says, as she looks past me toward Sandi. "Sandi?"

"Well," Sandi says, "the jury's touring the crime scene today and then Pamela's office, and I guess the judge was debating with the lawyers on some point and they will probably work it out after the jury's tour."

Dad leans over. "So I guess that's it for today, then."

"Guess so." Sandi answers.

I'm still confused, as I watch the bailiffs escort Pam out. She shuffles past us without a look. The room fills with a nervous, excited chatter as we stand and file out the courtroom. As I walk through the doors, my head is finally clearing. I turn briefly to look over at the empty jury box. I can't help but wonder if, as they tour the crime scene, any of them will step on Gregg's bloodstain, just as Pam did.

Chapter 21

The Brutal Beginning

At first, it seems like a replay of the day before. The bailiff calls out, "All rise." We stand as Judge Gray enters the courtroom and then we take our seats. The lawyers converge at the judge's bench and I hope there won't be another postponement. I sigh and look at Dad but see that he looks confident. I lean back against the wooden bench and watch the lawyers disperse.

"Opening arguments can proceed," the judge says firmly. I let out a low whistle of relief.

Diane Nicolosi stands up, and I think to myself, *Finally, after waiting so long, the trial is really beginning.* She walks around the table directly in front of us and turns to face the jury. Her delicate features soften a bit and she breaks into a slight smile.

"The State of New Hampshire alleges," she says in her soft voice, "that Pamela Smart, the media coordinator for the Hampton New Hampshire School District, was having an affair with William Flynn, a sixteen-year-old high school student, who attended Winnacunnet High School, where Pam Smart supervised him."

The crowd in the courtroom is silent as Nicolosi continues. "The state also alleges that not only did Pamela

Smart have an affair with Billy Flynn, but she also convinced him to murder her husband, Gregg Smart. The state also alleges that Pam Smart not only convinced Billy Flynn to murder her husband, but she in fact also helped Flynn and two other Seabrook teenagers in the planning of the murder. The jury will hear the testimony of the other two teens, Patrick Randall and Vance Lattime, as well as Billy Flynn, the triggerman in the murder."

Nicolosi pauses and steps a little closer to the wooden jury box on the side of the courtroom. "Pamela Smart and William Flynn began their affair in February of nineteen ninety, and it wasn't long afterward that Pam asked Billy to kill Gregg. When Billy asked Pamela why she wanted her husband killed, she answered that Gregg didn't treat her well and she even showed Billy bruises that Gregg supposedly gave her." I feel my anger rising as she speaks. I look over at Dad and see that he, too, is fighting back rage.

"When Billy Flynn asked Pam why she didn't just get a divorce, the defendant Pamela Smart answered that even if she did divorce Gregg that he would follow her around and never leave her alone." *Yeah right*, I think to myself, *Gregg never, ever, had to follow or chase any girl.* "And that she would lose her dog and her condominium in Derry and all of her furniture." There is a loud gasp in the courtroom but the lawyer pushes on, "The state will prove beyond a doubt that Pamela Smart planned and was an accomplice to the murder of her own husband."

As Nicolosi finishes her opening statement and turns away from the jury, there is silence in the court. All eyes are on Paul Maggiotto, but the state's other prosecutor seems to be taking his time. Judge Gray stares down in annoyance. "Mr. Maggiotto?"

"Yes, Your Honor," Maggiotto answers back calmly, as he looks down at some papers on the table. At last, he rises from his seat and walks slowly toward the jury box. His wire-framed glasses shimmer in the courtroom light and his dark moustache twitches slightly as he draws in a deep breath and begins.

"The state intends to prove beyond any reasonable doubt that Pamela Smart is a deliberate and premeditated accomplice to, and conspirator in, the murder of her husband, Greggory Smart." He pauses and continues, raising his voice slightly. "For it was Pamela Smart who masterminded this heinous crime — a crime admittedly perpetrated by Billy Flynn, a sixteen-year-old boy, who had developed a crush on his young, attractive, very hip media teacher, Pamela Smart." Maggiotto pauses again and turns away from the jury to face Pam. He raises his arm and points at her, then turns back to the jury.

"You see, Billy Flynn's crush — his fantasy about his teacher was encouraged by Pamela Smart, it was nurtured by Mrs. Smart, and indeed it was fulfilled by Mrs. Smart. The defendant initiated the affair, and she freely admits that she had sexual intercourse with sixteen-year-old Billy Flynn." He pauses for dramatic effect. "Several times, in fact," he says, moving in closer to the jury. "In his house — in her car — even in her office at school. But it was after the very first time they had sex in her home — in the bed she shared with her husband, Gregg — who was away on a business trip — that she drove Billy back to his house, and on the way, she informed him that they would have to break up, because Gregg was getting suspicious. There wasn't anything else that could be done."

Maggiotto stops pacing and looks up at the jury. "Except to murder Gregg—and for the next twelve weeks, she manipulated young Flynn. Mrs. Smart relentlessly urged and systematically instructed Billy Flynn to take her husband Gregg's life. Whenever Billy protested and pleaded to find another solution and he cried like a baby, she berated him, she denied him, she humiliated him. When he finally went along with her plan and plotted with her, she lavished him with gifts, with attention, with gratitude and with—sex." He looks at the jury, nodding his head silently. "Billy Flynn pulled the trigger that night—but it was Pamela Smart who was responsible—for that one fatal shot."

Maggiotto pivots away from the jury and takes his seat, and I hear Mom crying softly next to me. I turn to see Dad put a protective arm around her shoulder. He looks past her at me and shakes his head in approval. I give him a silent nod of agreement. *Maggiotto is good.*

Now it's the defense's turn, and Mark Sisti stands up and struts around the table. Wearing an out-of-date suit and tie and a vacant expression, he looks somewhat comical as he waddles past with all the grace of a drunken penguin. *I hate him already, and he hasn't spoken one word.* My blood rushes faster as he begins to address the jury.

"In the coming days, weeks, you'll meet the witnesses for the prosecution, each of whom has already made a very beneficial deal, arrangement, bargain with district attorneys. These so-called witnesses will be paraded before you in succession. They'll sit right there—" He points to the witness stand next to Judge Gray's bench. "Yes, they'll sit right there, and they'll recite to you a vile and preposterous concoction of toxic soup."

I turn my eyes away from him and look over to the jury. I'm dismayed to see that despite his rumpled appearance, he has their full attention. My fists clench up and I start shooting my serious look at him. "Mr. Maggiotto will try and convince you that what you hear from them is fact. But, in truth, it is based primarily on innuendo and speculation. What we have here, ladies and gentlemen, is a series of witnesses that not only conspired and acted together, to brutally and cold-bloodedly murder a twenty-four-year-old man, but now also, they have conspired and plotted again—to save their hides."

The courtroom murmurs as people whisper to each other and shuffle in their seats. Mom fidgets, as Dad rubs his eyes. I look over at Pam and she has turned in her seat to face the jury. Her dirty-blonde hair is pinned to the back of her head by a black satin bow. She writes notes on a yellow legal pad on the table in front of her. I stare at the bow in her hair and clench my fists repeatedly, wondering what she's jotting down. *Her lawyer's good,* I think to myself, *uh-oh, this could be a battle.*

Sisti steps forward and continues his argument, "You've heard the prosecutor characterize Billy Flynn as 'poor Billy Flynn,' 'young Billy Flynn,' 'vulnerable Billy Flynn.' Mmmmmmmm—how vulnerable I ask you is a person who not once, but on three separate occasions, admittedly set out to kill Gregg Smart—a person who admittedly lay in wait for his victim for an hour—with his best buddies by his side and another waiting patiently, coolly and calculatedly in the getaway car—a person who admittedly put a .38-caliber revolver to the head of another human being—a human being who begged for his life—" Mom sighs heavily as Sisti says, "Without much of a thought, Billy Flynn pulled the trigger, watched the blood splatter – and then simply left his victim to die!"

Mom lets out a loud "ohhh" into the courtroom and even Sisti turns to see what the matter is. I shoot him my death look. Dad puts his arm around Mom and she nestles her head on his shoulder, sobbing. "It's all right, Judy," he whispers in her ear. He looks at me with his jaw clenched and his eyes tightening.

The courtroom is silent and Sisti sighs and paces back and forth in front of the jurors. He stops pacing and continues, "Now, one of the sidelights here, and it is only that – a sidelight – despite the prosecution having dwelled on it in the opening – is this affair, so called. You'll hear all about it in vivid detail, I'm sure. Fine. But, ladies and gentlemen, you cannot let it cloud your evaluation of the case. Each of you told us directly, a number of times during the jury selection process, that the affair, in and of itself, does not offend you. If it did, you would not be sitting here. That being so, the affair plays a very singular role. It provided the motivation for the obsessed teenager to kill the husband of the woman he loved."

Sisti turns away from the jurors and walks toward the defense table as if he's done, then turns back to face them again. "Billy Flynn had convinced himself that he and Pam could live happily ever after once Gregg was out of the picture. It is, then, a murder fueled by obsession, jealousy and mental illness. Did Pam in any way engage in the planning of the killing of her own husband? We will prove she absolutely did not. But we will only prove that if you all keep an open mind to the facts. The Constitution grants each citizen the right to a fair trial. You must now see it, then, that it happens in Rockingham County. It is in your hands, and you must listen to everything in context—*context*," he emphasizes. "Not little bits and pieces that give you a kernel of truth. No, you must take it in the context of the person from whom it is coming. If you do that, if you give Pamela Smart a fair trial, if you do not jump to conclusions, but rather let the process play out before you—then you will return a not-guilty verdict—and you might even end up a little angry—as I am—that this case was ever even brought to trial."

Dad removes his arm from Mom's shoulder, and by the look on his face, on both of their faces, I can tell they are thinking what I'm thinking: *Sisti is good. We've just lost round one.*

After recess, the parade of witnesses begins. Patrick Randall, the teen who held the knife to Gregg's neck, is the first to be called. *He doesn't even have a suit on*, I think to myself, as he walks down the aisle in a maroon sweater and tight black jeans. He walks right past us and it's hard for me to even look at him.

As he walks up to the witness stand and takes his oath, I force myself to study him. The first thing I notice is how young he looks. I look at his hair fashioned in the mullet style, black, wavy and too long on the back of his head. His frame is thick and I wonder about the fight he and Flynn had with Gregg, and I think, *Well, no wonder Gregg couldn't take the both of them — he's bigger than I'd imagined.*

Maggiotto begins his questioning of Randall with the basics: "What's your name?" "How old are you?" "Where do you live and go to school?" I hear Randall as he answers in a nonchalant almost-monotone voice, heavy with a

Massachusetts accent. I start to lose focus and I wonder when Maggiotto is going to get down to it. He asks him how he was acquainted with Pam, and Randall answers, "From the school and the self- esteem program she ran." I reason to myself that this isn't going anywhere and it seems like Maggiotto is going to drag it out forever.

Suddenly he gets to the point, and his question catches Randall off guard. "Did you have any knowledge of the love affair between your best friend Billy Flynn and your teacher Mrs. Smart?"

"I did," Randall snaps. "They were together all the time."

"Well," Maggiotto responds, "just because they were together all the time doesn't mean they were having an affair — how do you know they were having an affair?"

"I know because Billy told me he was in love with her and that they were sleeping together and he said the sex was great — and I had seen them hanging all over each other one night after Billy drank a bunch of Southern Comfort."

"How did Billy feel about Pam's husband, Gregg?" Maggiotto asks.

"Billy hated Smart because Pam told him over and over again that Gregg treated her bad — and Billy said to me that Pam had shown him bruises that Pam said were from her husband." Randall answers. I look over at Dad and we shake our heads. We both know Gregg wasn't like that.

Maggiotto steps toward his table at the front of the courtroom, takes a sip of water from a paper cup and walks back toward Randall and the witness box. "Tell me, Mr. Randall, what did you do last May first?"

Randall pauses and seems hesitant to answer. Maggiotto prompts him, "Please, Mr. Randall, start at the beginning and tell me what you did on May first of last year."

Finally, Randall begins describing how it happened: How Pam and Billy were lying in the back of her car as they drove to Haverhill to pick up the getaway car. How Pam suggested that they not use the knife because the blood would get on the sofa and the carpet. How Pam said she would leave the bulkhead unlocked for them.

The bulkhead. The word triggers a memory and suddenly the courtroom fades away as a scene flashes into my mind. *I'm standing, just a kid, in the graveled driveway of the old white Victorian house in Hudson. We've decided to go in, even though we're scared. We quietly drop our bikes and tiptoe around the back of the house. Ronny leads and heads closer to the basement doors, taking a few steps at a time, as we, in turn, follow him sequentially, like spies, infiltrating the enemy's stronghold. I lean against the old house, hiding in its shadows, as the four of us encircle the wooden doors of the bulkhead. I kneel down, my heart pounding with adrenaline. Ronny grips the handles to the double wooden doors and silently gives them a pull. The doors don't budge, "Locked," he whispers.*

I come back to the courtroom. Randall is explaining how Pam asked them how she should react when she discovers Gregg's body. Should she run from door to door or should she call the police? Randall says they told her to act natural—like someone would act when they find a dead body.

Maggiotto holds up a plastic bag with a large black-handled butcher knife in it. He shows it to Randall and asks him if he recognizes it. Randall answers yes. Maggiotto places it on the evidence table in front of the witness stand.

Maggiotto holds up a silver revolver and asks Randall, "Do you recognize this?" Randall shakes his head yes.

Maggiotto asks Randall to explain exactly what happened in the condo on the night of May first: Randall explains how he and Flynn staged the house to look like a burglary and how they set the Kenwood speakers near the door. How they loaded jewelry and compact discs into a pillowcase, how they rifled through the drawers and tossed clothing everywhere, how they threw the dog, Halen, Gregg's little tan and white Shih Tzu, down the basement stairs. "We waited near the front door for him to come home," he says, his voice lowered slightly.

As the crowd in the courtroom strains to hear, Randall continues to convey what happened next: How he waited on the stairs with the knife, as Flynn stood in the foyer behind the door with the gun. How Gregg finally came home and hesitated, after he opened the front door and called out for Halen. How Flynn pulled him into the condo and the two of them overpowered him. "I grabbed him by the hair and slammed his head in the wall as Billy hit him," Randall says, his words echoing through the courtroom.

Mom sighs next to me. She drops her head down on her hands and starts crying softly. Randall continues, "I tell Gregg to get on his knees and I ask for his wallet. He gets on his knees and gives up the wallet. I hold his head still and put the knife to his throat, as Flynn stands behind him holding his head, too. I ask for his ring and Gregg says, 'No, I can't—don't take my ring—my wife will kill me!' "

The crowd in the courtroom seems to let out a collective gasp as they realize the irony of Gregg's statement. Mom's hand slaps down on mine and at once I'm in a state of shock. I can't believe what Gregg said. I look at Mom, a deep frown on her face, as if she is in pain. She squeezes the top of my hand as Randall continues, "I was supposed to cut his throat, but I couldn't do it—because of what he said. I just couldn't do it. I told Flynn I couldn't do it, and he points at his pocket with the gun and I shake my head yes. He pulls the pistol out of his pocket—puts it to the back of Gregg's head—he says, 'Forgive me, God'—and he pulls the trigger and shoots Smart in the head."

Mom squeezes the top of my hand so hard I think she might break my fingers. I look down at her hand, red from the pressure, she lets go and stands up, letting out a loud "ohhhhh" into the courtroom. She turns and runs, crying, her hands flailing in the air, down the aisle and out the doors. Dad and I look at each other, as the courtroom goes from an excited chatter to a shocked silence. We're both relieved when Judge Gray calls a brief recess.

We hurry out of the courtroom and search for Mom and find her with Sandi, in a side waiting room. My brother Rick is there, too, and he and his wife, Sue, are doing their best to console her. Mom seems better, so I decide to head out for some fresh air.

I walk out the front doors and stand at the top of the steps. A gentle snow flies and litters the lawn with patches of white. I spark a cigarette and watch the smoke swirl past the floating flakes, so light in the air. I stare at the shadows of the cameras on the lawn. Over and over in my mind, I hear Gregg saying what were supposedly his last words. *"Don't take my ring, my wife will kill me."* I keep shaking my head at the incredibleness of it, the sheer madness and randomness of his statement, the truth of his last words rippling through me. *"My wife will kill me."* *It's like he knew.*

I stomp my cigarette out on the steps and head back into the lobby. I stand and lean against the wall, watching people come and go through the security gates. I end up staring off into the glimmering little white tiles on the lobby walls. *It's like he knew*, I think to myself again. I start to fade away in my mind and see Gregg sitting on the tweed couch in Derry with his beads in his hands. People are rushing hurriedly past me, making their way back to the courtroom, but I feel like I can't move. Finally, when they're nearly all back inside, I manage to head in and take my seat. Sisti is already rising from his chair. He bows to the court and waddles around toward Randall to begin his cross-examination.

"Mr. Randall, tell the court what you told the police you wanted to be when you grew up."

"I wanted to be an assassin or a hit man." Sisti turns to the jury with a mock-surprised look on his face.

"Months prior to the murder, Mr. Randall, were you stealing cars and ripping off stereos?" Sisti asks.

"Occasionally." Randall answers.

"Were you ripping off motorbikes?"

"Occasionally."

"And you were drinking and buying dope, right?"

"Yes."

"And after the murder — on that very night — you went to Hampton Beach to trade the jewelry you got for killing a guy, for money to buy cocaine?"

"Right," Randall answers slowly, "I wanted to get my mind off of what happened."

"Would you say that after the murder you and Billy Flynn's drug and alcohol use increased?"

"Yes."

"Is it your opinion, Mr. Randall, that Billy was obsessed with Pam?"

"Yes, he was madly in love with her."

"How did Billy feel about Pam's husband, Gregg Smart?"

"Like I said earlier, he hated him—because of the things Pam said about him."

"Did Billy talk about murdering Gregg?"

"Yes, he did, a lot, because he hated him and wanted Pam."

"And Vance Lattime, Jr. stole the gun from his dad's collection and stole hollow-point bullets because they are deadlier and explode on impact, right?"

"Right."

"On the night of the murder, Pam wasn't there, right? She didn't send an instruction booklet?" Sisti asks, leaning closer to Randall.

"No, she wasn't there and didn't send a booklet." Randall answers. "But we were with her on the ride to Haverhill to pick up my grandmother's car, the getaway car, and she told us not to get blood on the sofa, and kept on asking us what she should do when she found Gregg's body—so we, I, told her to act normal—like if someone walks in and finds someone dead."

Sisti quickly changes the subject. "Prior to the night of the killing, you had been to Pam's condo, so you knew the layout of the place and where items of value were kept—without Pamela Smart's assistance—right?"

"Right, I knew the place, but, she did assist us—she left the bulkhead unlocked for us, she told us what to do with the dog, she told us where the jewelry was and how to set it up so it looked like a burglary." Randall says.

Sisti sighs and shakes his head to express his disagreement. "You took CDs and jewelry and put them in a pillowcase and took it with you after you killed Smart, right?"

"Yes."

"What happened after the murder on the way back to Seabrook in the car?"

"Billy said something about the thrill of killing—about the power he felt after doing it. He just kept repeating how he couldn't believe he just killed a guy." Randall answers.

"Right, so Flynn couldn't believe he just killed a guy. How HE just killed a guy—Gregg wasn't killed by Pam, right? It was Billy who killed Gregg, right? Billy put the gun to his head and shot him, right—not Pam?" Sisti asks, facing the jury.

"Right." Randall answers.

Sisti walks confidently from the witness stand and says, "I have no further questions, Your Honor."

That night I can't get Randall's words out of my head, and I have trouble getting to sleep. I finally fall into a dark slumber and have the dream again, the one where I'm floating over Gregg's truck, yelling as loud as I can, "Don't go home! Don't GO!" but as before, Gregg just ignores me and drives on. I wake up, my body shaking and drenched in a cold sweat.

I look at the clock flashing 3:03 on the bureau. I can't seem to cool down, so I pop open the skylight and step out.

The cold air hits my face, and I lean my head back and look up, high into the darkness. Just then, in the sky, I see flashing lights moving about. I rub my eyes, wondering if I'm seeing things. I look up again and they're everywhere—glowing orbs moving slowly across the night sky. They flash red and orange, then green and gold, and seem to dissolve away into an electric blue. *What the hell*, I think to myself. I rub my eyes again and shake my head. I look back up and they keep popping up and flashing deep in the sky.

I'm freezing as I stand out of the skylight, but I start thinking it might be a sign from Gregg, so I don't want to go in. Maybe he's trying to tell me something. I shiver and my jaw rattles in the cold. I stare at the lights in amazement until it's so bitter I can't bear it. I step in and pull the skylight shut. I lie back down and stare into the night, watching the glowing lights and wondering to myself if I could be going crazy. *If I am, there is nothing I can do about it.* I close my eyes and finally drift off into a deep sleep.

Chapter 22

Fathers and Forensics

We're driving to the courthouse again and we pass the ice clusters. I watch each section of the blown-out rock as we pass by, staring at the outcroppings. The ice is clouded in the overcast sky, but I notice that the blue center is still visible, glowing dimly. I remember the flashes I saw last night before I drifted off to sleep and I tell Mom and Dad I think they may have been a sign from Gregg.

They both start laughing. "No, really," I say, "I'm serious. I swear they were real and they went on forever—they kept sparkling in the sky."

Dad looks back at me again and says, "You're overtired and stressed out, so you're starting to see things."

"Dad, I'm totally serious, I swear."

"Well, maybe it was shooting stars or something, or maybe—" he smiles at me in the rear-view mirror, "just maybe, it was—aliens!" He starts laughing again with Mom, and this time I join in.

It feels good to laugh about something, but the mood slips away as we pull up in front of the courthouse and stare at the wild scene in front of us. "Holy shit!" I shout out in disbelief. It seems as though the crowd has quadrupled. There are dozens of cameras on tripods, lined up on the lawn, and throngs of reporters everywhere. *It's a circus,* I think to myself, as we survey the scene from the car. We sit for a moment and stare in disbelief. Finally, we decide to make a run for it and I rush past Mom and Dad, past the photographers and reporters who chase us up the stairs, making my way inside. I let out a sigh of relief and suddenly realize I feel like a celebrity, but not in a good way.

I walk through the security scanner and into the white-tiled lobby. As I wait for Mom and Dad and stare at the lobby walls, the little, randomly placed and brightly colored tiles suddenly remind me of the shooting stars I saw last night. *This is too strange – is everything connected?* I wonder. Finally, Mom and Dad come through the scanner and I see the cameras flashing behind them. *More lights, more flashes.*

We walk down the hallway toward the courtroom, and I can't seem to get these thoughts out of my head. I start thinking to myself, *It's like we're stars, shooting stars,* and the cameras keep flashing and the video cameras follow us, and the thought lingers with me, *We're stars, shooting stars,* as I walk down the hallway. I follow the multicolored wires, repeating in my mind, *We're stars – shooting stars – because of a shooting – we're stars.* I open the courtroom doors and walk in.

If it's a circus, I think to myself, *then Pam is the main attraction.* Today, she enters the court taking small steps, deliberately going slowly and sucking in the attention like a sponge. I decide not to look at her; instead, I watch the crowd watching her. She gets so close to us as she passes; I think I could, from here, just jump up and grab her. She sits at the defense's table and I see the same black satin bow in her hair. Someone is called to the stand, but I can't focus, so I just stare at the back of her head, thinking about the things she asked Randall and the others to do. Finally, I look up at the witness stand and see that it's a father of one of the boys. I reason to myself it must be Vance Lattime's dad, the one I read about in the paper. I turn my attention to what he is saying.

"Ralph Welch, who lives with our family, heard about the murder from Randall and Flynn." I hear the tension in his voice as he finishes answering Maggiotto's question. "Ralph heard the boys talking about how a guy came in during a robbery that they were committing, and how they might have shot him. I looked through my gun collection and noticed a revolver was recently cleaned." He sighs and slows down his speech, "So, I brought it to the Seabrook police station and said, 'This might sound crazy, but I think this gun might have been used in a robbery, somewhere around Salem, New Hampshire, involving a teacher named Smart.'"

I think, *Wow, that must have been so hard to do, to turn his own son in.* Suddenly, I feel for the first time in a while that there may actually be a glimmer of hope in the universe — that some people actually do the right thing.

Vance Lattime, Jr. is called next and Maggiotto gets through the initial questioning quickly. I pay close attention as the teen confirms all of Randall's earlier testimony: the gun, the getaway car, the hollow-point bullets, Pam and Billy in the CRX, on the way to Haverhill. Pam saying not to get blood on the carpet or the sofa. Pam leaving the bulkhead unlocked. Pam telling them to set it up like a robbery. He confirms the affair and even Flynn's failed attempt to kill Gregg in April. *It's the same story Randall told, I think. No difference.*

Lattime looks down at Maggiotto from the witness stand and looks nervous through his large square-framed glasses. "I thought it was a joke," he continues. "I knew they were going there, but I figured they would take the stereo and leave, before Gregg came home. I didn't think either one of them—umm—had the guts to kill someone." *Yeah, some joke,* I think. He goes on to describe how they tried on latex gloves and pressed their fingers on the window of the car, and realized their fingerprints came through, onto the window. "I figured with all that Flynn was doing for this murder he would have gotten better gloves." He explains how Flynn bought Scotch tape and taped his and Randall's fingertips so they wouldn't leave prints.

Lattime goes on to describe how he waited awhile in the shopping plaza and then drove around looking for Flynn and Randall. How he drove toward the condo and they came running through the field. Randall had a black pillowcase in his hand and Flynn still held the revolver. They jumped in the car, excited.

Lattime's voice fills the courtroom as he describes what happened next. "Randall screams, 'Get moving!' and yells 'Go!' I ask him, 'Why?' and he says, 'We just killed a guy.' I thought it was a joke—but as we drove away, I could tell Billy was serious. He was really nervous—really, really scared. I tried to change the mood, so I sang a song that we heard on the radio, 'Shoo Fly Pie,' and he started laughing." *I can hardly believe what I'm hearing. They just killed my brother and they are laughing and singing? What the fuck. Shoo Fly Pie?*

Maggiotto looks at the jury and stands still, letting Lattime's words sink in. "Did you see Pam after the murder?" he finally asks.

"Yes. A few weeks after the murder, I went to Pam's office and asked about the five hundred dollars she promised me and Randall. She said she would pay one hundred a week, fifty to each of us, and that she might take it out of her paycheck. She said it would have to be in fifty-dollar amounts, so the money wouldn't be noticed missing."

Maggiotto says, "No further questions," and the crowd remains silent. Lattime's words hang like thick dust over the courtroom.

Mark Sisti stares up at the witness box. "Vance Lattime, why don't you tell this jury whom you said good night to last night?"

"Billy—Billy Flynn." Lattime answers. "We're roommates at the prison."

"Isn't Patrick Randall in the same prison as you and Billy?"

"Yes, he's two cells down from Billy and me."

"What did you and Billy talk about last night?"

"We were up all night talking—talking about how life was before we got arrested—you know—different girls—and we talked about the conversation I had last night, with my ex-girlfriend."

"Did you talk about the case—because you are not supposed to discuss the case—did you and Billy talk about it?"

"Yeah, we talked about it, little by little we talked about it—about different parts of the case," he admits.

"Tell us what you and Flynn had planned, after you got suspicious that you might get arrested."

"We wanted to take off to Connecticut, but Billy asked Pam for money, and she said no, because she couldn't have any money disappear."

The crowd appears to be waiting for more, but Sisti is done with his cross and heads back to his table. I think, *Wow, that was fast,* and it seems like Sisti didn't really get the answers he wanted. Then I realize that maybe he was just trying to show the jury that the boys are liars.

I look over at the back of Pam's head and can't help thinking about how she turned her back on the boys after she got what she wanted from them. I mean, she wouldn't even give them money so they could run, after they killed for her. I hear the people behind us murmuring to each other, and it's almost as if I can feel the people in the courtroom turning slowly against her as the trial moves on.

After recess, a table is set up in front of the courtroom with a row of physical evidence: the revolver, the hollow-point bullets, the butcher knife, and even Gregg's Kenwood. I think how Gregg would be upset to see his magnificent stereo covered with white fingerprint dust. I sigh to myself as it shimmers in the front of the courtroom and find myself unable to look at it. In the center of the table standing upright inside of a large plastic bag is the brass candelabra I saw lying near Gregg's body through the screen door. It's bent slightly and looks like it could topple over if someone brushed up against the table. Even that night, I wondered what it was doing there. I hope to find out.

Maggiotto calls the state medical examiner, Dr. Roger Fossum, and then walks over to a tripod that has been set up in the front of the courtroom and covered with a sheet. He pulls the sheet off to reveal a huge photo of Gregg lying dead in the foyer and an x-ray photo of Gregg's head. There are several gasps in the room, and Mom and Dad both rise and hurry down the aisle and out of the courtroom. I decide not to join them.

Maggiotto asks Dr. Fossum about the cause of death. He answers, "A single, .38-caliber, hollow-point bullet to the head caused the death of Greggory Smart." He continues, "The bullet entered Smart's head, high above the left ear canal and pierced his brain. The hollow-point bullet began to fragment before entering the skull. The bullet caused extensive damage to Smart's brain; it struck the occipital bone in the lower skull and then bounced back into the brain area. The position of the bullet and entrance wound are consistent with Smart kneeling as he was shot, as described by the teen assailants, William Flynn and Patrick Randall." As the doctor speaks, Maggiotto is walking back and forth, avoiding looking at the images of Gregg on the tripod. The doctor says, "The ballistics tests showed the bullet taken from Gregg Smart's brain definitely matched the gun supplied to police by Vance Lattime's father after he learned of his son's involvement in the crime."

The sudden harsh ringing sound of the fire alarm interrupts the doctor's testimony and everyone jumps up from their seats and hurries to exit the courtroom. I hold back, for a bit, waiting for them to escort Pam past our row. *Maybe this is the moment, the perfect moment, to get my hands on her,* I think to myself. But even though she passes directly in front of me, I remain still, letting another opportunity slip by.

We head back into the courthouse, rushing past the reporters and video cameras and into the lobby that is so packed it's hard to walk through. As I walk past the rows of electric wires, I can't help but think, *What is the fascination, why is this trial the biggest story on the news?* The crowd just seems to get bigger every day, and I can't stand all the people staring and gawking at us as if we are freaks or the criminals. As I stare at the patchwork of wires, I suddenly realize that at this exact moment they are transmitting data, sending a picture of us, hurrying down the hallway, and that I'll see this exact moment later on the newscast.

I shake my head as I open the courthouse doors and walk toward our front-row seats. *The row reserved for the shooting stars.* We sit and wait for Judge Gray to appear, and he finally enters the court and the trial is underway. Maggiotto calls William Flynn to the stand, and all heads turn to the rear of the courthouse to catch a glimpse of Gregg's killer.

Flynn is slighter than I imagined. He doesn't have a tie on and he sort of struts by us quickly and takes his oath. He sits in the witness box, and as I stare at him with my evil look, he suddenly looks over at me, right into my eyes. Time freezes for a moment, as we look at each other, and then his eyes seem to soften, and he looks down, sadly. *He's trying to tell me that he's sorry*, I realize. I don't know how to react and my mouth just hangs open as I look up at him.

Maggiotto starts asking the preliminary questions, and as I listen to Flynn answer I'm surprised by how soft spoken he is, unlike his buddies. *He's almost polite,* I think. He talks about the affair and the bikini pictures and the love letters and the music he and Pam loved. He describes a pendant they made together at the beach that had engraved on it

Dean J. Smart

"Pam and Billy forever." Amazingly, I find myself softening toward him. The anger that I first felt when he entered the courtroom—the anger I still want to feel—seems to have vanished, and as he continues to talk about Pam, I know for sure that she put him up to it, that he was in love with her. Maggiotto's opening questions are over and he moves to the tough parts.

"Tell me, Billy, how did the affair start?"

Flynn answers, "Well, we were in her office around February, and she asked me if I ever think about her, I answered yes, and she said, 'I think about you all the time, too.'"

"Did you fall in love with her instantly?"

"Yeah, I wanted to sleep with her the first time I saw her."

"When was the first time you had sex with Pam?" Maggiotto asks.

"When Gregg was on a business trip, we hung out at her condo in Derry with Cecilia Pierce and we watched a movie called 9½ Weeks—it had lots of sex scenes and we copied some of them upstairs in the bedroom. She stripped like in the movie and we used an ice cube. We had sex everywhere, on the bed, on the floor." Flynn says.

"Did the affair intensify after you had sex?" Maggiotto asks.

"Yeah, I realized I wanted to spend the rest of my life with her, and she was saying that she wanted to be with me, too, but the only way we could be together, she said, was if I killed Gregg—and then we planned everything out." Flynn answers.

"After you were arrested for the murder, Billy, did you want to tell on Pam?"

254

"No, I told her I would never tell on her—I loved her."

Maggiotto questions Flynn about the planning of the murder and the ride to get the getaway car in Haverhill. Flynn goes on at length to tell his version of what happened and it's identical to Randall's and Lattime's versions. I wonder why Maggiotto is having him repeat all of this again, and then it dawns on me that he wants to show that the murder was planned—that Pam put the boys up to it. Finally, he gets to the night of the murder, and asks Flynn to step out of the witness stand and show exactly how Gregg was killed.

"Can you show us what position Gregg was in, Billy?"

Flynn looks pale as he kneels on the floor. "He was kneeling like this—" he says, his voice quivering a bit, as if he might start to cry. He stands back up and Maggiotto asks, "Can you show us where you were standing as Gregg was kneeling?"

Flynn takes a step back and points to a spot that is a step behind where Gregg would have been. His hand is trembling. "I was behind him, as Randall held his head and had the knife at his throat." He shakes his head and lets out a heavy sigh. He clenches his jaw tightly and his eyes well up with tears as if he is reliving the murder.

Maggiotto directs him to sit down and Flynn, obviously relieved, heads back to the witness stand. But Maggiotto isn't done. "So you have Gregg on his knees, Randall holds his head and has the knife at his neck—then what happened?" Maggiotto gently drops a box of tissues on the stand in front of Flynn.

"Well," Flynn answers softly, his voice breaking, "it was obvious we weren't going to be able to cut his throat. We weren't going to bring ourselves to do that. So, I motioned to Randall like this—" Flynn puts his hand up toward his jacket pocket. "That's where I had the gun, and Randall nodded his head yes." Flynn is crying now, and the tears stream down his face. The courtroom is silent.

Flynn says softly, "I took the gun out of my pocket. I cocked the hammer and pointed the gun at his head, and then I just stood there." He dabs at his wet cheeks.

Maggiotto asks, "How long did you just stand there?"

"A hundred years," Flynn answers, sobbing, "it seemed like—then I said, 'God forgive me.'" He starts crying and gasping for breath. He looks over toward us and says, his voice barely above a whisper, "Then I pulled the trigger."

I look at Flynn and I almost understand. *It's not you — it's her, Billy. She did this to Gregg and now she's doing it to you.* I nod up at him, trying to let him know I understand, but his head is bowed. I realize that the hate I've held inside for him, the anger I felt toward him, was somehow wrong, and now, somehow, it has all shifted, all faded and changed into a strange new sorrow. I drop my head, thinking that somehow I've let Gregg down. *I can't believe I feel for him. I can't believe I actually feel sorry for the kid who killed my brother. I can't believe that I would even think it.*

Sisti opens his cross-examination of Flynn with a surprising question. "Tell me, Billy, why were you upset with the media the other day after your buddy Randall testified?"

"They said he didn't look emotional, but that's because he was scared. On the news they nailed Randall, but it wasn't fair, because they don't know him." Flynn's eyes well with tears again.

"Do you care what the media thinks, Billy? And why are you crying?"

"I don't care what the media thinks. I care what Gregg's parents think, and I'm crying because I wish I never did it." I stare up at him in stunned silence. The courtroom buzzes around me. I watch as he wipes his tears away and I think, *He must have been so in love with her to do this.*

"Have you been talking about the case in prison, as you were instructed not to?" Sisti asks sharply.

"I've been trying to think about the case as little as possible, but we never said, 'This is what you're going to say' or 'You say this, and I'll say that.'"

Sisti comes back at him. "Why did you kill Gregg?"

Flynn answers, aggravated, "I killed Gregg because Pam said if I didn't do it— we couldn't be together—and I loved her—so I did it because she told me to."

Sisti looks angry. "Did you do whatever Pam asked you to do?"

"Yeah, I probably did—back then."

"So, you had no brain?"

"I had a brain—but I was in love."

Sisti looks puzzled. "Didn't Pam break off the affair with you?"

"Yeah, a few times, but we got back together. We were at a car dealership with Randall and Lattime because Pam wanted to buy a car with the insurance money. She asked me to get her a lollipop and I didn't. I thought she was being bossy, you know, to show me up in front of the others. She got mad and said, 'You don't love me, because if you did, you would have gotten me the lollipop.' She threatened to break up with me and asked me if that's what I wanted—I told her no."

"Did she break up with you another time?"

"Yeah, after we found out the police were looking for us, she kicked us out of her car and said she didn't want to have anything to do with me anymore."

I listen to the last few minutes of Flynn's testimony, but all I can think of is how he was used. *She used you, Billy, and spit you out. No wonder you turned on her, and gave her up to the police. How could you have known that she has no love, just schemes?* Pam the scammer. You fooled everyone. *Well, not everyone.* I smile to myself, as Flynn steps down and recess is called. We all rise to leave the courtroom.

As we file out, and I pass the wires again, I think about tonight's newscast. I wonder how they will portray Flynn— as a coldhearted killer or as someone to be pitied? Outside the cameras flash and the reporters are shouting questions: "Do you feel bad for Billy Flynn, Mr. Smart?" "Do you think the teens did this on their own, Mr. Smart?" We push through and make it to the car. As we pull away from the courthouse, I look out the rear window and see some guy mugging for the cameramen and grinning ear to ear. He is wearing a big sign around his neck that reads "Free Pam."

Chapter 23

The Tapes

There is a buzz of excitement in the courtroom. We sit in our front row, waiting, while technicians set up dozens of pairs of headphones. Rick walks in a few minutes behind us and sits next to me. He looks excited about something.

"What's up?" I ask him.

"Well, you know the guy out front with the 'Free Pam' sign?" I shake my head yes at him. "Well, I just ripped the sign off his neck, ripped it in half and threw it to the ground." I start laughing and smile at him. I reach my hand out to him and he shakes it. "What did the guy say?" I ask.

"He said, 'Do you always destroy other people's property?'" Rick then says, "I told him, 'No, just yours.'" I smile at Rick but wonder if the bailiff will escort him from the courtroom if they find out.

They set up the tripod again in the front of the courtroom, and I wonder if they plan to show more disturbing photographs. The law clerks are handing out sheets of some kind, and I'm excited to see that they contain the transcripts of the secret tapes. All the jurors and some others, including my parents, are being furnished with headphones; the rest of us are expected to follow along with the text. But, as soon as the tape starts playing, everyone in the court is able to hear the sound of voices coming through the headphones. As I recognize Pam's voice, I can't help but think she sounds like she is practicing, just like she used to do before her television interviews. I can almost picture her sitting at the kitchen table talking about how she has to get on with her life.

I give up trying to follow along with the transcript and lean closer to Dad's headphones. The voices sound tinny and mechanical and remind me of the speaker boxes at the drive-in movies, when I was a kid. As the tape drones on, I begin to drift away from the courtroom, and I'm suddenly back at the drive-in movies as a kid, taking the long walk to the concession stand, walking by the cars in the darkness, listening to the tiny speakers blaring. I hear the sound of all the little speaker boxes reverberating off all of the vinyl and plastic — *like a thousand news reports playing in sync from every television in town.*

I flash back to the courtroom and look up at the jurors with headphones strapped to their heads, as the voices continue to float in the air. Maggiotto is standing at the front of the room next to the tripod where the entire transcript is displayed on large poster boards. Some of the text is highlighted in bright yellow. He points to a highlighted section of text and I listen as Cecilia asks Pam, "Did you know — having seen what happened — wouldn't you rather have just divorced Gregg?"

"Well, I don't know, you know. Nothing was going wrong until — until they fucking told — Welch," Pam answers.

"Lattime is going to say you knew about the murder before it happened, which is the truth."

"Right, well, so then I'll have to say, 'No, I didn't.'" Pam says. "But even if I asked someone to kill somebody, you'd have to be fucking deranged to say, 'Okay, I will.'"

Cecilia asks Pam, "As far as I can see it, Billy did it because he loved you, I mean, you didn't pay him, right?"

"Yeah, right—no, I didn't pay him." Pam answers.

I can't get over what I'm hearing. As the tape keeps running, I search the text in my hand for confirmation.

Pam's voice continues as she tells Cecilia not to talk to the police and not to take a lie-detector test. "Don't think it's the end of your problems if you confess, because your whole family's like going to be like, 'You knew about a murder? How could you have lived like that?' And the newspapers are going to be, like, all over you—you're going to be on the witness stand a million times."

The crowd is rustling about excitedly, and I have to strain to hear Pam say, "If you tell the fucking truth, you are probably going to be arrested—and you're going to have to send Bill, you're going to have to send Randall, you're going to have to send Lattime, and you're going to have to send me to the fucking slammer for the rest of our entire lives."

The crowd mumbles and shuffles, and as the room stirs I think to myself, *I know I have heard Pam say that line about the slammer before.* I search my memory and the fog lifts: I see Pam standing in the galley of Dad's boat and she is sliding the glass door open and closed over and over, as she looks up at us and says, "Look, I'm in the slammer."

The tape is still running and I hear Pam say, "They're going to believe me or they're going to believe Lattime—the sixteen-year-old in the slammer. And then me, with a professional reputation and a course that I teach. Why would a twenty-two-year-old woman, like me, be having an affair with a sixteen-year-old student? That's just ridiculous and people will not believe that. They are going to get torn apart on the witness stand. I have the best lawyers anywhere—they got a guy off for murder even after he confessed." Pam pauses for a minute as if she's thinking of what to say next. "You know, I'm afraid one day you're going to come in here and you're going to be wired by the fucking police and I'm going to be busted. Cecilia, give me a hand signal if you're wired."

The tape is over and everyone in the court with headphones removes them at the same time, turning to each other with stunned looks. Dad and Mom are shaking their heads in disbelief.

"She's done," I say to them, and Mom gives my hand a little squeeze.

I feel light as air as we file out of the courtroom, until I notice a longhaired kid in the crowd in front of me. He is wearing a tee shirt covered with mock bullet holes that reads "I survived the Pam Smart Trial." I wince, thinking, *it's not over yet.*

After recess, Cecilia Pierce walks toward the witness stand. She's wearing a light cotton dress with a small flowery print, and everyone in the courtroom strains to look at her. She is pretty but a bit overweight, her dirty-blonde hair parted to one side and curled. She has a white bow in the back of her hair, like Pam's, and for some reason that aggravates me, as she sits down after taking her oath. Maggiotto questions her about the preliminaries and then gets right to the point.

"Cecilia, why didn't you go to the police when you knew they were planning to murder Gregg?"

"I didn't think they would really do it. I had known Billy for a couple years, and I didn't think he would kill someone."

"Well, what about the failed attempt by Flynn in April? What did Pam say about Flynn getting lost—and Gregg already being home?"

"She said she couldn't believe how stupid they were to get lost, and she was angry."

"Why didn't you go to the police then?"

"I still didn't think they would really do it."

"What happened on the night you stayed at Pam's with Billy Flynn?"

"After we watched the movie 9½ Weeks, Billy and Pam had been upstairs for hours, and I was getting bored. So, I ran upstairs and yelled, 'I hope you guys are done,' but when I opened the door, I saw Billy on top of Pam, and they were having sex—I just ran downstairs."

"Cecilia, when did you find out they were going to make another attempt?"

"On May first, Pam said to me, 'Tonight's the night they go to Derry for the murder.'"

"When did you find out they went through with it?"

"The next day at school they called us to Guidance and told us Pam's husband was killed. I was shocked—I didn't think they would do it."

I stare over at Pam to see if Cecilia's testimony is having an effect on her, but she sits impassive and still.

"Pam said she had a choice to get a divorce or to kill Gregg," Cecilia continues. "I told her to get a divorce, but

Pam said she would lose the condo and the furniture, and Gregg would take Halen, the dog, and she wouldn't have any money or anyplace to live."

"Did you hear Pam talk about the murder?" Maggiotto asks.

"Yeah, she told Billy to tie his hair back and to wear dark clothes and to make it look like a burglary."

The courtroom murmurs as Cecilia continues. "She told Billy not to kill Gregg in front of the dog, because it would traumatize the dog. She told him not to hurt the dog."

There is a groan from the crowd, as Maggiotto turns to face the judge. "I have no further questions, Your Honor."

Mark Sisti begins his cross by asking Cecilia to tell the court why she agreed to do the wiretaps for the police. She explains that the police told her she could be in trouble if they found out she wasn't telling all she knew about the murder.

"I was told I could be indicted for hindering an investigation and withholding evidence, so I told them the truth—I told them what I knew. They asked me to work for them and record Pam."

"So you lied, the first few times you talked to the police, and you agreed to tape Pam—and they said you wouldn't be arrested?" Sisti asks.

"Yeah, they said that I wouldn't be arrested, unless something comes up." She answers.

"Yeah—like if you change your story again?"

"No. It's not a story—it's the truth." She smiles and looks straight at Sisti. *Good girl, nice move, Cecilia.*

"So you sold your story for a movie for one hundred thousand dollars?" Sisti asks, changing the subject.

"Yes," she answers, without flinching.

Sisti walks over and stands directly behind Pam. "Was Pam a better friend than Flynn?"

Cecilia pauses and tilts her head to the side as she thinks, then cracks a slight smile. "I don't know if Pam was ever really — my friend."

There's a slight chuckle from the courtroom. Sisti says, "I have no further questions, Your Honor." He sits down next to Pam and they whisper to each other. His face is impassive, but I can't help but wonder if he thinks he just lost a round.

I drink and smoke alone in the bedroom loft. Beer after beer, I flip through the *Boston Herald* and read and reread an article from Pam's parents. Her mom calls the trial a circus and complains that there is never a nice story about Pam in the papers. I swig back another beer, and I read it again. "Not a single nice story about the plotter of murders?" I mumble out loud.

I look at Gregg's trophy as it sits on the black lacquered bureau under the skylight. *The trophy she put in a trash bag,* I think. *Not a single nice fucking story, huh? Well, there hasn't been any fucking nice story about Gregg, has there? No one talks of Gregg — they only talk of sex and teenagers and murder. All we have left of him are pictures from a murder scene. Yeah, and it is a circus, but it's your circus, Pam — you are the originator of this production. It's the Pam circus.* "Fuck, man, you couldn't have just divorced him and taken Billy and ran off," I say to myself. "Well, you should have, no one would have fucking cared." I slide back a sip of beer in the stillness of the loft. I stare back at the newspaper laying on the end of the bed, the space I used to reserve for Gregg. *Turn the Kenwood up.* I think to myself.

I drink and drink and smoke. I'm dizzy, as I sit down on the bed, my head beneath the skylight. The newspaper and the trophy and the circus filling me, I sip the beer and smoke some more and I watch the smoke swirl away.

Forgotten, I think, *and while he is gone forever, his wife's mother complains about circuses and unfairness. And she can still hug Pam and talk to Pam and see Pam and smile with Pam. And I sit alone where Gregg and I used to talk and sit and listen to music.* I look up into the skylight, in silence, for him and he is not there. *And it is a fucking circus, yes, it is. And you know what? You still have your daughter. And we have nothing, no son and no brother.* I finish another beer and pop open another.

I look up into the skylight and stare at the night sky. I sip and smoke and the haze fills my mind. Everything fades away and I'm alone with Mom at the indoor pool so long ago. She pushes me off from under my shoulders and I swim, barely. The sunroom fills with moisture and I look back at her blonde hair in the dim haze, the water rippling, as I struggle to stay afloat. She sits at the concrete edge of the pool, looking at me, smiling. I swim in it, across the pool, in the greenhouse, in the middle of winter. She says something, smiling, but I can't hear her. I swim and look back and she is gone, and the room is dark.

The water thickens, browning like mud. I grab onto the concrete edge. Holding on, looking back for Mom, as the watery mud bubbles around me. Hundreds of multicolored electrical wires pop out, near the corner of the pool. Joint roaches and cigarette butts float in the darkened liquid. The wires snake and spin in the mud. I close and tighten my eyes, but the pool doesn't disappear.

I look back at the pool and black satin bows ride the sludge. The bent brass candelabra buoys and bounces in the muck. Televisions emerge and on the screens is Pam's photo of her in a bikini. In the center of the black pool, rising out of the sludge, is Gregg's body lying on a carpet, floating and spinning in the circles of the forming whirlpool.

A spotlight shines near the glass double doors and circus music fills the greenhouse. The spotlight revolves on the concrete floor and then steadies.

Reporters on roller skates, laden with cameras on their necks, video recorders on their shoulders and microphones in their hands, glide through the doors, double file and split, skating away to each side, spinning in synchronization around the whole of the pool, flashing pictures and whirling in the spotlights.

A car driven by a straight-faced clown with large glasses glides through the entrance and parks in front of the doors. The back door opens and another clown steps out with an evil grin painted on his face. He carries a large butcher knife, and a black sack is draped around his shoulder. The passenger door swings open and another clown emerges. His face is painted in a perpetual frown with a red, upside-down, heart-shaped tear, painted on his cheek. He waves a glittering revolver in his hand and walks solemnly toward the clown with the knife. The pool-house doors swing open and Pam makes a robotic entrance, her face blank and her eyes red. Applause fills the room.

Suddenly, the mud in the pool bubbles, waving and spinning. I feel the wires touching my feet and moving up my legs, but I'm frozen and I can't move. The wires wrap and twist around me, pulling me under, into the black mud. I struggle, gasping for my breath, and pull my head out of the mud, but in one quick motion I'm jerked under, deep into the dark.

My eyes flash open and I'm looking up at the skylight in the smoke-filled loft. I sip my beer and stare up into the dark sky.

Chapter 24

The Ringleader

I watch the sun rise ahead of us on the horizon, as we travel down the highway to the courthouse, again. I stare out the window at the ice frozen on the rock on the side of the road. *Today's the day,* I think to myself. *Pam is going up on the stand.* Dad drives silently and Mom's foot shakes nervously as he drives.

I watch the ice glide by, and stare at my reflection in the window. I look tired and I can't stop thinking how different everything is now, ever since the night I ran to Gregg's and found him dead. *So different,* I think to myself, and I realize that everything from now on will be divided, into two separate sections of my life, of our lives. Every memory, every thought, is either the before, or the after, that night.

We drive by the ice-covered rock. I notice I can see the copper-colored Jaguar flashing by in the reflection. I watch closely and manage to see my silhouette, in the backseat of the Jag. I see myself in the ice, confined, isolated and trapped. I think about how things were before that night. I think about how I used to dance and DJ at the club, how we used to party in Londonderry, how we used to crank the Kenwood so loud that the windows would rattle. I see the car flash by again in the glimmer of ice, and I think to myself, *I'm trapped and frozen in this whole thing, like that heart of ice, glowing blue. I'm in here. Can you see me?* But no one sees me, no one can. I'm different, separated from the rest, a colored tile in a white-tile world. No one knows what it's like, to be stuck, inside the ice, staring out at the moving world. I know they can't hear me, the world can't hear me. But fuck them if they can't understand. I know I'm stuck in it, trapped in the blue glow, and I know that I'm going to wear that blue, that electric blue forever. And I want to go back to how it all was before, but I can't. I'm trapped in the reflection, in the ice that's as blue as Gregg's eyes are, as blue as Gregg's eyes were, as blue as Gregg's eyes used to be. I keep calling out, but no one answers. I look at my reflection in the window and my eyes are tired, as if I've seen too much.

"Your Honor, I call Pam Smart to the witness stand." As Sisti utters the words, murmurs fill the courtroom. Pam rises, steps up from around the table where she has sat for the whole trial. She walks to the front slowly and my heart races. I watch as she stands in the witness box with one hand on the Bible and her other raised in the air. I look at her, while she swears to tell the whole truth and nothing but the truth.

She sits down and the courtroom quiets. Sisti approaches and begins his questioning by asking her why she married Gregg Smart.

Pam answers quickly and without emotion, "Because I loved him—I wanted to spend the rest of my life with him."

"Could you keep your voice up? I couldn't hear the last part of what you said." Sisti asks her to repeat it.

"I said, because I loved him and I wanted to spend the rest of my life with him."

"What was it about him that you loved?"

"He was a really kind and gentle person—and he was a lot of fun to be around."

"Was the marriage happy?"

"Oh yes—extremely happy," she says, as cold as ice.

"How did you feel after Gregg had a one-night stand, Pam?" Sisti asks and looks at the jurors.

"I was devastated, very hurt. It had an effect on how I felt about myself. I didn't feel as important anymore. It affected my trust."

"There were allegations from other witnesses that Gregg was abusive. Is that true—did Gregg ever hit you?"

"No," she answers.

"You had an affair with William Flynn—is that right?" Sisti asks.

"I didn't set out to have an affair with him, but I did," she responds to the question with a blank look in her eyes. "I didn't want to have an affair with him—I didn't even like him, at first."

"What attracted you to Flynn?"

"He was easy to talk to and he was nice." She says without emotion.

"When was the first time you and Billy had sex?"

"When Gregg was in Atlantic City in March."

"Is this the night you watched the movie 9½ Weeks and Cecilia Pierce was there?"

"Yes."

"Did you and Billy reenact scenes from the movie?"

"Well, I wore a negligee, but I didn't dance, and we didn't use ice cubes—Billy's having a problem remembering where reality began and where the movie ended."

"You saw the photographs that were entered into evidence earlier—do you recall?"

"Photographs of myself, you mean?"

"That's right, what's the story with those?"

"My friend took photos of me—I took photos of her—for a modeling session we were going to do."

"Did you ever give Billy Flynn any of those pictures?"

"No, I did not. I was embarrassed by them," she says coolly.

Sisti walks to the evidence table and grabs a few sheets of multicolored paper. "Now, did you ever come to write love letters and notes to Billy—do you recognize this note?" He holds up one of the colored papers.

"Yes—but it's not a note. It's just lyrics to a song."

"Did you give it to Billy?"

"No, I didn't."

"How often would you say you saw Billy?"

"At a certain point—about every day." She answers.

"Did you encourage the affair?"

"No—I tried to break it off continually. I broke up with him several times in the spring."

"What did Billy do—after you broke up with him?"

"He said he was thinking about killing himself." She says matter-of-factly, with no trace of concern.

"Did you ever just end the affair completely?"

"Yes, four or five days before Gregg died, I told him it was over. I couldn't have two relationships at once, and I loved Gregg. I loved Billy at one point—but I never stopped loving Gregg."

"Were you and Flynn lovers after Gregg's murder?"

"No."

"Did you lend your car to Flynn in April—when Billy made a failed attempt at killing Gregg?"

"Yes, but I didn't know he was using it for that."

"Did you go over plans to murder Gregg on the ride to Haverhill?"

"No."

"Did you have anything to do with the planning of your husband's murder?"

"No."

"What happened on May first when you came home to your Derry condo?"

"I saw Gregg lying in the foyer. The first thing I thought of was to get help. I thought someone might still be in the house. I went next door, and I was ringing the doorbell, but they didn't come fast enough. Maybe they did, but it seemed like forever." She looks slightly disturbed for a moment but composes herself.

I'm listening but my mind is spinning. There is no emotion in her voice, no hint of sadness or regret, and I wonder if she is capable of any feeling or if she is truly the robot she appears to be. *How is it possible that she can describe that scene so coldheartedly — that scene that has been burned in my mind — that scene that I can't stop thinking about — and she doesn't shed a tear?*

Just as Sisti is about to ask another question, the fire alarm sounds throughout the courtroom. There is confusion and relief on Pam's face as she is whisked from the stand, out the side door, while everyone else jams the aisles in an effort to exit the courtroom. Minutes later, after the police dogs have been brought in and out of the building, we're called back and allowed to return to our seats. "Most likely a bomb threat," Dad says to me, shrugging his shoulders.

After the interruption, Sisti begins again, unfazed. "On the tapes, Pam, why were you questioning Cecilia Pierce about the investigation?"

"After the arrest of the students, Cecilia was calling me on the phone. She was very nervous, very excited. She seemed to indicate to me she knew more than she was saying. I thought she had more information, and I was totally obsessed with finding out who murdered my husband and what happened in the house that day — I figured if she knew more about the murder, she would tell me — if I acted like I knew more about it. In my mind, I thought I'd play a game with her to say I knew more. All the information I was getting seemed to indicate that Billy did it — but in my heart, I didn't want to believe it."

She's done, I think to myself. I smirk up at her, giving her my best Gregg grin. *You just beat yourself, Pam, with your own pride, your own overconfidence. If that's all you've got to say in your defense, it's over. We win.*

Sisti continues, pushing for more. "So, you were just trying to get information out of her about the murder because you thought she knew more than she was saying?"

"Yes."

"And the police had shut you out of the case and wouldn't tell you anything, so you played a game with Cecilia Pierce trying to find out what really happened?"

"Yes."

"I have no further questions, Your Honor."

I watch Sisti take his seat and I wonder what he's thinking. *Does he think the jury bought what she said? Come on, no way! Well, okay, maybe your little act did fool the jury, Pam, but it didn't fool me. Whatever the jury thinks, we both know what you did.*

Pam steps down from the stand, and all eyes are on her. She looks calm, unfazed. I grin up at her like Gregg. *Yeah, you still get what you always wanted, don't you, Pam? You're a TV star, Pam, the center of attention. On the news every day, just like you always dreamt. You're on the news, baby. You ARE the news. See, dreams do come true.* I can't help but smile slightly, as I watch the bailiffs escort her from the courtroom.

After recess, it's Maggiotto's turn. I watch Mom and Dad lean forward in their seats as he gets up and walks toward Pam on the witness stand. I'm hoping he tears her apart slowly. He pauses in front of Sisti and Twomey, then looks up at Pam, then glances toward the jury. He turns around and faces Pam. "Do you know why Billy Flynn killed Gregg?" Maggiotto asks calmly.

Pam tilts her head slightly and looks off into the distance. For a moment, she appears distracted, but when she turns back to face him, her confidence returns. "I don't know why Billy Flynn killed Gregg. I can just come in here and give my testimony." She gives Maggiotto a challenging look as if preparing to do battle.

Maggiotto raises his voice a notch, "So, even as you sit here today, you still have no idea why he might have done this—is that it?" He looks back at her sternly.

"I didn't say I had no idea." Pam answers.

"You didn't—oh—well, I'm sorry—then what did you say? You *do* have an idea?"

"Well, no—not specifically." She looks down at him, her lips tight, then raises her hand in the air as if to ask a question.

"So then you don't have an idea—I mean, which is it?" He smiles up at her.

"I would guess he did it because he probably thought—we could be together." She tilts her head and squints at him.

"And what, do you suppose, might have ever given him that idea?" I smile to myself, and out of the corner of my eye, I see Dad quietly patting the top of Mom's hand in approval.

"I couldn't tell you. I tried to break it off with him several times." Pam says, void of emotion.

"You tried—but you didn't. I mean, you testified this morning that you were having sexual relations with him at least until the end of April. That's usually not the best method of breaking up an affair—especially with a fifteen-year-old."

Twomey jumps up from the defense table and shouts, "Objection! Your Honor, he's making speeches—he's making statements and not asking questions."

Judge Gray remains calm. "Mr. Twomey, Mr. Maggiotto, approach the bench, please."

The courtroom rustles with excitement as the lawyers approach the judge's bench and then confer with him for several minutes. I turn to Dad and whisper, "Wow, Maggiotto is magnificent, isn't he, Dad? He's nailing her, huh?" Dad nods his head in agreement. *His eyes are shining again,* I think to myself. *He's more like his old self.* He pats Mom's hand and I see that she, too, has a little glimmer of light in her eye.

The conversation at the bench ends and Maggiotto continues his cross-examination. "Mrs. Smart, tell the jury again, if you would, in as much detail as you can remember—how is it that you tried to break off your relationship with Billy Flynn?"

"A few days before Gregg was murdered, I told Billy I loved Gregg and that's why I was ending the relationship. He told me he was going to kill himself. I told him I didn't want a relationship anymore. He started crying and he said he couldn't live without me."

"Seems, you have all the answers—do you know what my next question is going to be?"

Pam looks confused, as if she doesn't know what to say. *Yes! Throw her a curve ball.* She doesn't answer; she tilts her head to the side as if she can't quite compute his words and looks at him blankly.

Maggiotto asks, "Right after the murder, you talked to the captain of the Derry police. Well, see, this is what I don't understand. The police captain, who is heading the investigation into the death of your husband, asks you in no uncertain terms not to go to the press—because it will hamper the solving of the case—and the very next day, you appear on television. Why?" he looks at her and waits.

"Okay—see, they were going on the assumption that drugs were involved—and I wanted to clear the air and get them to concentrate on the burglary issue." *Exactly! That's how you get people to do what you want. You wanted the police to concentrate on the burglary — the fake burglary that you plotted — so they'd think the murder was just some random event.*

"I see—you wanted your husband's murderer to be apprehended, I take it?"

"Of course." She gives him that look that's designed to convey "what, are you like dumb or something?"

"Well, then did it ever occur to you to mention the affair with Billy Flynn to the police? Pretty logical motive there, no?"

"I didn't think so at the time. Also, I was trying to hide the affair. I was ashamed." She answers unattached, her eyes vacant.

"Well, how about after Billy was arrested? Ever occur to you to mention it then?"

"They never asked." Dad and Mom shoot me a look.

"What, I couldn't hear you—could you repeat that?" Maggiotto asks.

"They never asked me if I was having an affair with him." Pam looks back at Maggiotto who turns to the jurors and grins.

He looks back at Pam and says, "Oh, so they never asked—no reason to tell them. Well that makes sense—" He looks at the jurors again. "If you told the police about Billy Flynn and your relationship, that would mean Flynn had a connection and a reason to kill your husband, right?"

"No," she answers coldly and stares at him.

"It would also give you a connection to the murder of your husband—and to Flynn—if you told them about the affair, right?"

"NO." She says emphatically, raising her hand up, as though she has had enough of his questions.

"And that's the real reason you didn't want to talk to the police about Flynn and his affair with you?" *Attaboy, Magg.* I think. *Go get her!*

Pam is flustered now, her anger rising. "The real reason is the truth—I think if the police knew I had an affair with Billy—they would automatically conclude—that I was party to the murder." *Oh, so now it's a different story, huh, Pam?* I turn to look at the jury to see their reaction.

Maggiotto hammers on. "You knew all of these things and consciously decided not to tell the police?"

"My honest-to-God truth was that they couldn't have done it—all I knew was that they were arrested. That doesn't mean they committed the crime."

"Did the police ask you about possible motives for the murder?"

"Yes."

"The police asked you if you had a motive and you didn't tell them about the affair?"

"I didn't think—having an affair is a motive to murder someone."

"Maybe you didn't mention it because you were involved in the murder?"

"No, if I was guilty—I would have plea-bargained like the rest of them." She looks down at Maggiotto.

"Do you think not mentioning the affair to the police was a mistake, Pam?"

She looks off into the air again and stares at the courthouse ceiling as if hoping to receive an answer to the question.

Maggiotto steps closer to her and says, "You made a lot of mistakes—didn't you?"

"Yes," she admits.

"Was killing your husband one of those mistakes?"

"No," she answers.

"Was not getting divorced one of those mistakes?"

"NO," she repeats.

"Tell me again, Pam, why didn't you tell the police about the affair?"

She sighs and says, "I didn't consider the police my allies."

"Oh, I see—do you remember the tapes, what about the tapes, where you incriminate yourself—how do you explain what you said on the tapes?"

"I was stressed, on medication, confused, scared, in a state of hysteria and desperation," she says in a monotone.

"Oh, so you just added medication and hysteria as two more things which would explain what you said." She looks stuck again as if stunned by his odd question. She is frozen in the witness stand and makes no attempt to answer.

Maggiotto paces and waits, then says, "The truth of the matter, Mrs. Smart, is that you didn't want Cecilia Pierce to go to the police because she was the only person out there that could link you to the murder—isn't that right? You didn't tell the police about the affair, before or after the killing, because it would link you to the murder—isn't that also right?"

"No, I didn't want to go to jail for a crime I didn't commit."

Maggiotto looks over at the jury, cocks his head slightly and raises his eyebrows. "I have no further questions, Your Honor."

Chapter 25

Closing the Case

We drive down the highway in the morning, toward the beach and the courthouse. I look down at the *Boston Herald* on the empty backseat in the Jaguar, next to me. It reads:

THE ICE PRINCESS

Next to the headline is a photo of Pam on the stand from yesterday. I smile and watch as the trees and rocks pass on the side of the road. Dad drives the Jag faster than usual, and I have a feeling that the end is near as we approach the exit to the courthouse. I can't help but think that I want to leave it all behind. I want it all to end.

I'm still having these feelings as Twomey rises and steps in front of the jury box. He stares at the jury and recites his closing argument, barely pausing to catch his breath.

"The boys are vicious animals," he hisses. "They're human beings not worthy of belief. They were bad people who did horrible, horrible things. This was a thrill killing. You heard the testimony of Flynn talking about the power — the thrill of killing. What happened on May first was an abomination committed by vicious animals — petty thieves and burglars who do not have a shred of moral decency."

Twomey rambles on, and I struggle to follow him. "It was not Pam's planning that caused the murder. It was Billy Flynn's lust and sexual urge that was the driving force behind his actions. I contend that something else happened in the condo that night, something no one has heard — something the boys don't talk about — something unspeakable. They tortured that man in some other way they won't talk about. They're lying, that's the point."

My mom sighs and deflates in front of me onto Dad's shoulder, a look of unrelenting horror on her face. She lets out a long, loud sigh and crumbles in his arm. I look at Twomey in disgust. Dad shakes his head at him with Mom crying in his arms.

Twomey looks away and continues. "If Flynn and Randall's friend said that they make him sick, they should make you sick, too. And, as far as Cecilia Pierce is concerned, she testified against Smart because she knew that the police could charge her with conspiracy to first-degree murder.

"My client was ashamed of her affair, and she feared she would be wrongly arrested. I ask you, as you listen to those tapes, to imagine Pam as a basket case who has something she desperately has to prove, that she desperately has to hide that affair. If Smart believed Flynn committed the crime, she would have had to believe that her affair led to her husband's death. Would you embrace that and say, 'Good, I'm happy they solved that,' or would you shrink from that and pray and hope it wasn't true, and try and find a way to show that it wasn't true?

"She snapped. She was a woman who had been emo-tionally drawn and quartered—ripped by her love for Billy and her fear of being arrested. She was torn in every which way. Is she guilty of an affair? You bet she is. Is she guilty of having an affair when she's in a position of authority? Absolutely. Was she guilty of having an affair with someone only sixteen years old and six years younger? You bet. Does that make her guilty of murder? No, it does not."

Twomey struts away from the jury box and sits down next to Pam who has no reaction. As Twomey confers with Sisti, she sits there, staring in front of her, barely moving.

Maggiotto stands and walks toward the jury. He looks at the jurors lined up in the box. He scans across their faces, rubs his chin and begins speaking. "Ladies and gentlemen of the jury, I want you to listen to those tapes, and listen closely to Pam. Listen to her tone—listen to the pace of her voice—listen to how she talks to Cecilia Pierce—and then you make the determination on who's controlling the conversation. You make the determination if this is a woman who's about to snap—or is this a woman in a panic. On the tapes, she complains that everything about the murder was undetected—until a teenager went to the police with information. Pam tried to say that she was hunting for information; she said the things she said to get information from Pierce, but it's just another one of her fabrications, a last-ditch effort to somehow, someway, explain away the evidence in the case.

"What choice does she have? She can't deny those tapes. She's got to come up with an explanation. Look at her past character. Think about her history of deception. Think about how she had no problem lying to her family about her affair. Think about how she would lie to the police right in their face and say, 'Honest to God, I don't know why they did this.' All the while, she's not admitting the affair to the authorities just because they didn't ask. Think about how witness, after witness, got up there on that stand and testified about a bullet being put in her husband's head. She shed not one tear of remorse—not one tear of grief. She wasn't shaken up, one time. Think about her rapid-fire answers to our questions, like a programmed robot. She had every possible answer you could think of, before the question was asked!

"I'm not suggesting she killed Gregg Smart for the insurance money. We're not suggesting she killed Gregg for the furniture. She was very concerned about her professional reputation. If she got divorced, the affair would come out. It would ruin her reputation and she would lose her job. So, she manipulates the situation—she is good at this. You can decide for yourself, if this is a frantic woman, desperate and about to snap, or a cool, calculated operator rallying the wagons around her, talking to lawyers and talking to Cecilia.

"What you will see is that the circle was closing in on Pamela Smart, as one of the teens went to the police. She was doing everything in her power to set up her defense, to keep Cecilia quiet, to keep the police off her tail. She manipulated Flynn, too. This was torrid. It was the kid's first sexual experience and he's in way over his head. And that's the way she liked it. She was in control. Was Flynn a killer, yes—but, he was not a perfect recorder of everything that was happening. That's why there are a few minor discrepancies with the boy's testimony. You saw Flynn testify—you saw the emotion coming out of him. That's a thrill killer? You think that kid was masterminding a vile concoction of lies to get this woman? If Billy Flynn was a liar, that was one of the greatest performances of all time. Flynn testified that when she threatened to leave him, he was all too willing to do anything for her, even murder. By the time her hook was so far into that kid's psyche, so deep in his hormones, he was willing to participate. Ask yourself: How did these teens know how much life insurance Gregg had? How did they get into the condo that night when there was no sign of forced entry? How did they know when Gregg got home every night?"

Maggiotto walks away from the jurors and stands directly in front of the table for the defense. He points directly at Pam, his finger aimed straight at her face. She doesn't flinch or move. He says in a voice that booms through the courtroom, "Pamela Smart has counted on that, from day one, putting herself on the stand, and with her background, intelligence and her ability to answer questions—but, if you apply common sense to the defendant's preposterous testimony of the last two days, you'll see it was a last-ditch, calculating effort by this woman trying to distract you. She wants to manipulate you, the jury, as well—don't let her put one over on you, too."

Maggiotto finishes and I wish I could rise to my feet and congratulate him. Pam is escorted out of the courtroom by the bailiffs. As the crowd begins to file out, Maggiotto walks over to us and Dad stands up and shakes his hand. They exchange words and smiles, and I hear one of them say, "Now, we just hope for the best." We walk out of the courtroom, and all around us the cameras are flashing and the videotape is rolling, and the crowd in the lobby is gawking and staring at us. Dad and Mom are surrounded by the press. A large circle forms around them. I step off to the side and listen as they make their comments.

"Everyone wishes for a son like Gregg." Dad says into the cameras. "They took one of our stars from us, and we will never be able to see him, hug him or kiss him again." He pauses and the room is silent. "I hope to God," he says, looking into the cameras, "that justice is served."

The room is quiet for a second, then one of the reporters asks, "Do you think the jury will find her guilty?" The cameras flash and the videotape rolls.

"There is no doubt in my mind," he answers.

"Mr. Smart, why do think the trial has been so publicized?"

"I know why there is so much coverage—it's because it's sex, adultery, someone murdered and teenagers involved with an adult. I know what the draw is here, and the only thing we don't want anyone to forget is that she and these boys took a star out of our lives."

A reporter shouts, "What if she is acquitted?"

Mom steps forward and says, "She has other charges with the state pending against her and she will not get away with this." The crowd falls silent and then Mom says, "I was horrified by Pam's testimony. I felt violated because of what she did to us; my emotions were so mixed. It's so hard to explain your emotions when something like this happens to your children. I just can't explain it. It's just a horrible, horrible feeling. I sat there. I watched her. Most of the time, I sat in disbelief, in shock. I couldn't believe how cold and calculating and manipulating she is. She's nothing but a—a manipulating b-i-t-c-h, in plain English."

"What about Flynn, Mrs. Smart, how do you feel about Flynn?" a reporter shouts.

"I would tell him that I'm very, very sorry for what's happened to him. But, I believe he deserves everything he gets. At one point when he was on the stand, I felt some sympathy for him, but now, I hope he gets everything he deserves, and the other boys, too." She looks up at the reporters with her tough look.

"What would you say to Pam?" A reporter asks.

"I don't think . . . I could say that . . . on television," Mom answers.

"Do you have a comment on Pam's planned freedom party if she is found innocent?" A reporter asks.

"No, I just know we are not planning to have a huge party after the verdict, as Pam's family is." Mom answers sternly.

"What about the defense's allegations of torture?" Another reporter asks.

Mom steps away from the cameras and Dad shelters her under his arm. Dad waves his arm to signal "thanks" and "no more," but the reporters keep shouting questions at them. I watch as they push their way through the courthouse lobby, the cameras flashing behind them.

I look up at the white tiles for a moment—the hundreds of gleaming white tiles and the tiny colored ones mixed in with them. The cameras keep flashing, and I think about the shooting stars again and about Gregg, flashing and disappearing, like a flashbulb, flashing and disappearing, bright and fading, dissolving into echo, lingering and then gone, and then I follow the reporters out of the lobby and through the courthouse doors.

I watch from a distance as Dad hurries Mom across the lawn and the parking lot toward the Jag. Photographers are scurrying behind them, snapping pictures. I catch up to them, jump in the car, and Dad drives away, with several photographers chasing after us down the road.

Chapter 26

The Verdict

We sit at a large round wooden table in the side room at the courthouse, playing cards to pass the time. I flip through the *Boston Herald*. The newspaper is taking a poll to see whether readers think Pam will be found guilty or innocent. I try to envision the headline in tomorrow's paper. I go over everything in my head and wonder if there is any way that Pam is going to get off. *It could be a hung jury,* I think to myself. *They could find her innocent and she could just walk away, free.* Then I think, *No juror in his right mind could deny the evidence against her.* Back and forth, I go in my mind, until I have to stand up and walk around for a bit just to calm down.

I end up leaving the waiting room and start walking around the courthouse by myself. I stand in the hallway and listen to the Japanese reporters talking to each other, even though I can't understand a word they are saying. I notice the wires that run along the hallway are thicker now than when the trial began. I start to imagine that they are thick with mud, the sludge that everyone is so attracted to—the hate, the sex, the murder, the evil that is flowing through the wires. I think about the mud from my water carnival dream and all the evil circus images, and I picture all of these images, choking the wires, pushing to get through. I have the urge to kick them, to cause the cameras to go down. I notice that people are looking at me and whispering to each other. I wonder what they are saying — *Look, that's his brother. He looks sad. He looks angry. He looks like he wants to get Pam.* I wander around the lobby, going in and out and lighting cigarettes and smoking them down to the stubs. I wait for hours and there is still no verdict, and with every moment that passes, I wonder what the jury is doing and if, as time passes, a guilty verdict is less likely.

I head back to the waiting area and watch my family play cards. I would join them, but I'm too keyed up to sit down. I stare at the door willing the bailiff to open it and call us into the courtroom, but it doesn't happen. The day goes by and there is no bailiff, no verdict, so we head home, Mom shaking her foot the whole ride and Dad rubbing his eyes with exhaustion.

The next day, we wait again. We wait all morning but still nothing happens, and then, after lunch the waiting-room door suddenly swings open and the grey-haired bailiff sticks his head into the room and says, "Judge Gray has called everyone in." For a moment, no one moves. After waiting so long, I feel my knees wobble a bit as I stand up. Mom and Dad let out a huge sigh and slowly rise to their feet.

I push through the crowd that is rushing toward the courtroom doors. We walk through, make our way to the front row and sit down, as people scurry for seats and flood down the aisle. After a few minutes the courtroom settles. The bailiffs escort Pam down the aisle, and I can hear the crowd rustle as she enters. I turn and look back at her. I notice the small cross pendant that hangs from her neck and I shake my head a firm no as she walks by. From there, it is all in slow motion—Pam taking her seat, the judge moving toward the bench, the jury filing into their box, the judge reading the charges.

Time stops and the room is frozen. A juror, sitting closest to the judge, rises from her chair so slowly it hurts. We all hold hands down the entire front row. The juror stands, motionless, and hesitates. I stare at the back of Pam's head and notice she has no black satin bow in her hair, just a pair of plain barrettes. I stare at the foreman of the jury, waiting for her to speak and it seems like forever. I watch her lips as they take in a breath of air. "Your Honor," she says softly, "we have a question."

"Go ahead." Judge Gray answers.

"If our verdicts are identical, for all three charges, may I read them all at once?"

"I don't see why not—yes, you may."

I glance at Mom and she has her hand over her mouth, her eyes wide. Dad rises to his feet and looks up toward the ceiling. The juror lifts the sheet of paper and begins to read.

"We the jury find Pamela Smart—guilty, guilty, guilty."

Mom screams, "Ahhhh!" Dad drops his head in relief and the whole courtroom fills with noise and excitement. The cameras flash as we all rise in the front row and hug each other.

Judge Gray calls for order and the courtroom eventually quiets. He looks down at Pamela from over his glasses and says sternly, "I hereby sentence you, Pamela Smart, to the New Hampshire State Women's Prison for the remainder of your life, without the possibility of parole."

We cheer and clap for a brief moment and I feel like the whole scene isn't real, the relief I feel isn't real. We stand and wait for Pam to be escorted out in front of us. She shows no sign of any reaction. The bailiffs take her in a different direction and walk her out a side door. I imagine them handcuffing her and driving her off, forever.

Outside, in front of the courthouse, Dad and Mom are surrounded by hundreds of reporters and spectators. Dozens of cameras and video recorders encircle them. They stand on the podium in front of what seems like at least fifty microphones. I watch from the back of the crowd and an odd feeling comes over me — that I will never be here again, behind this crowd, in front of this courthouse. *Pam is guilty — it's over.* I should feel relieved, but I feel nothing, as though the life has drained out of me. My mind drifts as Dad's words enter the microphones and echo across the lawn.

"As a family, we're very, very happy with the verdict. Thank God, the justice system works and thank God for Paul Maggiotto. We're going to go to the cemetery just to tell Gregg what happened today."

He pauses, sighs and looks up into the sky. "We've said from the beginning that this woman was cold and manipulative — the justice system has proved it without a doubt. She thought she was going to control twelve jurors through her manipulative power. This time it didn't work." He sighs and grabs Mom's hand. "Pam never looked at me once during the whole trial — in my life and with twenty-five years of experience in the insurance business, I have never met such a cold person."

The Verdict

Dad then shows the reporters Gregg's "lucky paper clip," explaining that he retrieved it from Gregg's suit pocket after Pam dumped Gregg's belongings in a trash bag on our doorstep. "Gregg took it on all of his appointments for luck and now I carry it everywhere." He raises it in the air toward the cameras, in triumph.

Mom steps forward, a huge smile spreading across her face, and I see that most of the reporters are smiling along with her. *They're happy for her, happy for us,* I realize. She says excitedly, "It feels great to smile again. She got what she deserved—we have been praying and praying—and it came true." She turns and looks at Dad and winks.

She fields several more questions, the smile never leaving her face. When a reporter asks what it's like to lose a son like Gregg, she reaches for the necklace that hangs low near her heart and holds it up for the cameras. I watch the golden heart pendant spin on the braided chain. The etching on the heart spiraling, shining and sparkling, as she holds it in front of her smile. "I keep his picture and a lock of his hair inside. I've got to have something of him left—something I can hold on to."

We walk across a thin layer of snow on the grass and make our way to Gregg's headstone. A few reporters have followed us here, and they stand off to the side on one of the small winding cemetery roads. They keep their distance. We walk toward the grave. Cars keep pulling up and parking all around us. As we arrive at Gregg's grave site, I see a set of lone footprints in the snow that appear to be from a child. I walk to the back of the headstone and read Gregg's name and birth and death dates; under his name, Mom's and

Dad's. I think to myself, *I wish they could have waited to have their names carved on the stone.*

Dad stands in front of the marker with his head down and holds Mom's hand. One by one, each member of the family walks across the snow and joins us in a circle around Gregg's gravestone. We hold hands and Dad says a prayer, and we linger around the stone, hugging each other under a grey sky, quiet and cold. Eventually, we separate and only Mom and Dad are left, standing alone, holding each other, in front of Gregg's granite stone. I watch them from a distance, wondering if they will ever be the same and if anything will ever be normal again.

"Morning, guys, looks like we aren't heading to the courthouse today, huh?" I laugh, as I plop down in my usual seat in front of the sliding glass door.

Mom and Dad smile at me, then Dad flips the newspaper over and slides it in my direction. "Well, not today, son, but take a look at this." I stare down at the headline:

SMART TO APPEAL LIFE SENTENCE

I let out a groan and drop my head in my hands. "Wow, it won't ever end, will it!" I sigh and stare out into the bright morning sun. Suddenly, an idea occurs to me.

"Dad, let me take the Jag to the beach today, please?"

"All right, son, sure — go ahead," he says, tossing me the keys. I smile and race upstairs.

I open the black lacquered drawer where I keep Gregg's stuff that I salvaged from the trash bag. I throw on my grey faded Led Zeppelin tee shirt and grab the old *Bad*

Company tape he left behind, when he moved out. I throw on my Levi's and run down the stairs, open the garage and put the Jag in reverse.

I cruise down 101 toward the beach, the same road that leads to the courthouse. I slide open the sunroof and the sun hits me. The car quiet, the wind floating in through the windows, I look to the side of the road at the rocks. I look for the ice. It's there, cloudy, unclear and melting, and I try to catch my reflection in it, but I can't see it. I look again and again and still can't see myself.

I look back again and in my mind I see not my face but Pam's, trapped in the ice, frozen. She is straight faced and impassive, her face stuck in the ice as it melts away onto the grass below, and I think, *The ice princess – now she's frozen and stuck.*

As I get closer to the exit for the courthouse, images of the courtroom fill my mind. I see myself as I walk through the white-tiled lobby, down the hallway with the wires and into the reserved front row. I see Flynn crying in front of the witness stand, in position, signaling for the gun. I see Gregg below him on his knees. The gun goes off and Gregg slumps to the foyer floor. I shake my head, trying to escape the scene in my mind. I think to myself, *I got to stop thinking about it. I got to look for anything with any hope, anything that can make it stop. Why did it all happen – what did Gregg die for? Well, at the very least, he died for* LOVE *– Billy must have really loved her, or he never would have done it.* I start crying again, thinking about the craziness of it, the absurdity of it all. The wind comes through the windows and the sun shines through the roof, and I watch in the rear-view mirror as the courthouse exit disappears behind me.

I think back to the night it all started and the white mist fills my head again and I see myself running, through the dark, toward Gregg's condo. I stop and breathe with my hands on my knees and I look up toward the parking circle and the flashing sirens. I stare up at his street sign, Misty Morning Drive. I look back for Mom and Dad, but instead I see Gregg running behind me in the woods in Hudson, chasing me through the wooded path under the trees. He looks so young, smiling and laughing, as he runs behind me in the wind of that lost spring. I smile, the thought breaks, the mist rises, and I'm back, driving again.

The old Jaguar hums down the highway and I remember that I've brought along Gregg's tape. I look down at it, lying on the passenger seat. The lettering is almost worn off with wear and I can't remember the last time we listened to it. I grab the cassette and hold it, thinking it feels good to hold something of his in my hand, knowing he had touched it. I slide the tape in and turn the volume up, letting it play from wherever it was left last. A soft guitar riff fills the car and I stare out the windshield at the sky widening before me, as I get closer to the shore. *It's the "Seagull" song,* I think to myself, as it plays on.

The lyrics come through the speakers, "Seagull, you fly—across the horizon—into the misty morning sun—" When I hear the line about the *misty morning sun*, I can't believe it. I hit rewind on the tape and I play it again.

"Seagull, you fly—across the horizon—into the misty morning sun—nobody asks you—where you are going—nobody knows where you're from—" *So weird, the connection,* I think, and it brings me to tears.

The lyrics continue, "There is a man asking a question—is this really the end of the world?—" Instantly I think of Gregg and it's almost as if the song were written for him. *It couldn't have been*, I think to myself. *It was written way before Gregg*. I keep listening, "Seagull, you must have known for a long time—the shape of things to come—" As I hear it, I can see Gregg sitting on the couch in Londonderry with his beads in his hand, worry in his eyes.

The music widens and the chorus plays, "Now you fly—through the sky—never asking why—and you fly—all around—until somebody—shoots—you—down—" As I hear the words, they wreck me and I slump and sob in the driver's seat, thinking, *Unreal. It's like it was written for him, before the whole thing even happened*. The lyrics repeat, and as I listen through the song, I cry the whole way.

I get to the strip in Hampton Beach that runs along the shore. I open the glove compartment and grab a napkin, wipe my eyes and look at myself in the rear-view mirror. "Tired," I mumble. I stare at the casino on the strip and the arcades, pizza places and the shops that are all closed and boarded up. I drive down the strip, slowly cruising the Jag, as if it's the middle of summer. I get to the end of the strip and slow down, looking to pick a spot to park in. In front of McDonald's I see a newspaper box. I stare in at the headlines:

SMART TO APPEAL LIFE SENTENCE

"There's no escape," I say out loud, as I pull the car away from the box and into a spot facing the beach. I turn off the ignition, sigh and think to myself, *I'd like to appeal my life sentence, too*.

I stare out the windshield toward the ocean. *Yeah, I bet Gregg would like to appeal his life sentence, too*. I pull the handle and swing open the door. I turn and put one foot on the ground, and I sit there staring at the newspaper box behind me, then walk toward the beach. A metal railing separates the sidewalk from the sand, and I sit on the railing and stare at the water. The silver sunlight reflects off its surface, flashing and glimmering in the waves.

I lean back on the railing a little, trying to take in the whole scene. I can feel the newspaper box behind me and I wonder what Gregg was thinking as they put him on his knees. I cry, my eyes blur, and I squint at the sun as it stretches across the water. I turn around and look back at the Jaguar, expecting Gregg to be sitting in the driver's seat. I look through the windshield and my eyes end up stuck again on the newspaper box across the street.

I turn back to the sun. I feel it almost pulling me toward the water. I jump off the railing and head toward the light in the waves. I look over at the pavilion with the stage, where we used to dance so many summers ago. I see myself smiling and spinning to the music, with the crowd watching. "Remember that?" I mumble, as I make my way to where the water meets the land. I stare up at the sun, closing my eyes, feeling its warmth.

I step to the edge of the beach, the expanding light spread out before me on the water. My sneakers are mud soaked, as the water washes over them with each ripple of the current. I watch the light's reflection; it reminds me of the shooting stars that I saw that night in the skylight. I start to think again that maybe it's Gregg. Maybe he's there, inside the flash, inside the light.

I look down at the water, searching for him, and all I see is my own reflection shifting and moving in the sun, mirrored back at me. I stare at the watery reflection of the angel on my Led Zeppelin tee shirt. As the ocean moves, it's like the wings are moving. I look down at the angel, his wings spread and stretched, his chest pressed forward, pushing his heart out ahead of the rest of him. *He's rising with it,* I think, *floating above everything, his hair long and curled like Gregg's, flying over the surface of the water.*

I look down at my sneakers and watch the water flashing and dotting white light around my feet. I see Gregg standing on the white pebble-filled stairs in Londonderry, on the day we moved. He grabs me in a hug, and when he lets me go, I see a tear slide down his cheek, "I wish we could stay," he says softly to me, "I don't want—to go." I bend down and kneel before the glimmering water. I see Gregg perfectly, reflected in its surface. He opens the screen door and walks through it. He stands behind it and says slowly, "It'll be all right, Dean." He holds out his hand to me, his eyes expecting. His reflection shimmies and shifts in the water, breaking up and reforming in the waves and light. I reach out for him. My hand touches the sparkling sun as it shines. I touch his reflection for a moment, trying to grasp at his hand, and as I do, his image fades and echoes away in the waves. I pull my hand from the water, cold, wet, the drops on my hand sparkling in the sunlight. I drop my head and watch, as my tears fall into the glint of the sea. *He's gone,* I think.

I stand up, raise my head high and stare off into the sunlight. "It's all right, Gregg," I say out loud, looking toward the horizon. "Yeah, it's all right, Gregg—you can live through me—you can just live through me—and I'll live for you."

Acknowledgements

To Wendy Lazear, whose guidance and dedication have made this book possible, thank you Wendy for having faith in me. To Art Gutch, for giving me a shot and for all his hard work that was essential to the book. To Cathy Kessler for an outstanding job on the copy edit. To Penny and Sherrie from Author Marketing experts for all their help and guidance. To everyone at WMUR television in Manchester NH, and especially to Jean Mackin for her assistance, her kindness and for her journalistic professionalism. To former WMUR reporter Bill Spenser, who was both a great reporter and a trusted source of help to our family. To Franci Richardson from the *Derry News* for the use of part of her article from June 20th 1990. To Lauren Collins from NECN. To everyone at the Derry, NH police department, and especially to Captain Loring Jackson and Detective Pelletier, who both went beyond the call of duty to help me and my family. To Paul Maggiotto and Diane Nicolisi for all of their efforts before, during and after the trial. To Sandi Matheson for her kind guidance and assistance, throughout. To Charles Simic for helping me find my voice and for inspiration. To the people of New Hampshire who were always there for our family with kind words and support. To all of my former students who helped me during the tough times, and especially to Dun, his brother and family for always being there for me. To my family and friends who have put up with me while I wrote. To my beautiful wife, Brooke, whose support allowed this all to be possible. To my two beautiful children, I love you both. Finally, to my three angels, Gregg, Mom and Dad, I miss you all dearly.